Based on an original idea by Nigel Trevena.
Additional material by Tony Wakefield
Edited by Dr Alan Earnshaw

Printed by Troutbeck Press, Mabe, Penryn, Cornwall

ISBN 9 780906 899519

PUBLISHED BY

ATLANTIC TRANSPORT PUBLISHERS
TREVITHICK HOUSE · WEST END · PENRYN
CORNWALL TR10 8BE · ENGLAND

THE COMPLETE STORY

Barry Top Yard in 1967, a common scene of the era as a fine mixture of LMS, GWR and SR rest together before going to the Scrapyard. In the centre of the picture No.5322 dominates the view, this however was one of the few that escaped, being eventually obtained for preservation at Didcot.
Derek Short

CONTENTS

ACKNOWLEDGMENTS

The compilation of this book is the work of many hands, in fact so many people have been involved that it would take a page or more to list them individually. From Nigel Trevena's conception of the first volume in the series, down through the two subsequent books, to this compendium, our readers have willingly volunteered their efforts to ensure the story is brought right up to date. To all of these we must say a special thanks, but I must offer particular thanks to Phillip Atkins, Oliver Carter, John Corkhill, Peter Hands, Norman Preedy, Gerald Robinson and Peter Trushell. This book has also involved a lot of behind the scenes work, it is appropriate therefore, to say thankyou to:-
Barney Trevivian for all his skilful work in merging the new text with the original photographs, to Sarah Earnshaw for her mammoth task in collating and typing out the new material written by Tony Wakefield. Also I must pay tribute to Alan Earnshaw for the countless man hours spent of sifting through the text and photographs, enabling this volume to be presented in a logical sequence. My thanks also go to Michael Eltham, Janet Wakefield and Larraine Earnshaw for proof reading. Finally may I say thankyou to all the long-suffering readers who have supported Steam For Scrap for so long, and made the series such an undoubted success both by their kind patronage and their assistance in the supply of information.

David Jenkinson

FOREWORD

IN 1985, NIGEL TREVENA wrote and published the first instalment of one of the most interesting and controversial series of books ever to come out of the Atlantic stable - *STEAM FOR SCRAP*. The books looked at a subject which hit right into the hearts of railway enthusiasts world-wide, the end of steam in Britain! Many thought it a depressing and macabre topic, others considered it insensitive. However, astute readers would have recognised that it was a dedicated record which chronicled one of the most important eras of British railway history. Never had such a fascinating over-view been presented on the demise of steam, and never had so many facts about locomotive disposal been made available. Since the initial books in the series, hundreds of readers have been prompted to supply further information, in particular a host of disposal records and photographs.

When the third volume of the series went on sale in August 1987, it had already become evident that a fourth book would be required to tell, as best we know it, the story of how British Railways disposed of its steam locomotive fleet. Many readers have looked forward to the arrival of that concluding work but, incredible as it may seem, some five years have elapsed since the promise of a fourth volume. The reason for this partly lays in the managerial and editorial changes at Atlantic, and the exhaustive work which has gone in other fields. However, the real reason behind the delay has been the desire to provide our readers with the most comprehensive account of the subject, coupled with the need to amend a number of minor errors which appeared in the earlier volumes.

Since Volume three, Tony Wakefield has faithfully compiled a whole new area of supplementary information to round out Nigel's original account. Yet the problem has been in how this new material and the amendments could be presented, without seeming to be going over old ground which would be essential to set the background for a fourth volume. As the earlier volumes are now almost unobtainable, and would have to be reprinted, we have decided to take the opportunity to produce a single volume detailing the *STEAM FOR SCRAP* story. Much of the original information has been retained, but new material and amendments have been inserted. Meanwhile, a large number of 'grey' areas have been coloured in. In addition, the whole subject has been treated in chronological order and the various chapters have been re-arranged to facilitate this. Making, what is essentially, a new book - which will undoubtedly become an essential work of reference rather than a compilation of tragic or depressing photographs.

It has been a rather difficult task to blend the work of two writers, but with such a fascinating story to relate, I have found this one of the most absorbing projects with which I have ever been involved. I hope you will have as much enjoyment reading, *STEAM FOR SCRAP - THE COMPLETE STORY,* as I have had in editing it.

Alan Earnshaw
Shepley, West Yorkshire
December 1992

Ex-Somerset & Dorset Joint Railway 2-8-0 Class 7F pictured at Woodham's Barry in 1974, preserved in 1975 and then steamed in 1980 on the Midland Railway. Before its departure the engine has been suitably identified and given a nebulous shed code - 55G (Huddersfield Hillhouse), the culprit still has to be identified!!!!!
Alan Earnshaw

INTRODUCTION

IN JANUARY 1990, THE weed covered sidings of a South Wales scrapyard saw the departure of a large rusting hulk, a remnant of a bygone era. Though such establishments, throughout the length and breadth of the land, daily disgorge large pieces of industrial machinery for re-cycling; this consignment was no ordinary one. In fact it was the last survivor of the 213 steam locomotives which had gone to the scrapyard of Woodham Brothers in Barry for disposal, an ex-GWR 2-6-2T, No.5553. As it left for the Forest of Dean after a sojourn of 28 years in the yard, the *Steam For Scrap* story came to an end. The preservation miracle in which Dai Woodham played such a significant part, is perhaps one of the most glorious sagas in the entire history of railways. For twenty-one years, the interest and enthusiasm surrounding events at Barry stimulated a thirst for knowledge on what had happened elsewhere concerning the disposal of steam. Interestingly, the prominence and celebrity enjoyed by Woodham's tended to obscure the fact that at least 134 private scrapyards were once involved in identical operations. In 1985 Nigel Trevena set out to answer some of the outstanding questions, as well as presenting a pictorial record of the events in *Steam For Scrap*. This spurred on a number of researchers to contribute additional information and many unpublished photographs, then all this data was meticulously compiled by Nigel and (later) Tony Wakefield.

But why did so many people find it necessary to preoccupy themselves with, what on the surface appears to be, such a negative episode in railway history? The answer must surely be found in the locomotive scene itself, for though the end of operational steam was a major change on the railways, dare I say it was only a change. Just one of the many changes that have taken place, since the Stockton & Darlington Railway's first crude locomotives pounded down inferior track secured by stone sleeper blocks. Some of these changes were minor ones, others were more significant and some, like the end of steam, were quite revolutionary. Yet, most changes are for the good, as technological advances are gradually applied to every-day working practice. As the *Times* put the demises of steam railways on 3rd May 1966, 'Change is the law of life. If things do not evolve, they die.'

To most enthusiasts the change from steam-powered traction was both unpalatable and ill-advised, therefore steam's demise was the greatest issue ever to appear in the pages of the popular railway press. Yet, would it not be accurate to say that the majority of people who enthuse about the steam railway never had to work on it. It was a hard, dirty and physically demanding life and, in many ways, dangerous. Steam locomotives were often wasteful and inefficient; in environmental terms an ecological disaster with their high levels of pollution and smoke emission. But surely, some may counter, they were well loved? Perhaps, but as the original Volume in this series pointed out, 'for every railwayman who mourned the passing of steam there were probably a hundred whose reaction ranged from indifference to delight.' As one Western Region driver said in 1962, 'Many of the engines we work are in a deplorable condition and I can only hope that we get regular diesel work soon'.

The advent of diesel and electric traction in Britain may have been an anathema to steam fans, but in many ways it was a change which was long overdue. In Europe and the USA progressive steps had been taken to revolutionise rail transport, and as early as the 1930s the LNER had seen the financial and operating benefits of electrifying steeply graded main lines such as the route over Woodhead. The real problem lay in the fact that steam locomotives were so robust, and therefore had an exceptionally long life. As a technical assistant to the Eastern Region Traffic Manager said in July 1961, '...there is no such thing as a 'life-expired steam locomotive, repair costs climb slowly in the first ten years or so of life, then remain fairly constant. There are examples of steam locomotives remaining on certain restricted duties, which they perform perfectly satisfactorily for upwards of 50 years.' The great argument therefore, is whether diesel and electric traction should have been introduced en-masse (and without proper testing and evaluation), or if transferring to such forms of traction should have been part of a more costly but gradually progressive conversion plan. Leaving aside this question, the fact remains that (with a few notable exceptions) the new locomotives brought with them much superior traffic availability, increased dynamic efficiency and a greatly improved working environment - all things greatly appreciated by those accustomed to the vagaries of steam.

The withdrawal and scrapping of a steam locomotive would seem, at first, to be a simple process: life expired, it was condemned and cut up. Nothing, it would seem, could be more straightforward. Not so! There were, for a start, a lot of engines to be dealt with. At the end of 1958, when the torch really began to burn in Britain, BR was running a fleet of 16,108 steam locomotives and was still building more. But the writing was firmly on the wall: already, after four years of building, there were 2,417 DMUs and diesel railcars and 105 main line diesel engines. Five years later, the steam engines had been decimated to 7,050 and the diesels were in full flood: with 2,009 shunters, 4,145 DMUs and railcars, whilst the main line locomotives had increased almost twentyfold, to 2,051 units. Another five years of

Identifying the fact that locomotive cutting was an age-old pastime, this view at Dinton in June 1948 shows the end of A12 Class, No.615. Note the apparent orderliness of the scene.
Lens of Sutton

The scene at Barry Docks on 19th November 1967, with No.53803 in a somewhat better condition than the previous view. It is surrounded by Nos.7802, 35011, 80072/8, 80100 and other unidentified engines. *Alan Sommerfield*

upheaval and the BR standard gauge steam locomotive fleet had ceased to exist.

Over 16,000 locomotives, then, in a little under ten years. Just consider the breaking process alone: as a general rule of thumb, a team of two men could cut up an average size steam locomotive in about one working week. Projected to cover the ten year programme this gives a figure of 1.28 million man hours to dispose of the British steam fleet. Clearly a significant industrial operation. But when other factors are considered, the scale becomes inestimably bigger. Many withdrawn locomotives were stored for months, occasionally for years, and they took up a lot of space. Once their final destination - BR works or private scrapyard - had been finalized, they had to be found a path in traffic patterns: sometimes they disgraced themselves en-route and were shunted into limbo; sometimes they waited for weeks or months at a concentration point, presenting a sombre picture for the enthusiast and a cause of puzzlement for the frustrated passenger cooling his heels behind a failed diesel.

Even at the scrapyard itself, it might be some time before final extinction. Private yards usually dealt quickly with the locomotives for that was the way in which profit was made, but some went bankrupt or cut up something more lucrative or easier. Some hapless engines, partly cut up at one location, were re-sold and travelled to another yard - often in a state of embarrassing dismemberment in a rake of mineral wagons. Those enthusiasts who saw and witnessed these events, and spent months chasing the last few steam locomotives before they too disappeared to the scrapyard will know the great sadness that many feel about the end of steam. As the RCTS Journal stated in 1966 'One feels that the real significance of much that is happening will only be appreciated some years hence by many railway enthusiasts.' Some two and a half decades those words certainly ring true!

Through the following pages, the complex account of *Steam For Scrap* unfolds and tells the stóry as best we know it. Sadly the record will probably never be complete, too much happened in too short a time - with disposal work assuming 'production line' status. We hope this work, which completes Atlantic's commitment to complete our *Steam For Scrap* series, will provide a comprehensive overview of the demise of British Steam. This can not be a locomotive by locomotive account, it would be too large a task to cover in any single volume. So we begin with a portrait of locomotives in store, withdrawn from traffic and facing an uncertain future. Next we had the locomotive dumps, where condemned engines often waited for several months or more, whilst a decision was taken about their eventual means of disposal. Once it was decided, the locomotives would be towed to their final destination as a dead engine movement. We present a detailed analysis of both the BR works and the private scrapyards, as well as a comprehensive look at the demise of the giants of steam. Steam For Scrap also investigates some of the myths and legends behind the disposal of steam, and what really happened to the hundreds of disposed locomotives. Finally, we look at the happy few, those, which like No.5553 escaped to fight another day!

By contrast the picture taken at Buttigieg's yard in Newport two decades later, shows the production line method of disposing with steam engines. Here the cabs of Nos.34032 and 34005 have been stripped away from the boilers, whilst No.34009 awaits its turn next.
N.E. Preedy

Chapter One

The Road to the Scrapyard

THE REAL GENESIS OF the scenes of railway carnage in the scrapyards of the 1960s was a political event; one which had its origins in The Labour Party's victory in the 1945 General Election. The subsequent Nationalisation of Britain's railways which took effect from 1st January 1948, being a political solution to the exceptionally difficult post-war situation that faced the Big Four railway companies. At this time locomotives, rolling-stock, track and infrastructure were virtually worn-out after six years of hostilities. This move into full state control of the railways provided the centralised decision-making process essential to force through desperately needed modernisation and renewal, but it also opened the door to haste, insensitivity and Government pressure.

The Railway Executive arm of the British Transport Commission almost immediately launched its plans for a new fleet of 999 Standard steam locomotives - a policy contrary to that of other nationalised railway systems in the industrial West most of whom were already heavily investing in a diesel and electric future. So the common sights that became evident a decade or so later begs the question, rather than being scrapped too early, were not these Standard Classes built too late? Problems in the post-war recovery of operating efficiency and time-keeping on the steam railway were exacerbated by difficulties in the supply of quality steam coal and the growing dissatisfaction of the BR work-force with dirty and outmoded working conditions.

Thus all was far from well on BR when the 1955 modernisation plan was unveiled. The bulk of the proposed £1,240 million expenditure was to go on motive power, rolling stock and electrification, and when the first stage of this plan was approved in January 1957 it clearly signalled the beginning of the end for BR steam. Diesel locomotives were to be ordered in quantity, and electrification was to take priority on the most heavily used routes, but the end of steam still appeared to be a considerable way off. It was not until 1958 that the BTC's worried re-appraisal of the 1955 Plan sealed steam's fate within the decade. Faced with a rapid decline in freight traffic, encouraged on to the roads by the 1953 Transport Act, and by rising wage demands and material costs, the BTC made the decision to accelerate the disposal of the steam fleet (despite its operating deficiencies contributing only a small part of BR's problems); with the hopelessly optimistic aim of overall profitability within five years. A carefully designed and protracted range of pilot schemes to evaluate competing diesel designs was all but abandoned and, with brand new steam locomotives still leaving the workshops, BR was forced to embark on a mad scramble for modernisation with little knowledge or experience of diesel traction. A situation unparalled on any national railway system before or since!

The immediate and heavy increase in the scrapping of steam locomotives quickly convinced BR that its own works would no longer be able to cope. So, throughout 1958 they conducted discussions with the scrap metal industry, laying the basis for an extraordinary series of transactions which was to ultimately involve many thousands of engines being sold to private scrapyards for breaking.

The road to the scrapyard was a long tedious affair, with engines being consigned in convoys from one convenient point to another. The last journey often taking days, sometimes weeks and occasionally months. As journey's end draws near, a batch of taper-boilered Ivatt 2-6-0s, with Nos.43158/41350 leading, wait to be consigned to the yard of King & Co. Norwich.
Dr. Ian C. Allan

Steam for Sale

IT FELL TO THE Western Region, in the vanguard of dieselisation, to start the ball rolling. At 5.20am on 25th March 1959 the first procession of dead BR engines left Swindon, headed for a private scrapyard. These were Churchward 53XX Class Moguls, Nos. 5312,60,92,97, bound (with astonishing appropriateness) for the scrapyard of Woodham Brothers, Barry, South Wales. By August a number of other yards, primarily located in the steel-making areas, had also commenced purchasing engines, notably T.W. Wards of Sheffield. The early 1960s saw a rapid increase in both the size and number of sales to private yards and soon there over 100 locations throughout Britain where ex-BR steam locomotives were being broken up.

Transaction was by competitive tender, the highest bid secured the sale, but the scrap merchant had to add the cost of movement by rail from the holding BR works to his yard and this could add as much as £200 to the price. As transactions increased in number, however, locomotives were no longer passed through BR works but sent direct to the scrapyards from their last running sheds; this broadened the scope of operations considerably as it reduced the cost of transit and encouraged more local yards to bid for the engines being made redundant in their own areas. As the number of yards involved increased (and became more proficient) supplies of engines ebbed: in such circumstances scrapyards would bid for engines from more distant sheds, viable if only to keep the cutters fully employed.

By August 1968 BR had terminated standard gauge steam working, but several months were to pass before they had disposed of all the locomotives unceremoniously dumped around the system. But no sentimentality, for it would fit uneasily into a book on this subject. Yet it would be an insensitive reader who could peruse the photographs which follow without a stab of regret, a moment of mourning for a fine machine, unwanted in its last hours, dismembered and forlorn - once a living, breathing steam locomotive and now nothing but a frozen image on a printed page! So, as he turns the pages which follow, the reader must steel himself for the sight of the legendary giants of the steam age (the Kings, Bullieds, Stanier Pacifics, A4s, and Britannias) along with more humble locomotives, stored, redundant, unwanted and in pieces. These photographs will not be to everyone's liking, but they do two things and do them well: they fix precisely in time when an engine ceased to exist and they do it with a compelling power. In fact, they bring together the twin themes of the story - the statistical and the emotional. While the withdrawal dates of virtually every BR steam locomotive are now a part of documented history, records of arrivals at scrapyards and the crucial cutting up dates are much harder to pinpoint.

Whatever the emotions that are stirred, the mixture of re-used and new photographs in this new volume of *Steam For Scrap* provides a valuable historic record. In stark contrast with the vast plethora of railway picture books, most of which strive to accentuate the romance of steam, the aim of this publication is to detail as comprehensively as possible a specific part of railway history - albeit a tragic one. Too many publications look with a rose-tinted perspective on the days of steam, however the running of trains was not as romantic or as trouble free as some might portray. Regretfully things happened, sometimes dramatically (as readers of our *Trains In Trouble* series will appreciate), and a locomotive's days were suddenly ended - that, like life expiry, was a normal part of railway operation, but in this book we look at another aspect of railway management - waste. Things have frequently happened in the past which hindsight shows as being regrettable, poor planning, bad judgements and hard decisions often taken to satisfy the dictates of business, and astute readers will wish to question the reasons which led to these circumstances occurring. However, though some courses of action may have been lamentable, sentimentality has no place in a serious analysis and the two intangibles of heritage and tradition scarcely figure in the calculations. This is certainly true in our over-view of the demise of steam, but the serious enthusiast concerned with the complete picture will want to know about these things too.

Traditionally, the only reason for the premature destruction of an engine was that it had been involved in an accident and was therefore beyond viable repair. Yet by the early 1960s even the most trivial damage became reason to condemn an engine. This was the case with No.9737, seen after the Pontrhydyfen accident on 24th November 1960. It was condemned on 14th December and despatched to Caerphilly Works on New Year's Eve - 14 weeks later it was completely cut up.
the late Eric Mountford

ONE OF THE MOST significant aspects of the scrapping process, and that most in evidence to the travelling public, was the storage of withdrawn steam locomotives on shed, at works or at concentration points throughout the system.

This lengthy line-up has just arrived at the 'withdrawn' road at Westbury shed, WR, and comprises condemned southern and Western engines. SR Class U Moguls Nos. 31798/31792 have just completed several weeks in store at Yeovil shed and will leave shortly for Bird's scrapyard at Bynea, Llanelly.
Photo: Ovo Peters

RIGHT: Saturday 31st December 1966 was the last official day of steam on the Isle of Wight and eight of the surviving Wight 02 0-4-4 tanks were withdrawn. On 18th February 1967 they were photographed at the closed Newport station awaiting transfer to the nearby scrapyard of H. B. Solliffe, where they were cut up in May. Nos. W12, W31 survived at Ryde until the following March whilst W24 escaped into preservation on the Isle of White Steam Railway. *Photo: John Bird*

BELOW: Darlington North Road scrap sidings on 13th March 1962 with a variety of NER classes awaiting the torch. In the foreground are five of eighteen Class J72 0-6-0Ts withdrawn in October 1961, the oldest of which had a working life of 63 years. Condemned the same month was the Class J26 0-6-0 No. 65769, and in the distance are members of classes L1 and B16/1. Note, on the right, the pile of tyres for Class 2MT tanks. *Photo: P. J. Lynch*

26th August 1967. The end of steam on British Railways is only a year away and this batch of LMS motive power is in store at Carlisle Upperby MPD, its useful life almost at an end. Class 8F 2-8-0 No.48451 will survive only until the following May and 'Black Five' 4-6-0 No.44812, behind her, will never steam again. *Photo: the late Derek Cross, courtesy D. M. Cross*

DEAD ENGINE MOVEMENTS

DEAD ENGINE MOVEMENTS — an ineffably evocative part of the 1960's railway scene — ebbed and flowed and gave enthusiasts one last chance to 'cop' their favourite engine.

A high proportion of SR and WR locomotives were sold to private scrapyards in South Wales and as the towing of dead engines through the Severn Tunnel was not permitted, Gloucester became one of the focal points for such movements, originating on the Southern, Western and London Midland regions.

TOP: On 9th June 1965 this woebegone procession was entering Gloucester Central en route for South Wales. Comprising GWR Hall, 2-8-0 and 0-6-0PT plus a Standard 9F, it is hauled by GWR 4-6-0 No.5042 *Winchester Castle* on her saddest — as well as her last — duty. In deplorable condition, without smokebox number and shed plates, right hand cabside number plate and safety valve bonnet, the once proud Castle will be cut up at Bird's yard, Bridgend. As a last salute to her Great Western pedigree, someone has painted her number on her buffer beam, Great Western style. Only twelve Castles lasted into 1965: of the last four, three — Nos.7034, 7022 and 5042 herself — were condemned in June while No.7029 *Clun Castle,* purchased for preservation, worked until the year's end.

BOTTOM: Tramway Junction, Gloucester, on 6th August 1967 and BR Standard 2-6-4Ts Nos.80019/80154 and 2-6-0 Nos.76058/76063, newly arrived after a period in store at Salisbury, depart for Buttigieg's yard, Newport. No.80154, the last engine built at Brighton Works, has 'Steam for Ever' chalked on her tank and No.80019 has her rods secured on her tank top. Gloucester Horton Road MPD is in the background: closed in December 1965, it is already dilapidated. *Photos: N. E. Preedy*

ABOVE: Falkland Junction, Ayrshire, on 22nd April 1963. A condemned locomotive special from Ayr MPD heads for the Arnott Young, West of Scotland Shipbreaking Company's scrapyard at Troon Harbour. LNER Class B1 4-6-0 No. 61243 *Sir Harold Mitchell* (one of 18 of the class named after LNER directors) is in charge of three Caledonian 0-6-0s, Nos. 57262, 57392 and 57364. Sixteen months later the B1 made the same journey again: she, too, had been bought by Arnott Young. Photo: the late Derek Cross, courtesy D. M. Cross.

OPPOSITE, TOP: The familiar western portal of Twerton Tunnel, Bath, and another scrapyard-bound special, photographed on 2nd April 1965 and of exceptional interest. The engine in steam, No. 34006 *Bude*, was ironically the only one of these five Bulleid Light Pacifics to be cut up, at Cashmore's, Newport, in September 1967, a sad end for a locomotive which performed with such distinction in the 1948 locomotive exchanges. Her four sisters were being towed to Woodham's, Barry, and all still exist: Nos. 34058 *Sir Frederick Pile* (purchased privately); 34067 Tangmere (Mid Hants Railway); 34073 249 Squadron (purchased by Southern Action Group) and 34081 92 Squadron (Nene Valley Railway).
Photo: Ivo Peters

OPPOSITE, BOTTOM: Far to the north a few months later on a bitter New Year's Eve 1966, another dead engine movement is seen approaching Goole station headed by the pioneer LMS Class 8F, No. 48000 (then with three month's life left). Bound for Draper's scrapyard at Hull are LMS engines 'Black Five' No. 45063 and Class 8F No. 48080 (both from store at Leeds Holbeck) and Ivatt Moguls Nos. 43135, 43030 (from store at Manningham).
Photo: Gavin Morrison

A Matter Of Record

AT THIS POINT IT is pertinent to say a little about how we have set about compiling the information for this book. As noted above, some scrapping statistics are on record and readily accessible, some are hard to find and scattered across the length and breadth of the country, others have ceased to exist. It would be difficult to think of few relatively modern railway subjects where there is such a dearth of reference material: many of the official BR and BTC records are unavailable due to a variety of reasons, but others have been lost or deliberately destroyed. Take the case of one shed in the last stronghold of steam where, when the last dead engine was towed away in August 1968, its chimney belched smoke for the last time - the entire stock of loco-record cards having been dumped in the smokebox and set alight: amusing at the time as a sort of two digit gesture at officialdom, but sadly a valuable source of archive material was lost for ever.

Once a locomotive had been sold to a private scrapyard, its documented history became very vulnerable. Some yards kept precise and detailed records, others did not; to most commercial operators one engine was much like another, its value being gauged by its weight and scrap (particularly copper) content. As for the cutters, unless they were enthusiasts, numbers and cab plates were of no importance. In any case most of the yards have now ceased to exist, whilst others have been absorbed into much larger groups, meaning that the few individual records that were kept have now vanished into obscurity.

This lack of accessible information has been compounded by another crucially important factor, the actual movement of certain engines purportedly acquired by the yards concerned. Some locomotives, by error or failure en-route (such as hot boxes), never got to their intended destination at all. Meanwhile several 'grey' engines moved unrecorded from one yard to another, some were re-sold others passed on to a subsidiary firm; several were partially cut at one location and after being stripped of the more valuable items, were then disposed of to dealers in ferous metals. On a practical level this means that *Steam For Scrap* has relied on the individual records, photographs and sightings of a small band of enthusiasts who, with notebooks and usually meticulous dedication, carried out a marathon detective operation. In the original books a few errors, largely in numbers being misread (a 3 for an 8 being the most common) and so on, were presented as fact, but our generous readers kindly offered corrective notes, and those have been included in this revised edition.

The activities of the various yards is something of a paradox, for a small, unimportant yard may have been well documented by virtue of the fact that an enthusiast lived nearby and popped in daily to see what was going on, while some large yards with several locomotives arriving every week went unrecorded as it was company policy to exclude visitors, frequently on safety grounds. Occasionally, enthusiasts did manage to wangle their way in to even the most secure scrapyards, making a record of what was happening at the time. But, as such visits were generally few and far between, and then often at weekends, what routinely went on within their gates remains a mystery.

So, whilst it is very true to state that the end of steam and the transition to diesel and electric traction was traumatic, problematical and wide-open to criticism, *Steam For Scrap* is much more concerned with the 'how' of the demise of British steam rather than the 'why'. In the chapters that follow our stance will be consciously objective: recognition of great achievements of steam should in no way compromise or obscure the change and evolution so fundamental to a credible public transport system. Indeed, it should not be forgotten that the following scenes and descriptions depict not only an ending, but a new beginning also.

To wander round the back of shed could bring a surprise or two in the 1950s, even at locations as small as Hawick. Here ex-North British Class C15, still in LNER livery, was captured by Frank Alcock facing an uncertain future.
the late Frank Alcock

The same sort of scene was also captured at some depots late into the final years of the steam era. Looking like a dinosaur from a forgotten age, an ex-L&YR Barton Wright 0-4-4T stands at the back of Newton Heath Depot in an embarrassing state of dismemberment. Used for steam raising purposes, this engine was not one that vanished to the private yards for disposal.
V. Bamford

Chapter Two

Locos In Store

ONE OF THE MOST significant aspects of the scrapping process, and that most in evidence to the travelling public, was the storage of withdrawn steam locomotives on shed. During the 1950s and 60s, every shed seemed to have its own line of 'stored' engines. Some contained just one or two locomotives, others had dozens - the prelude to disposal.

Locomotives have been 'stored' almost since the beginning of the railways, as engines which were redundant, defective or 'surplus to requirement' were temporarily laid up. However, laying up a steam engine was no simple task, and a number of procedures had to be adopted before the mothballing process was completed. If the period in storage was likely to be protracted, it was customary to first drain off the water, clean out the fire- and smoke- boxes and generally tidy-up the locomotive. Having taken care to eliminate the possibility of frost damage or the solidification of dust, sludge and ash, the main protective work began. The motion would be heavily greased, chimney stacks would be covered and rust patches given a quick lick of paint or daubed with grease to prevent the problem worsening.

The process was not a quick one, but as steam engines had such a long life, it was generally

Withdrawn and facing the least palatable of futures, this pair of 4-4-2 tank engines Nos.41929/75 stand at Devons Road on 23rd July 1950. *Oliver Carter*

considered worthwhile as it was expected that they would eventually return to revenue-earning duties. Their durability and overall strength, was such that a visit to the works would make them good for another round of service. Yet it was not only those locomotives needing attention which went into store, but also many which were in perfectly good condition. They were, quite simply, not needed at the time due to a decline in traffic. Where it was expected for the availability or demand to return, locomotives were placed in store rather than being moved elsewhere - unless it happened to be a rogue engine or a bad steamer, which the Shed-foreman would then be quite glad to pass on to some other unsuspecting depot.

Scrapping an unwanted locomotive was generally not a process which was automatically considered, unless 'the powers above' had decreed it to be so. As a result, it was not uncommon to see locomotives in store for considerable periods of time. This situation was particularly noted with 'non-standard' types both after the grouping and again after 1948 - a typical example are the London Tilbury & Southend tank engines which we will meet later. Yet, by the early 1950s, this situation had changed considerably. Thereafter, rather than being an interlude before returning to service, a period of protracted store usually meant that an engine was bound for the scrap. True, in the first years most of these were old engines which should have been scrapped in the 1940s and had only been kept in service to meet the war traffic demands.

However, as the 1950s progressed, it became increasingly evident that engines which could have been restored to service were going into store as the first stage in the disposal system. As the accompanying photographs well illustrate, the vagaries facing locomotives in store were many. Some may have earned a temporary reprieve but, for most, the undignified shunt into a back road or a weed covered siding was the beginning of the end.

Meanwhile, other engines that had been taken out of revenue earning service continued to play a useful role in the life of their home depot. Such as ex-NBR Class N15 0-6-2T No.69128 which has found gainful employment in steam raising duties at St. Margaret's shed in July 1964.
John Corkhill

The Early Storage Dumps

FOR OVER A CENTURY and a quarter, there have been concentrations of out of service locomotives, or to use the vernacular ‘dumps’. Such dumps originated because large numbers of engines were ‘in store’, primarily because they were either redundant or in transit. Though the dumps mainly tended to be centred around the various locomotive works or depots, some were situated in isolated or unusual locations. One of the large works dumps was at Crewe, and those who have read the ‘Chronicles of Boulton’s Sidings’, by Alfred Rosling Bennett, will be familiar with the fact that Isaac Watt Boulton used to make regular visits there during the late 19th century. From there he would select old locomotives for complete rebuilding, and sometimes re-gauging, mostly for industrial use.

Some of these would get lost during transit and he would go out looking for them, others were actually driven down the cobbled streets into his Ashton-Under-Lyne works, a sight which must have caused a bit of a sensation if not hysteria at the time! However, probably the best example and record of a group of engines in store during the last century will be the massive dumps of broad gauge locomotives at Swindon after the GWR’s final conversion to 4’ 8½” gauge in 1892.

The next large concentration of dumped

An example of one of the early works dumps, pictured at Eastleigh with Nos.2224/6/3775 and three more sister engines in various stages of demolition. *John L Smith*

Ex-War Department locomotives returned to the Great Western at Swindon. These former Shropshire & Montogomery 0-6-0s wait disposal, with No.8236 at the front of the queue on 23rd August 1950.
Oliver Carter

locomotives appears to have been at the end of World War One, when hundreds of engines were returned from overseas service with the Railway Operating Department (a story which is more fully told in Atlantic's Britain's Railways At War series). On their return to England, usually via the Southampton or Richborough train ferries, many were in appalling state of repair. At this time there was already a huge number of locomotives needing drastic attention at the country's workshops, due to a backlog which had built up by the repeated deferal of non-essential maintenance. By 1919 the Railway Executive's short-sighted approach meant that just under 1,800 locomotives were stopped awaiting repairs, a fact which meant that all the overhaul work on these engines alone would not be completed until the end of 1921. The prognosis for the repatriated locomotives was much worse, and many remained in store until the grouping. The GWR for example were very reluctant to accept many of its 'loaned' engines back at all, and a large number of these went to scrap.

After the Second World War the situation was somewhat similar, with a large number of battered and bruised locomotives being returned from war service

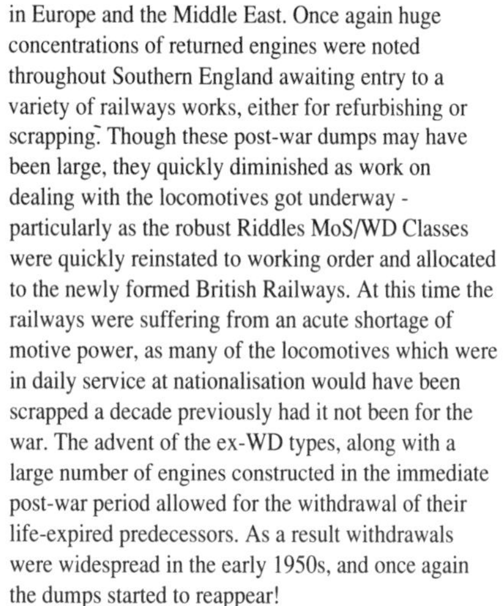

in Europe and the Middle East. Once again huge concentrations of returned engines were noted throughout Southern England awaiting entry to a variety of railways works, either for refurbishing or scrapping. Though these post-war dumps may have been large, they quickly diminished as work on dealing with the locomotives got underway - particularly as the robust Riddles MoS/WD Classes were quickly reinstated to working order and allocated to the newly formed British Railways. At this time the railways were suffering from an acute shortage of motive power, as many of the locomotives which were in daily service at nationalisation would have been scrapped a decade previously had it not been for the war. The advent of the ex-WD types, along with a large number of engines constructed in the immediate post-war period allowed for the withdrawal of their life-expired predecessors. As a result withdrawals were widespread in the early 1950s, and once again the dumps started to reappear!

'Unloved, unwanted, and nowhere to go', these four ex-LT&SR tank engines are pictured at the back of Durran Hill shed, in June 1954. Carlisle is a long way from home, but Nos.41971-4 had been consigned to Scotland, though they weren't wanted there either. They were sent back to Skipton, but as it happened the convoy of engines never got any further south than Carlisle, at least not until they went to the scrap.
Oliver Carter

Depots & Other Locations

A FAIRLY TYPICAL EXAMPLE of the early-1950s was to be found at Dukinfield on the Great Central line from Sheffield to Manchester [London Road], where a number of these engines which were stored on sidings off the main line. Not a large dump, only a line of locos tucked away at an odd location, tantalisingly just far enough away for the individual identities not to be discernable. Apparently, Gorton Works had an acute labour shortage at that time and were unable to cope with cutting. Withdrawals were exceeding the rate of disposal, and locomotives cluttered the works sidings to such an extent that it was difficult to move stock around the yard. This was remedied by despatching locomotives to Dukinfield, where men from the carriage works would strip off all the non-ferous fittings and remove the coupling rods. The maximum number of engines at any one time rarely exceeded ten, and all were usually returned to Gorton for cutting - two or three being towed back to the works at a time. Most were ex-LNER Classes J10, J11 and N5, though one interesting resident was the Metropolitan-Vickers Gas Turbine Co-Co, No.18100. On 8th February 1957, the following locomotives were noted there:- Nos.64431, 65182, 67431, 69270, 69277, 69318, 69345. The problems at Gorton stemmed back to 1955, when it was decided to send two engines per week to Darlington for scrapping. This situation certainly continued into 1957, and it is interesting to note that Doncaster Works had also adopted this pressure-relieving operation from time to time. A notable example were three Class S1s, Nos.69900/2/4, which went north in December 1955.

Perhaps the strangest small dump of this era was that at Durran Hill, the former Midland shed at Carlisle, where the sidings contained four 4-4-2Ts from the London, Tilbury & Southend section of the LMS (LMS Nos.2153-6). On nationalisation these Class 3Ps, now re-numbered 41971-4, were transferred to Dundee in January 1948. However, they were intensely disliked by the Scottish crews and by June they were heading back over the border. Officially transferred to Skipton (20F), they never progressed further south than Carlisle where they remained for almost seven years. Though Durran Hill's fitters carefully 'mothballed' them, they were essentially redundant. Thus, un-wanted, and a long way from their home-territory on the Thames Estuary, they were left to decay. Their sojourn was endured by another pre-Grouping locomotive, an L&YR Aspinall 3F No.52418, which had found its way to Durran Hill via Workington. On 10th February 1955, the 4-4-2Ts were towed to Derby, but no resurrection awaited them - only the cutter's torch during the month of March.

In passing, perhaps we should mention the stores at some of the Scottish sheds. At Arbroath, the small three-road shed was used between 1955-1958, though the inmates were constantly changing as locomotives left for Inverurie. During May 1955 the shed was host to Nos.55169/73, 55217, 55227, 62672/82/87/88, other members of the Director Class followed, with Nos.62673/4/80/4/6/7/9 all being noted. Dundee West was another location where engines were stored, the pigeons doing a good white-washing job for free!

To complete the picture of the middle part of this

The old for the new: As Class EM1 1500v DC Bo-Bo No.26023 emerges from Gorton Works as Class Y3 No.68164 prepares to go in for the last time.
Oliver Carter

The dump at Spondon where five ex-L&YR 2-4-2 tank engines are pictured on 25th July 1959. These engines were among a group that were shuffled from one location to another, the first being the back of Mirfield Shed in West Yorkshire - the last being Spondon, where the firm of A. Loom would ultimately dispose of these hard-working Aspinall engines.
Oliver Carter

With the build up of unwanted/out of service locomotives growing daily, the problems of space at some sheds became quite acute. This is the situation at Sheffield's Darnall shed on 28th February 1959, with Nos. 69294, 61761, 61747, 62668, 61728, 61760, 62664/7/70, 64746, 64804/8/78, 69258/86/90 69314 and 64388, whilst a number of others skulk inside.
N.E. Stead Collection

decade we will add just two more examples. In 1956, the back roads of Manchester's Trafford Park shed were filled with stored locos from the former CLC lines. Among those noted were Class J10s, Nos.65140/45/46/56/70, 65208; Class C13s, Nos.67400/13; Class N5, Nos.69274, 69332/58; Class D11, Nos.62661/5/8, several ex-LMS compounds, Nos.41066, 41116/23/50/59/63/68; and a solitary Class C14, No.67449. The emergence of this dump was presumably due to a lack of duties and the afore-mentioned situation at Gorton - by 1957 this total had increased to nearly 30 locos. Meanwhile, at Llandudno Junction shed, quite a selection of 2Ps and compounds had been put in store; including Nos.40495, 40548/49/80/89/671; 40925, 41086/93, 41106/11/19/20/24/53/57/58/64, some of which were in a very sorry state. However, the decree had been issued to rid BR of the 4-4-0s and the older Classes of locomotives as a part of the progressive introduction of the 999 standard locomotives which had been ordered as part of the 1955 Modernisation Plan.

After 1957 this policy was gradually beginning to have a pronounced affect, as the withdrawals of older locomotives accelerated. Shed closures were also beginning to produce a knock-on effect, with the storage lines swelling as condemned locomotives started to accumulate at the works. An example of how this affected the motive power situation was seen in Sheffield. When Millhouses shed closed, most of 41C's allocation went to the more modern shed at Darnall, but a large number of engines became surplus to requirement. Coupled with the fact that there was a general decline in freight after the 1956-7 Suez Crisis, more and more engines slid quietly into the store sidings. This lack of work was not just confined to freight types, but passenger locomotives such as Directors, Patriots and Jubilees also went into store at Darnall. As the shed roads gradually filled up, a number of locomotives were eventually removed to create room. Many were sent to Staveley, where a dump was established; in October 1958 engines stored there included Nos.62660/1/5/6/9, 63581, 63621/4/48/61/82/5, 63702/20/71/87/90, 63882.

To solve the problem of over-crowding at the operational depots, a number of less well-used locations were identified as points where supplies of surplus locos could be concentrated. One such location was Staveley, and large numbers of engines from the Sheffield area were dumped here, including several of those pictured opposite.
N.E. Stead Collection

The Large Dumps Emerge

IT IS DIFFICULT TO say precisely when the large dumps began to form, but early in 1959 a large build-up of ex-GNR Class 02s had formed at Doncaster South shed, with Nos.63939/41-3/54/6/63-4/7/9/81/3/4 together with Class J39s, Nos.64876, 64981 all being present by 12th April. A similar situation was taking place at other depots, particularly Plaistow and Rugby. During the latter 1958 preliminary discussions had taken place between BR and several scrap merchants, as the railway works began to buckle under the strain. Consequently, much of this redundant stock was moved to little-used sidings or disused branches, in preparation for their despatch the private yards which would take the burden. To categorically pin-point the first real dump is difficult, but that at Heapley (near Horwich) must have been one of the fore-runners. Locomotives were sent there in December 1958, and the last one left sometime early 1962. The list in Appendix 1 summarises the main occupants but it may not be complete.

The real turning point was in mid-1959, as the build up of withdrawn locomotives at Crewe and Derby was proving too much. At Derby, the timber sidings at Spondon Junction and Turntable Sidings at Chaddesden were having to be used to accommodate condemned stock. Crewe decided to use the old Over and Wharton branch near Winsford for storage purposes, whilst it is presumed that Badnall's Wharf at Stafford was similarly intended to ease the situation at Derby. By March both these sites were filling up, though many of the engines were slowly being disposed of by being put out to tender to the scrap industry. The Winsford site was relatively short lived, and though engines continued to arrive there until May 1959, by the following February the merchants had taken full delivery. At least 35 occupants were ex-LNWR 0-8-0s as well as 11 LT&SR 4-4-2Ts, as will be seen from Appendix 2.

The Badnall's Wharf dump was situated roughly two miles north of Norton Bridge, adjacent to the West Coast Main line and therefore conveniently placed to the south of Crewe. Most of the early arrivals were marshalled on sidings off the down lines, but later four others were occupied on the upside. Locomotives were constantly being removed as new arrivals came in, but (even so) the dump lasted into the middle of 1960. The initial residents included a dozen ex-L&YR types, 8 2-4-2 Aspinall Tanks, two 0-6-0ST and two 0-6-0 3F Tender engines; the tanks going en-bloc to Looms of Spondon. The remainder were of the Midland variety, Fowler tanks, Compounds and no less than 18 Johnson 3Fs. During October 1959 a Sentinel 0-4-0T, No.47191, arrived from Radstock on the Somerset & Dorset Joint. The removal of No.43613 to Scotland seems, in retrospect, to have been a strange move but the 3F's price must have warranted it. Sightings of at least 44 different engines were recorded but there could have been more, disposal details (where known) are given in Appendix 3.

To conclude that there were no more significant dumps in England and Wales would be wrong for, following the mass withdrawals which had commenced during September 1962, a number of locations were used for often extended periods of time as 'temporary stores'. In order to understand why this problem had assumed such significant proportions, we need to recall that at the time the Western Region had approximately 340 engines in store. Though BR's objective was to drastically reduce this figure, by the following autumn the tally had risen to 478 as dieselisation took hold. Traditionally, concentrations of redundant 'Western' engines were gathered at Swindon, but large dumps were already beginning to build up in South Wales. Stored locomotives awaiting disposal in the Principality were gathering at Briton Ferry and Barry shed, but these locations were not unique as numerous loco depots had their share of condemned stock on view.

The Eastern Region was in a similar state, and at Stratford both the works and the shed were full to the brim with 'dead' engines. To alleviate the problems which this caused, several depots, including Southend and Shoeburyness, were utilised to store the overfill. Around the same period the London Midland Region had about 500 engines in store, and the situation at Derby was becoming a controller's nightmare. We have already mentioned the dumps at Spondon Junction and Chaddesden, but these were quickly filled and several locomotives from Spondon had to be moved to Chellaston Quarry. Two storage lines had also been created behind Derby Station, with about 10 locos held in the St. Andrews Goods Yard. In addition over a dozen locos were stored by the side of the main line to the south of the city. Movements here are too complicated to list, and it was only the mass sales to the breakers which restored order. Though this might appear to have addressed the issue, by October 1963 over 242 redundant locomotives were still in store.

Meanwhile, in Scotland, stored engines were being shuffled around like playing cards. The Edinburgh depots were moving stock to Longniddry, Bathgate and Polmont, whilst Forfar was being used as a dumping ground for engines en-route to Inverurie

However as time passed by, even the interim dumping sites were too small and so additional areas were identified. One such location was the old Winsford & Over branch, where ex-LT&SR tank engines are seen on 31st May 1959. These being Nos. 41939/41/6/78.
Oliver Carter

Up in Scotland an appreciable dump was situated at Hurlford, and many of its early inmates were 4-4-0 types. On 22nd August 1960, Nos.440593/7 are seen languishing with a third (unidentified) member of the class.
Oliver Carter

It was much the same story around the great London sheds, but here the shortage of space was often critical and engines were quickly moved on. One location which held on to some of the withdrawn engines for a while was Southall MPD, where No.5041 *Tiverton Castle* is seen on 8th March 1964.
Gerald T. Robinson

Works. The Glasgow district was initially using outposts such as Greenock, Parkhead and Kipps, but a more permanent solution was clearly needed. By April 1961 a suitable site was selected at Bo'ness, where two long sidings were made available, essentially to clear the sheds in the Glasgow North district. It was estimated that over 100 locos would be sent to Bo'ness during 1962, but actually only about 85 appear to have been received. Before entering Bo'ness harbour, Polmont depot stripped the locomotives of all their backhead fittings in order to prevent petty theft of the valuable scrap. For most of the period in which the dump operated, dead locomotives were moved by the Bo'ness shunter, D3557. Two of the first residents were Pickersgill 4-4-0 3P's, Nos.54475/83. These had been stored at St. Rollox for 10 years, together with No.54474 which went to Arnott & Young's yard at Carmyle in February 1960. By November 1961 the dump housed two Black Fives, Nos.44956/77, possibly the first two Scottish members of the Class to go into store, however the following March they earned a reprieve when they were called into St. Rollox for overhaul. Numerically speaking, the largest Class to pass through the dump were the V1s, but possibly the most notable engines were three ex-GCR Class D11 Directors, Nos.62689/91/93 and No.62496 *Glen Loy*. A McIntosh 3F 0-6-0, No.56370, was sent in error and quickly removed! Those locomotives which are known to have been at Bo'ness are listed in Appendix 4 with disposal details. By the end of October 1963 only Nos.62031 and 62052 remained, these were cut up at Cowlairs Works the following March.

One cannot discuss Scottish dumps without mentioning the strangest one of all, that at Carnbrae sidings. This was situated to the south east of Glasgow at the terminus of the former NBR line from Coatbridge to Bothwell. Some 35 locos were dumped there, mainly from Polmadie and Motherwell sheds. With the exception of one ex-LNER loco., No.68717, all were of Caley origin. An eerie sight, rusting engines dumped in a mass of waist high vegetation, weeds and small trees together with old bolster wagons in an isolated location looking forgotten and neglected. What a pity it couldn't have been ignored by the authorities for a decade! Unfortunately it wasn't, and all the engines were gradually taken away to Arnott & Young's, Connell's, etc., leaving just a memory. It is believed that the following list presents a complete record between March 1962 and the end of that year when the sidings were cleared:- 0-4-4T 2Ps Nos.55201/20/65/67-8; 0-6-0Ts, Nos.56298, 56313/56; 0-6-0 2Fs, Nos.57239/68/71/88/92, 57303/17/19/21/25/63/67/69/89, 57417-8/36/61/63; 0-6-0 3Fs, Nos.57563/64/93, 57632/59/63/65; 0-6-0T Class J72, No.68717.

To complete the Scottish section we should not forget the other smaller dump on the former Glasgow & South Western at Lugton East Junction, where locomotives arrived mainly from Corkerhill (67A). Though this is probably not a complete inventory, Nos.40620/1, 42144, 42268/76, 45458, 45621/65, 45707/11/20, 55206/25/66, were all noted as being stored there. The Jubilees were sent to G.H. Campbell's scrapyards at Shieldhall and Airdrie during November 1963, whilst the Caley engines and the 2Ps went to Connell's at Calder.

At the back of Stockport Shed there always seemed to a motley assortment of stored engines, and it was always worth a visit - that was if you could manage to wangle yourself in. On 21st October 1963 Class 6P5F 4-6-0 Jubilee *De Robeck* awaits a decision on its future, but already bits have started to disappear. The engine was finally scrapped at Taylor Bros.
Keith S. E. Till

At Lostock Hall, one of the last bastions of steam working on British Railways, the end has finally drawn nigh. It is 11th August 1968, and at least two dozens engines have been condemned to death. The coal from their tenders litters the ground alongside, whilst chalk marks indicate 'COND' on their sides. Marks of affection scribbled all over the engines show that in the hearts of the enthusiasts, steam still lives. *Atlantic Collection*

The scrap line at another North-west stronghold in November 1967, as D7640 drifts past Carlisle's Upperby shed on a local freight trip. In the background Nos.41264, 44932 (now preserved), 45262 and 75027 all stand in the disposal line. *Peter W. Robinson*

THE TORCH

THE DESIGN AND CONSTRUCTION of a steam locomotive demanded skill, precision, method and a certain amount of pride. Its scrapping, by comparison, was brutally simple and not without macabre overtones.

There were, of course, a few basic rules to follow but, generally, two or three men armed with heavy duty torches, a sledgehammer or two, four or five dozen cylinders of oxygen and a couple of hundred pounds of propane, could reduce a once proud Pacific, barely cold from traffic, to a dozen wagonfuls of assorted scrap metal in something under a week.

It was usually piecework so the men worked fast. Arduous and filthy, the job was not without its hazards: from blue asbestos boiler lagging, flying splinters of steel and globules of molten metal. The accumulation of grease and oil on an engine's moving parts could cause spurts of molten metal so most scrapmen got rid of it by the simple expedient of setting it on fire, with spectacular results.

It was, of course, the non-ferrous content of an engine that paid the bills. The copper firebox was the real prize — at about 2½ tons this was a valuable item, representing at 1966 prices a selling scrap value of about £1300, and it was the rise in the price of copper (by some 75% in 1966 alone), that probably more than any other factor encouraged more and more private yards to bid for BR steam locomotives. Photographs of yards taken in the Sixties show rows of salvaged fireboxes neatly lined up ready for despatch, in marked contrast to the chaos of ferrous scrap and each representing a sale price more than enough to pay a workman's wages for a full year.

Smaller non-ferrous fittings on a locomotive could amount to something approaching the weight of the firebox and, usually easily accessible, they were rapidly stripped. The ferrous content — the engine's basic structure (frames, boiler, smokebox, cylinder blocks, etc) — was at once both more time consuming to cut up and financially much less valuable. Detailed methods varied from yard to yard but the end result had to be the same: pieces of scrap metal about 5′ x 1′6″, sized to fit the scrap pans at the steel works. Axles, their wheels cut off, made conveniently sized scrap charges, large driving wheels often had to be burned through, chimneys were usually left on the smokebox while boiler tubes left the scrapyard in bundles like drinking straws. Small fittings and dismembered fragments piled in confusion, their origin and purpose a mystery and fascination to those muddy-booted enthusiasts fortunate enough to gain access to these private places.

Behind their walls, one of the most bizarre and fascinating episodes in British railway history unfolded, unseen by almost everyone.

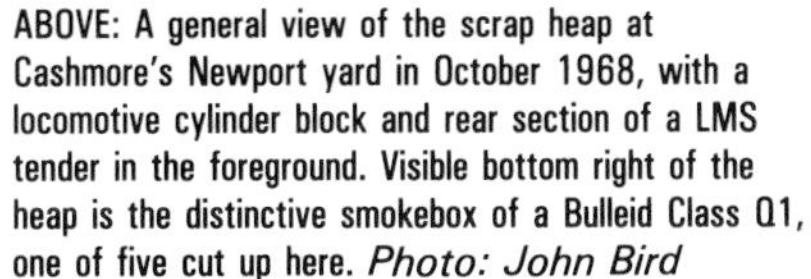

ABOVE: A general view of the scrap heap at Cashmore's Newport yard in October 1968, with a locomotive cylinder block and rear section of a LMS tender in the foreground. Visible bottom right of the heap is the distinctive smokebox of a Bulleid Class Q1, one of five cut up here. *Photo: John Bird*

LEFT: The debris of a locomotive scrapyard, photographed in August 1968. One of Edge Hill's Class 8F 2-8-0s, No.48249, looms over a bizarre collection of engine 'bits' and oxygen cylinders at Newport – one of the two yards of J. Cashmore Ltd which played a significant part in the mass scrappings of the 1960's. *Photo: John Bird*

TOP: At the BR scrapyard at Darlington Works on 11th February 1961 stands the hulk of LNER Class L1 2-6-4T No.67711, her cab dumped on her running plate. Notice that the bunker is still full: this was discouraged by BR as full coal stocks on 16,000 withdrawn locomotives amounted to a considerable expense but it was laborious and awkward to get out. A private yard would doubtless have salvaged it. *Photo: Ken Hoole*

ABOVE: A reminder that the destruction of the steam railway also involved the cutting up of many thousands of coaches. This is LNER articulated twin E1715E/E1716E, built in 1937 for the Coronation streamlined train, awaiting scrapping at Hull on 5th June 1963. The scrapman is only interested in their metal content: seats, panelling and unsalvageable fittings will be burnt off and the intense heat will be enough to melt the windows, leaving nothing except the steel frames and bogies, ready for the torch. *Photo: Ken Hoole*

Chapter Three

The BR Works

FOR WELL OVER A century, the traditional means of disposing of redundant, obsolete or life-expired locomotives or rolling stock was in a railway workshop. Prior to the Grouping of 1923 each company handled its own disposal, though not all the locomotives were cut up, as many hundreds were still quite serviceable. In an attempt to extract every last penny out of their investment, the companies sold off many of their redundant engines, for rebuilding and/or industrial use. These traditional methods served them well, so much so that it was only after 1923 and the subsequent rationalisation implemented by the 'Big Four' that significant changes were noted.

Thereafter a degree of centralisation was in evidence, as the GWR, LNER, LMS and SR began to dispose of their unwanted stock through specific works. Even so, many of the pre-Group locomotives were still cut up at their birth place and this trend continued down through nationalisation. For example on the LNER, North Eastern types were still cut up at Darlington, whilst GNR engines went to Doncaster and Great Eastern locomotives to Stratford. A parallel situation existed at the constituent works of the LMS and GWR, with only the Southern partially centralising its disposal system.

This position changed somewhat after 1948, and by the late 1950s 'foreign' locomotives in the scrap lines at BR works were becoming increasingly common. Thereafter, some classes travelled to workshops a considerable distance from their birth place in order to meet their end. During the modernisation years of 1955-65 the following BR loco works were involved in disposing of steam engines.

ex-GWR works	ex-SR works	ex-LMS works	ex-LNER works
Barry	Ashford	Crewe	Cowlairs
Caerphilly	Brighton	Derby	Darlington
Swindon	Eastleigh	Horwich	Doncaster
Wolver'ton	Ryde	Kilmarnock	Gorton
		St. Rollox	Inverurie
			Stratford

Additionally, some engines were also cut up at Halbeath Wagon Works, Dunfermline and the BR Carriage & Wagon Works at Heatheryknowe, Glasgow.

In the early 1950s, when the number of locomotives in BR ownership stood at around the

ABOVE: The last hours of 'Big Bertha'. The unique MR 0-10-0, No.58100, was designed and built for use as the Lickey Incline banker and had a working life of 37 years commencing in 1919. Here she is being cut up at Derby Works on 1st July 1956. A cylinder from this celebrated engine was supposed to have been preserved at Derby Works but all trace of it has long since been lost. *Photo: Gavin Morrison*

RIGHT: As the rate of withdrawals increased most BR works experienced serious problems with storage of dead engines and they overflowed beyond the works' boundaries into any available siding. In the Derby area large silent groups of rusting engines began to collect at Chellaston Quarry and Spondon. The former location is seen here on 10th April 1960 with a number of MR Johnson Class 3 0-6-0s, including Nos.43587/43237, in the foreground. Johnson 0-4-4T No.58065 and Fowler 2-6-4T No.42341 are also visible and in the distance are two Midland Compounds: Nos.40493/40534, which were stored for almost a year following withdrawal from Nottingham shed in July 1959. *Photo: H. N. James*

RIGHT: This view was taken at Crewe Works on 31st May 1947. LNWR 4-4-0 No.25373 *Ptarmigan* was one of the last three surviving engines of the 90-strong George V Class, built 1910-15, none of which carried a BR number. The last survivor was scrapped the following year. Also visible is a withdrawn LNWR Webb 0-6-0 Coal Engine, No.28100, a survivor of the 500-strong class which became extinct in 1953. *Photo: H. C. Casserley, Millbrook House Collection*

BELOW: The major overflow site of withdrawn engines despatched to Crewe Works was the Winsford and Over branch. On Sunday 27th September 1959 a number of veterans were there awaiting their fate: 0-6-2Ts Nos.41982, 41983, 41991 and 41992 were members of a 14-strong class built by the London, Tilbury & Southend Railway and the Midland between 1903 and 1912, while 4-4-2T No.41945 was also of LT&SR design, perpetuated by the Midland. *Photo: Gavin Morrison*

20,000 mark, withdrawals were comparatively light and largely compensated for by the new constructions. Due to the comparative longevity of most steam engines, it was often common to find some ancient locomotive in the process of dignified dismantling - a policy which contrasted starkly with what was to follow later. Generally, a dismembered engine standing in a works scrapyard would usually command little attention from the work-force, though a visiting enthusiast may be tempted to look for some form of identification if the cab and smokebox had disappeared. This was usually best done by searching out the stamp marks on the rods or slide bars, but often the whole macabre scene was like some giant jigsaw puzzle. The bits might be left lying around for months, probably scattered over a wide area, and this undoubtedly provided the privileged few with a unique opportunity. If there is a fascination for scrapped engines, it undoubtedly has its roots in the works yards, for even if they were hard to gain access to, they were far 'easier' than the private yards that followed.

During any works visit it could be a real highlight to disappear round to the scrapyard or wander along

THE MORTAL REMAINS OF an A3 Pacific stand at the rear of BR Cowlairs Works, Glasgow, on 30th August 1966. No.60041 *Salmon Trout* had been a St Margarets (Edinburgh) engine since July 1960 and was taken out of service in November 1965, the penultimate A3 to go. After arrival at Cowlairs the previous month she has been stripped of serviceable parts including her boiler (repaired, despatched to Darlington Works, and fitted to preserved A3 *Flying Scotsman*), before movement to Arnott Young's Carmyle yard for final extinction. She was survived in service for a few weeks by the last working A3 of all – No.60052 *Prince Palatine*, also from 64A.
Photo: N. E. Preedy

the disposal lines; leaving fellow enthusiasts fawning over the newer or refurbished machines which were on display. In this way it was not unusual to find a rare 'cop', an elusive locomotive from some far flung outpost of the railway system which had previously been just a number in our ABC books. Often it was possible to find the last member of a particular class unceremoniously pushed into a siding awaiting 'the call', looking for all the world as though it had been forgotten by the authorities. Those of us who took time to linger in these parts of the works were often given 'sympathetic looks' by our contemporaries, but to us it was just as important to see the last rites of an engine as it was to witness the out-shopping. It is impossible to present a complete picture of the work undertaken in all these yards as, for example Swindon, some work's disposal statistics would fill a book in their own right. However, we would like to take our readers into areas of the works which many never visited, presenting an over-view of both the scrap yards and the dumps.

ABOVE: The forty-five Class A8 tanks, Gresley 4-6-2T rebuilds of Raven's Class H1 4-4-4Ts – the NER's largest passenger tanks – were withdrawn between 1957 and 1960. The pioneer engine of the class, No.69850, must have been a good example as she was amongst the last batch to be condemned: eleven engines of the class going in June 1960. Two months later, on 14th August, she was already succumbing to the cutter's torch at Darlington Works, forty-seven years after building, 26½ years after rebuilding.
Photo: Brian Webb, via Ken Hoole

RIGHT: Another NER design in its last hours: this is Class D20 4-4-0 No.62387 at Darlington Works on 1st December 1957, some three months after withdrawal. She was one of the last six members of this famous Worsdell design to remain in service: Nos.62375, 62381, 62387, 62395, 62396, once regulars on Newcastle-Alnmouth workings, leaving Alnmouth shed for the last time that year. They had each served for almost exactly half a century.
Photo: Ken Hoole

THE GWR WORKS

SWINDON WORKS

AS THE MAIN WORKSHOPS for the Great Western Railway (and later the Western Region) Swindon, throughout its history, bore the main responsibility for the disposal of that railway's engines. The most significant scrapping work was witnessed in the late 1800s, with the change over from broad to standard gauge when the works were presented with huge dumps of redundant locomotives. The same situation was experienced in 1919/20, with large quantities of stock being returned by the ROD. after overseas service during World War I. If the truth is told, the GWR were not particularly keen to see these engines return, so many languished for a considerable time before disposal. A similar build-up of redundant locomotives was experienced after the Second World War, but this time the carnage was amongst the ancient classes which had been reprieved at the outbreak of hostilities in 1939. By 1945 most of these were, to quote one former Swindon manager, 'running wrecks' - though it is doubtful if many could run at all! The works had no sooner cleared the backlog, than the withdrawals began in earnest. The early 1950s were an interesting period at Swindon, with many of the pre-Grouping tank engines of Welsh origin being consigned to extinction.

'C' Shop at the west end of the works had opened in 1932, and thereafter acted as a focal point for cutting operations. There was always a large number of condemned locomotives in the vicinity, most of which were usually visible from the main line. By the late 1950s 'C' Shop was becoming increasingly busy as the first of the GWR standard classes were withdrawn. Then, in the early 1960s 28xxs, Castles, Halls, Granges, Kings and Counties arrived in force. In addition, dozens of tank engines and smaller tender locos were also disposed of. One of the features of a visit to the works at this time, was trying to determine whether a particular engine was in store or actually condemned and awaiting cutting. The main yard, dump, stock shed, turntable area and sidings behind the erecting shop all held prospective candidates - some awaiting a decision, others simply in store. Bits of locomotives which had met their end could be found scattered around 'C' shop, as might be expected, but also near 'A' shop and the Old Barn.

As we shall see elsewhere, it fell to Swindon to become the first BR works to despatch steam locomotives to a private scrapyard for disposal. This first batch left the Works at 5.20am on 25th March 1959, as a 'dead engine movement' - bound, appropriately enough, to Woodham's at Barry though few observers at the time would have appreciated the significance which we can see in retrospect. Thereafter the Works were regularly used as the assembling point for convoys of dead engines, all awaiting despatch to the scrapyards of South Wales. Accordingly, even engines which had been shunted outside 'C' Shop could be destined for one last journey, as opposed to the more immediate fate that appeared to face them within. As time went on, other Swindon locations were also used for storage; including the Gas Works Sidings, Stock Shed, the field end of the main yard, and the sidings to the north end of the works alongside the Gloucester line.

As might be imagined, the enthusiast wishing to collect information was hard pressed to gather it, and this has made our endeavours much harder; although we do have a fairly complete record of the engines which were gathered at Swindon for disposal. In the absence of any official records, to determine which locomotives were cut at Swindon, we have had to eliminate those which went to the private yards. Unlike many other works, Swindon continued cutting after the private scrap merchants became involved. The victims were predominantly of Western origin, but LMS types such as 'Jinties', 'Crabs', Ivatt 2-6-0s and even a 4F met their end here - a long way from home. During the summer of 1964 a batch of LNER V2s arrived for cutting - a rather curious occurrence worthy of note: the correct numbers of these engines were 60809/12/33/56/87 and 60904/16/22/5/32/41/5/64/75, and not as quoted in the original books. As a matter of interest, some of the tenders from these engines were reclaimed and sent to Eastleigh Works for conversion - snowploughs being the principle use.

Why Swindon had begun cutting up 'foreigners' is something of a mystery, but one former member of the disposal team writes that this was 'because they were so good at disposing with their own stock, they gradually ran out of work - rather than lay men off, the cutting of locomotives was undertaken on behalf of other regions!' Whatever the case, by May 1965 all the loco disposals were out to private tender. Thereafter the role of 'C' Shop was reduced to cutting up cranes, wagons and other redundant vehicles, and this remained the pattern until the older diesel classes began arriving on the scene.

The Swindon Scrapyard on 23rd September 1962, with No.6008 *King James 11* awaiting its final movement. Already the front bogie has been attacked, but the name-plates are still extant.
Gerald T. Robinson

ABOVE: A general view of the 'dump' behind the Great Western's Swindon Works. Photos of the Swindon scrap lines taken in the 1960's are common but this early view shows a number of vintage 4-4-0s whose passing was rarely recorded. In the foreground are Flower Class Nos.4163 *Marigold* and 4172 *Gooch*, the latter engine a most interesting rebuild which originated as Broad Gauge Convertible No.8 of 1894. The view is undated but the engines were both withdrawn in April 1929. Withdrawn members of the 100 Robinson ROD 2-8-0s purchased by the GWR 1919-25 are also visible: the 25 engines of Lot 240 being taken out of traffic 1927-30 after as little as 28 months service – interesting proof that failure to exploit fully an engine's working lifespan was not confined to the 1960's. *Photo: Millbrook House Collection*

OPPOSITE, TOP: This later view of the same location shows Class 850 0-6-0ST No.1925 and Bulldog 4-4-0 No.3447 *Jackdaw*, both withdrawn in April 1951. The little Wolverhampton-built tank was one of only 17 of the large class not to be modified to pannier tank and in concert with only 21 of the class passed into BR ownership. She went on to outlast all her sisters to become the very last traditional GWR saddle tank in traffic, with a working life of almost 68 years. No.3447 was also very much a survivor. The days when almost every English depot of the GWR had an allocation of Bulldogs had long since gone: only 34 of these pretty 4-4-0s lasted into Nationalisation and only four outlived *Jackdaw*. *Photo: P. B. Whitehouse, Millbrook House Collection*

OPPOSITE, BOTTOM: Four 0-6-0 tanks of fascinating pedigree at Swindon for scrap in August 1953. From right: Burry Port & Gwendraeth Valley Railway saddle tank No.5 (GWR No.2195) once named *Cwm Mawr*, GWR 0-6-0Ts Nos.2135 and 2122 of Wolverhampton-built Class 2021; and GWR Class 1076 No.1287. This latter engine dated from January 1878, was built as a saddle tank, rebuilt as pannier in 1925 and had been used as a stationary boiler at Newbury and Leamington for several years following withdrawal from traffic in April 1946. She was the very last double-framed GWR 0-6-0 tank in service and was finally cut up in October 1953 after a working life stretching from the age of the wooden-walled ship of the line to that of the nuclear missile. *Photo: Peter Hay*

1925
34 47

E 10372

ABOVE: By the 1960's, scrappings at Swindon included all the famous standard classes, many engines being of BR origin to GWR design. This line up of condemned stock on 23rd September 1962 is typical of the scene. Class 42XX 2-8-0T No. 4235 had arrived from Newport (Ebbw Junction) shed the month before and will be cut up in October, and a sister engine – almost certainly No. 4293 from the same shed – stands behind her. Also visible are a Class 73XX Mogul, a Castle and a Hall while a 14XX tank and Class 57XX pannier No. 5758 (in store and despatched to Cashmore's Newport yard a few weeks later) are visible in the distance. The hulk on the right is Class 51XX 2-6-2T No. 5187.
Photo: G. T. Robinson

LEFT: A reminder that 'foreign' locomotives were cut up at most BR works. ON Swindon dump on 6th September 1964 were LMS 'Crab' 2-6-0 (now a 2-4-0) No. 42760 and LNER Class V2 2-6-2s.
Photo: W. Potter.

BARRY WORKS

IN THE *STEAM FOR SCRAP* story, the name Barry is synonymous with the private scrapyards, particularly that of Woodham Brothers. However, whilst most enthusiasts tend to associate the majority of Western Region disposals with Swindon, the works at Barry were also a traditional dumping ground for withdrawn engines. In the pre-Grouping days a good deal of cutting went on here, but by and large the vast majority of small tank engines that were consigned to Barry still had useful lives; accordingly many were sold off into industrial use. A lot of ex-Barry Railway engines went this way, and the eventual destinations of these locomotives was both wide and varied.

After the Grouping, Barry became a dumping ground or concentration point for dead engines, the majority of which were then moved on to the huge scrapyard at Swindon Works. Just how many locomotives were cut at Barry after 1923 is something of a mystery, but the work appears to have been carried out with a sort of spasmodic regularity. A number of tanks engines from the Welsh valleys disappeared into the works for the last time in the post-World War Two period. Many of these were completely scrapped, though the boilers of some were carefully removed and retained for steam-heating duties elsewhere. Just five engines were disposed of in the 1950s, the last being 14XX Class 0-4-2T No.1461 in 1958. The following year Woodham Bros. commenced operations and their first cutting-up site was on a single siding just behind the BR Works.

CAERPHILLY WORKS

IN MANY WAYS, THE story of loco-disposal at Caerphilly is similar to that of Barry. The operation was always limited, and during the 1950s Caerphilly was probably cutting up just one or two engines each year. Between July 1957 and December 1962 the figures showed a modest increase, and about 30 locomotives were disposed of. These were mostly tank engine classes which were condemned after entering the works for repair; a good number of which were accident victims. Sometimes, engines which Barry Works had determined as being beyond economic repair were forwarded to Caerphilly for cutting, No.1141 in June 1952 and No.5792 in December 1956 being specific examples. In the early 1960s two dozen Western engines were cut up, but the actual breaking often took quite some time. For example, the frames of Nos.1143, 2213, and 9737 laid around for over a year before being finally reduced to scrap in 1961. The peak year was 1962 when 16 locomotives were disposed of, but by this time the private breakers had taken over much of the work. As a consequence operations ceased in 1963, with Nos.3719 and 8478 being the last victims.

Demolition at Barry prior to the days of Dai Woodham, with No.1368 sitting in the breakers' yard at Barry Works.
G. F. Balmer

WOLVERHAMPTON WORKS

Finally, before moving onto the LMS workshops, we will look at Wolverhampton Works which was second in importance to Swindon in the disposal of GWR engines. However, with the Western Region only cutting up 35 locomotives in the West Midlands in the period 1950-63, Swindon's dominance in the field is clear. Stafford Road mainly cut up tank locos but they also managed the occasional tender engine, notably 2-8-0s No.2850 in 1960 and No.2855 in February 1963. The following year saw the end of disposals at the works as only four engines were cut up, but these included two Halls - *Littleton Hall* and *Stanley Hall.*

Condemned at Caerphilly, the work on demolishing No.1404 is well advanced on 5th April 1956, just seven weeks after the engines was withdrawn. Once again, please note the orderly process of scrapping the engine.
The late Eric Mountford

THE LMS WORKS

CREWE WORKS

THE MASSIVE CREWE COMPLEX was arguably the most organised BR Works, where the management instilled a superb quality of structure-related performance which was clearly evident in almost every department. This orderly arrangement even permeated down to the scrapyard, and it was unusual to find locomotives in the process of being cut up in any location other than that around the old steel works. This area was some distance from the main offices, and was reached by a long walk alongside the access lines. Adjacent to the foundry stood a tall steel building in which locomotives were unceremoniously cut up, and for many it was the first port of call on a works visit. Condemned engines were lined up outside for all to see, but the dark interior largely concealed the terrible things which went on within. However, the flickering sparks from the cutters' torches would occasionally provide brief glimpses of two or three engines in various stages of dismemberment.

Over the years Crewe had performed its fare share of cutting up, principally old LNWR types, but later dismantling a variety of LMS standard classes. The last remnants of the LNWR fleet were dealt with during the 1940s and 50s, with the Class G2 0-8-0s particularly evident. Attention was then turned to other types, like the LMS Garratts which were disposed of in a relatively short period. A typical feature of some 'condemned' locomotives sent to Crewe, were the temporary reprieves they unexpectedly found. It was not uncommon for such engines to find a month or two's employment doing odd shunting duties before finally trundling into the scrap lines - it was almost as though every last bit of life was being squeezed out before they were finally given up for dead.

During the 1960s the sights became more dismal, as a host of express passenger types were vanquished. Forty-one Patriots went this way, accompanied by 57 Jubilees, 45 Royal Scots, 17 Coronations and 9 Princess Royals which Crewe went on to swallow up. Smaller tender engines and tanks followed at an alarming pace, at times at a rate of 20 locos per month. Perversely it was not just life-expired machines that went, but also some which had many years of service left in them. One example which comes to mind is a Patriot transferred to Sheffield Darnall from Millhouses; this was condemned the same day as refurbishment (including restaying the firebox) was completed. The shed staff were totally shocked, but off the engine went to Crewe. Among the very last steam locomotives scrapped at Crewe were Nos.45306 and 45327 (April), 70007 (July) and 44673 (August), all in 1965.

Inside the dim interior of Crewe Works, No.58921 stands in the cutting up shop, the former steel works, on 14th August 1951. The ex-LNWR 0-6-2 'Coal Tank' is illuminated by streaks of light filtering in through the broken corrugated iron sheeting, almost basking in the last hours of its retirement before it meets its end.
Oliver Carter

The end of a great lady, as No.46205 *Princess Victoria* stands outside Crewe works in her final days. No reprieve will be possible, so the superb engine will only ever make one more rail journey - ignominiously cut into bits and dumped into steel mineral wagons - on its way to the smelting hearth.
John Corkhill

Another main line high-flyer, Patriot Class No.45511 *Isle of Man* seen inside the works, its tender already stripped away as the demolition process begins.
John Corkhill

DERBY WORKS

Demolition Derby-style, with Nos.58045 and 41001 under the first stage of scrapping on 28th October 1951. The Compound has already been deprived of her tender, and the boiler cladding has been riven away - the future is all too obvious.
Oliver Carter

THE STRANGE THING ABOUT Derby Works was the fact that, although there were always dozens of locomotives stored out of use in the works yard and on sidings within a mile or so's radius, it was rare to see more than three or four actually being cut up at a time. Readers have confirmed that it was common practice to dismantle engines in the main fitting and erecting shops, when they were deemed beyond economical overhaul. This might explain why so many locomotives were never observed in the course of dismantling, they simply disappeared during routine stripping for general overhaul.

One basic plot of land was set aside for cutting, an area surrounded by a formidable steel fence with sharp, rusty spikes - giving rise to the nickname 'Spike Island'. There were two tracks in use but these were never cluttered with engines, as in some other works' scrapyards. Two or three engines at a time was par for the course, with a rake of wagons or skips marshalled alongside to collect the scrap. Incidentally, the same site was later to be used for the disposal of diesel locomotives.

Derby progressively scrapped a large amount of stock, mainly ex-Midland and LMS types; 2Ps, Compounds, 1Fs and the like. The busy years were the late 1950s and early 1960s, and the most common 'victims' were the LMS 2-6-2 and 2-6-4 tanks of Classes 2, 3, and 4, along with a few 'Crabs'. About this time condemned locomotives were also being stored and cut up in the main yard, adjacent to the diesel engine testing shop. Yet, despite the extra cutting area, Derby could hardly make any impression on the massive influx of redundant steam engines that arrived there during the onset of dieselisation. Consequently many of the stored engines were soon being sent to private yards in the North Midlands and South Yorkshire. This change of policy brought about the gradual demise of steam scrapping at Derby and the work was finished by the end of 1963. However, this was not with out the surprise arrival of a number of ex-LNER 04s, including No.63881 in August.

Unique Midland Railway 0-10-0, No.58100 awaits its turn in the demolition line. The great engine had given so many years of service up the Lickey Incline, it had literally reached the end of the road. The huge cylinders were reputedly saved from the scrap, but no trace has ever been found of them - could this story be just another of those great myths and legends that have grown up around the demise of steam locomotives.
Oliver Carter

HORWICH WORKS

SITUATED NEAR BOLTON, LANCASHIRE, the Horwich Works of the Lancashire & Yorkshire Railway had been established on a green-field site in the latter years of the 19th century. Throughout the LMS era, and well into nationalisation, the locomotives that were traditionally disposed of there were of L&YR origin. As many of these, particularly the Aspinall classes, were of considerable longevity, the disposal of Horwich-built engines lasted through the 1950s and into the early 1960s. Thereafter it was the LMS standard types which met their end at Horwich; 4Fs, 3F tanks, Ivatt 2-6-2Ts, various 2-6-4Ts, and no fewer than 53 of the 'Crab' 2-6-0s. A few 2-8-0s of the WD and GCR O4 Classes went to Horwich, but the most prestigious engines disposed of were four Jubilees and two Patriots, Nos.45507/18.

Horwich seems to have operated in a similar fashion to Derby, as the majority of scrappings were engines which had been sent for overhaul but, on inspection, were deemed to be beyond salvation. There are no obviously apparent large movements of locomotives being sent there specifically for disposal, particularly after local scrapyards (like Central Wagon at Ince) started buying bulk withdrawals. A visit to Horwich was like taking a trip back in time, there was always a miscellany of ancient 19th century engines on view. These were often stored down the side of the main erecting shop whilst a decision was taken regarding their fate. Most were of the Aspinall and Barton-Wright types and, to the uninitiated, it was often a mystery how these Victorian engines had lasted so long. The answer was their sturdy construction and a design which made them no nonsense 'work-horses', so they often survived yet another withdrawal and once again entered the shops for an overhaul. However, as the mass withdrawals began in earnest, 2-4-2Ts, 0-6-0 tender engines and other L&YR types began to disappear at an alarming rate.

Cutting up was concentrated on the sidings to the south side of the main erecting shop, and on 'the Moss' at the end of the yard. The latter area often had large bits of cut or partially cut locomotives laying around for some considerable time, exposed to the elements and looking for all the world like an 'elephants graveyard'. A little 18" narrow gauge system, with seven miles of sidings served the works and one spur ran down to 'the Moss'. It was not uncommon to see the last surviving 0-4-0 saddle tank, *Wren*, trundling down this line with some piece of a dismembered engine perched precariously on a small wagon. As early as 1959 redundancies were forecast, when loco-production fell to just six engines per week. Correspondingly disposal work also dropped, but the situation was partially alleviated by breaking up the Bury line electric stock during 1960. Locomotive cutting began again in earnest that November, with a batch of L&YR 0-6-0s and LMS 4Fs. As withdrawals accelerated during the early 1960s, many of the Hughes 'Crabs' were directed to Horwich. Time finally caught up with the Works and loco-repairs ceased on 6th May 1964, the last engine to be overhauled being No.48756 off Carlisle Kingmoor. The work's last victim was a Horwich-designed 'Crab' 2-6-0 No.42731 in March 1964.

On 9th August 1953, the works narrow gauge engine *Wren* shunts near the scrap line at Horwich. The engines in the background may have been destined to die at the works, but fortunately this powerful little locomotive was saved from an untimely end when it was acquired as part of the National Collection and it now resides at York.
Oliver Carter

Last days at Horwich, as ex-L&YR locos await their turn to enter the disposal line, pictured here is Aspinall 2-4-2T, No.50746, and three Aspinall 0-6-0 tender engines.
Alan Earnshaw

KILMARNOCK WORKS

THROUGHOUT THE SCOTTISH REGION, there were some fascinating scrapyard sights if you knew where to look. Even after the formation of the Scottish Region of BR, the old policies of the LMS and LNER remained strongly entrenched north of the Border. And, to a certain extent, so did the pre-Grouping traditions of an earlier generation. In the earlier years of BR it was decided to rationalise the situation, by centralising certain aspects of the region's operations on specific workshops. This policy also affected disposal, so by the early 1950s the bulk of condemned engines were being despatched south to the old Glasgow & South Western Railway's works at Kilmarnock. Here significant scrapping operations took place, with (for example) 61 of the 62 Scottish compounds cut up in just 45 months; commencing with No.41171 in 1952. To keep would be inquirers informed, the engine numbers were chalked up on a board, and to give an idea of the scale and scope of the operations, the following numbers were recorded during a visit on 6th August 1953: Nos.68551, 57410 and 41092 were all awaiting their fate, along with No.54481 which had sustained accident damage at Gollanfield near Inverness. Interestingly the board offered a running tally, listing all the engines which had been cut up since 1st January 1953 and that date: Nos.57339, 62411, 62281, 57332, 40918, 55136, 57387, 57471, 55175, 41182, 57322, 57423, 62457, 57454, 57397, 41109, 57388, 56237, 54636, 57395, 56258, 56276, 57438, 57464, 57439, 57450, 54445, 55143, 40911, 41184, 40922, 68111, and 55135 - evidence that many of the older classes - of which the Scottish Region had more than its fair share - were reaching the end of their days.

Scrapping at Kilmarnock ceased on 4th July 1959 when the works closed, and that date corresponds with the initial rise of the private scrapyards. Interestingly, the tally of engines cut up at the works quite probably exceeds the number built there - 392 between 1857 and 1921. One of the very last to go was LMS 0-6-0T, No.47331 in June 1959. Other types disposed of in the last years included ex-MR compounds, LNER K2s a fair number of Class J35s and some J36s.

The end of a sturdy Scottish servant, as No.57955 stands outside Kilmarnock Works in July 1952 - the engine had but a few more weeks left before it was reduced to a pile of scrap metal. An action justified as 'The conversion of an unwanted asset into a tangible resource - cash!'
Oliver Carter

ST. ROLLOX WORKS

Up to 1948, the St. Rollox Works of the LMS (previously the Caledonian Railway), handled a large percentage of the company's Scottish disposals - mostly Caley engines. The Glasgow works had been constructed in 1853 with major improvements in 1870 and 1884. By 1921 some 3,000 men were employed there, and all the Caledonian's disposals were done through the works, though few details have emerged about the how and why of operations. It is believed, that like many other workshops, St. Rollox purposely stripped down locomotives in order to salvage any re-usable components - a tedious, but cost-effective operation which would have pleased the thrifty Scots. The work continued under the LMS, and ostensibly one would have thought it would have done so after nationalisation. Yet, it is surprising to discover that very few engines were cut up at the works in the period under review. The vast majority of Scottish locomotives were directed to other works (including Darlington) or the private scrapyards, such as Motherwell Machinery & Scrap Ltd.

The Jubilee Class No.45718 *Dreadnought* certainly has something to worry about as it waits at the back of St. Rollox Works - along with three sister engines nearby, it has seen a final withdrawal from revenue earning duties, and its last journey will be to the scrapyard. *John Corkhill*

THE LNER WORKS

DARLINGTON WORKS

A SCRAPYARD IN DETAIL

ABOVE: LNER Class J26 0-6-0 No.65770 poses at Darlington scrapyard on 15th March 1959. Behind her is LNER Class K2 2-6-0 No.61757, one of no fewer than 33 of this 67-strong Gresley class made redundant that year, withdrawals having commenced in September 1955. *Photo: Ken Hoole*

ON 27th SEPTEMBER 1825 the first steam hauled train from Shildon to Stockton, headed by *Locomotion* driven by George Stephenson himself, stopped at Darlington to put off six wagons of coal, and to take up two wagons containing 'Mr. Meynell's Band'. The siding leading to the coal depot branched off the Stockton & Darlington Railway's main line adjacent to where North Road station now stands, and it was on the very site of this siding that the scrapyard for North Road Locomotive Works was established 107 years later!

As early as October 1900 the NER Locomotive Superintendent, Wilson Worsdell, had suggested that the cutting up of redundant locomotives currently caried out at Percy Main, Gateshead and York, should be concentrated at Darlington, on land at Hopetown.

The sidings leading to the coal depot on the west side of the Great North Road (later A1) originally crossed Hopetown Lane on the level, but they were cut back following the provision of improved facilities at Hill House (on the opposite side of the North Road) in 1872. In 1895 some of the sidings were provided with timber and earth platforms to handle livestock and implement traffic bound to and from the Royal Show, which was held in Darlington in that year, and these remained until the site was cleared by BR.

Eventually the area between Hopetown Lane and Station Road, adjacent to the 1842 North Road station, became the scrapyard, but this was not until 1932, when on 28th October Class D17/1 4-4-0 No.1625, withdrawn from Alnmouth shed on 3rd October, was placed in the yard ready for cutting up. This was the first of a long line of engines cut up there, those dealt with in the early years being of North Eastern and Hull & Barnsley origin, although three LNER-built engines — the short-lived Raven Pacifics *City of York, City of Durham* and *City of Ripon* — were cut up in 1936/7.

In 1947 engines from the Great Northern Section of the LNER were cut up at Darlington and included were some of the famous large Ivatt Atlantics. Following nationalisation engines from the Great Central and Great Eastern sections were also sent to Darlington for cutting up, with a few examples that had originated on the Metropolitan and Midland & Great Northern.

The onslaught of dieselisation brought many former LNER locomotives to the yard: D49 4-4-0s, V1 and V3 2-6-2Ts, J39 0-6-0s, etc, — not to mention the long-lived NER types, such as J27 0-6-0s, Q6 0-8-0s and B16 4-6-0s. The inclusion of former LMS sheds in the West Riding of Yorkshire into the North Eastern Region brought a smattering of LMS classes for scrapping. Due to the proposed closure of North Road Works, and the BR policy of selling unwanted locomotives to contractors for cutting up, the work at Darlington scrapyard began to decrease in 1964, and scrapping operations ceased in March, two years before the Works ceased to repair locomotives. The last engine cut up in the yard was J94 0-6-0ST No.68039. In this final period some engines were scrapped in the Stripping Shop in the Works Yard, where previously engines had been dismantled prior to overhaul. A few engines were stored in the scrapyard following its closure, but these were awaiting disposal. North Road Locomotive Works finally closed in April 1966.

The area adjoining the scrapyard was steeped in railway history. At the western end were the works of William and Alfred Kitching, and William Lister, both concerns that built locomotives for the Stockton & Darlington Railway in its early days, and the new North Road passenger station was erected nearby in 1842. This latter building was renovated for the 150th anniversary of the Stockton & Darlington Railway in 1975 and now houses Darlington North Road Station Railway Museum, with the BR services between Darlington and Bishop Auckland still calling at a platform inside the old building but outside the Museum portion.

In preparation for the opening of the Museum the area in front — formerly the scrapyard — was grassed over, but it is still possible to see the area where so many locomotives ended their days under the cutter's torch! KEN HOOLE

THE LNER WORKS
DONCASTER WORKS

THE REALISATION OF CHANGE increased during a visit to Doncaster for the Plant Centenary in 1953, with the sight of Sandringham Class No.61604 *Elvenden* being cut up - a named passenger locomotive being disposed of along with older veterans of GNR origins; with Classes C12, J1, J2, J5 and N15 in disturbing numbers. As may be imagined, Doncaster Works was responsible for the demise of a large number of withdrawn locomotives. With scrapping going on at the same time as out-shopping, the 'Plant' was always a fascinating place to visit. The back-roads usually being packed with some antiquated types awaiting the cutter's torch, yet for the majority of enthusiasts it will best be remembered as the graveyard of the large LNER express classes. The very first of the LNER Pacifics Thompson Class A2/2s Nos.60503/60505 were sent there in November 1959 and were duly cut up early in the following year. In the months and years which followed Doncaster cut up a seemingly never-ending procession of large locomotives, including one Thompson A1/1, four Thompson A2/1s, six Thompson A2/2s, 11 Thompson A2/3s, 8 Peppercorn A1s, 7 Peppercorn A2s, 35 Gresley A3s and an unlucky 13 Gresley A4s. To list loco by loco would be an endless task, but the notes which follow highlight a few of the arrivals to give a flavour of the carnage which went on there.

In December 1954 there were a batch of 14 locomotives waiting cutting, including Classes C13, J15, J21, J72, N1 and N5. In October 1955 Nos.68769, 68771, 68783/7, 68804-5/7, 68861/4, 68879, 68883 and 69451 were all awaiting 'a decision', but few survived any length of time and No.68861 was cut up within a month. The trend of cutting older, obsolete types continued in 1956, but No.68816 enjoyed a reprieve when it acquired the frames of sister engine No.68858 and a new boiler. Wandering through the cutting lines you were occasionally met by an engine bearing the legend 'Not To Be Cut Up' as was seen on Class B17 No.61636 *Melton Hall* in May 1958. Unfortunately the engine did meet its end later that year along with 13 other members of the class, whilst the first B17 'footballer' No.61667 *Bradford* was dealt with in June. Other 'footballers' to be seen were Nos.61650 *Grimsby Town* and 61669 *Barnsley* (both in September), and No.61648 *Arsenal* which was gunned down towards the end of the year. During 1959 a procession of two dozen B17s went to the 'Plant' for the last time, though at least the name-plates of some these engines were saved as they were presented to Sheffield United, Derby County, Darlington, Sunderland, Middlesbrough, Newcastle United, Sheffield Wednesday, Manchester United and Leicester City football clubs.

The end of yet another express type at Doncaster Works shows the decline in steam as early as 12th April 1953 whilst Sandringham Class No.61624 *Lumley Castle* waits for the cutters to resume work. Already the cladding has gone from the boiler, the cab has vanished and the burners have nibbled away at the front end. Meanwhile, to the left of the engine the boiler of No.65484 shows what fate has in store.
Oliver Carter

In January 1960 a visit to the scrap line saw the presence of *Lord President* with 'COND' and 'X' markings painted on its side. Whilst its fellow 'inmates' were *Honingham Hall, Wynard Park, Brancepeth Castle, Leeds United, The Essex Regiment, Manchester United,* and Class J39s Nos.64838/64960. The following week a number of ex-LMS types had been shuffled into the pack, with Nos.40025, 40582, 43665 and 43759 being the first arrivals. The pattern continued through the spring, but despite repeated trips I never managed to see No.61653 *Huddersfield Town* which had been withdrawn to Doncaster in January. To compensate there were a number of ex-L&YR types from Huddersfield, Mirfield & Low Moor sheds which I had so often seen working hard on my local branch. The scene now became a depressing one, with at least 182 engines being recorded as 'Cut Up At Doncaster' in 1960. This compared with109 in 1959 and 96 in 1958, and when only 160 were cut up in 1961 it seemed as though the peak had been reached. Yet the figures started to rise again with 172 in 1962 and 207 in 1963, when the last victim of the year was No.90453. Those who expected to see a repeat performance in 1964 got off to a good start with 17 engines in January and 20 in February, but by the time No.90161 was being dismembered, the bulk of disposals were going to the private yards and Doncaster's next victim was to be some time in coming.

GORTON WORKS

WITH ITS EARLY CLOSING date of 31st May 1963, Gorton cut up few of the more modern classes and none of the BR Standards. However, it did make a significant contribution in the disposal of a large number of LNER types, particularly classes associated with the former Great Central line. One or two 4-6-0s were handled, but it was mostly engines with an 0-6-0 wheel arrangement that became the work's most numerous victims. Most notable were all 37 of the J10s and all 137 the Robinson J11s. A few veteran 4-4-0s, K2s and 2-8-0s of Classes O4 and WD met their end at the works, whilst a few LMS types such as 2-6-4Ts and 2Ps were also handled. During a visit to the works one could always tell which locos were in store and which were due to be cut, for they were in the habit of painting a huge white cross on the condemned inmates.

As discussed earlier, after the second World War, Gorton began to experience problems in the storage of all withdrawn and condemned locomotives. As the works sidings soon filled up, dumping began at Dukinfield towards the end of 1946. However, when the practice started, it was engines waiting to go into the shops which went to Dukinfield rather than those about to be scrapped. On 1st September 1946 one B5, three J11s, four J39s, three O4s and a solitary Q4 were noted in the sidings - a month later locomotives of Classes C4 and N5 were also observed. John Duncan, a former apprentice at both the Gorton and Dukinfield works recalls. 'Locomotives were cut up at Dukinfield until 1951, when the EM1 electrics went there for fitting out. Scrapped locos were then cut at Gorton. Due to the cramped space, locos were often stored in sidings at various locations around the works and could be seen in various states of dismantling.' During the period of 1948-51 there were frequent movements of locomotives between the two works. It was not uncommon for engines in a stripped-down state (to boiler, frames and wheels) to be seen in transit to and from Dukinfield. Volume Two of the original series of Steam For Scrap stated that Gorton was handling about 15 locomotives a month, but former employees suggest that the figure was probably much higher in the period up to 1954.

STRATFORD WORKS

SITUATED DIRECTLY OPPOSITE THE large Jubilee steam shed, the ex-Great Eastern works complex covered some 60 acres. During the late 1950s and early 1960s it became cluttered with obsolete engines from all over the Great Eastern section, many of them of ancient origin; Classes E4, F5, J67, J68, J69, Y1 and Y4. Electrification and dieselisation accelerated the withdrawals, and soon express types like Sandringham and Claude classes were becoming evident. Disposals at Stratford seem to have been used as time fillers, one ex-employee, 'Tinker' Smith, who worked on the 'demolition' team recalls:- 'The work was often spasmodic, and we undertook the cutting when there was little else to do. We had a number of men who should have been made redundant, but they'd been retained to undertake what management called a "tidying up exercise", this included disposing of old stock. I recall one chap who always volunteered to strip out the coaches, it wasn't until months afterward we found out that he made a good supplement to his wages by recovering coins which had dropped down the back of the seats. Another man, a Polish immigrant, used to clear out the tenders by bagging the left-over coal and then dragging it to place where he could recover it later. Unfortunately management found out, and he was down the road.'

A fairly large batch of engines also went down the road in the summer of 1955, including No.67213 from Epping shed which was scrapped in error. A few red faces surrounding that debacle no doubt! Included in this batch of destruction was ex-LMS No.41976, whilst more ex-LT&SR types followed in December. As the 1950s progressed cutting was done on a number of sites, including the scrap road, stripping shop, the old works, the foundry and the field. Yet, it is surprising that when the withdrawal of the Class B17s began apace in 1958/9, none of the early withdrawals went to Stratford. Indeed the works only took 11 members of the class, and these in the first half of 1960. In the first month of 1960 an edict was issued for 12 locomotives to be broken up each week to provide work for men made redundant in the repair shop. The work, as might be imagined, proceeded much more quickly now and a regular procession of stock went through the works. It is difficult to see from the records how this figure could have been achieved, but some locomotives were only partially cut before being sent on. Yet even so, by the beginning of 1961, no less than 46 locos were stored on shed awaiting demolition. Despite the continued efforts of the cutters, and the forwarding of some engines to Darlington for disposal, there were still over three dozen locos awaiting attention at the end of August. A mild flurry of activity followed, then the well ran dry, with just 7 engines being cut up in the last three months of the year. By the end of 1961, the disposal of steam at Stratford had come to an end. Perhaps it was of little consequence any way for, as of September the following year, the withdrawal of steam from the Great Eastern Section had been fully accomplished.

Electrification of the Southend line in December 1956 resulted in a sudden influx of redundant steam locomotives to Stratford Works. Photographed on 16th February 1957 are Class B12/3 4-6-0 No.61512 (withdrawn January) and Class D16/3 4-4-0s Nos.62608/62609 (withdrawn January/February respectively). *Photo: R. C. Riley*

THE SCOTTISH WORKS

IN DISCUSSING THE FORMER LNER works, it was decided to group the two Scottish plants together because of the similarity in the way steam was disposed of there. Initially, after nationalisation both only handled ex-LNER engines, but by 1949 a variety of LMS types were also making a regular appearance. As the Scottish Region became a more self-contained organisation, the company identities began to gradually vanish. Thereafter a variety of locomotives with Caledonian, G&SWR, Midland and LMS origins began to arrive. Originally, Cowlairs opened in 1841 serving the Edinburgh & Glasgow Railway, until 1865 when it became part of North British. Up until the grouping of 1923, the works had produced a large number of locomotives, but the LNER's rationalisation scheme meant that few were produced thereafter. Once the batches of production planned before Grouping had been completed in 1925, the works concentrated on major overhauls, accident repair and routine maintenance. Significantly, around the same period scrapping began to increase. Hitherto it had generally been on a one for one basis, with roughly an equal balance between new and condemned locos being maintained. During the 1930s and 40s hundreds of life-expired engines were cut up, though a number of engines which were standing condemned at the works were repaired and reinstated into service around the end of 1939 due to war-time demands. From 1947 onwards a veritable flood of unwanted engines began arriving from all over Scotland, including examples of most of the Scottish-based tanks. LNER types such as K1s, K2s, K3s, J35s, J36s, J39s, and B1s became the scrapyard's staple diet.

As the 1950s progressed, they were followed by ex-LMS types mainly from the Glasgow area and other sheds like Hamilton, Motherwell and Carstairs. By the time cutting ceased, Cowlairs' LMS tally would include eight Black 5s, four Jubilees, four 'Crabs', along with a number of 2P 4-4-0s and 'Jinty' 0-6-0s. Seven WD 2-10-0s, over a quarter of the Scottish-based class, went to Cowlairs for disposal along with several of the 2-8-0s. One of the most notable engines to go there was A3 No.60090 *Grand Parade*. Cowlairs' scrapping operations dropped back dramatically in the 1960s, and with the end of steam in sight its reason for existence came into question; the plant itself was also found to be 'surplus to requirements' and it closed in 1966.

Situated just north of Aberdeen on the line to Keith, the works at Inverurie played a significant part in the demise of Scottish steam. Though the former Great North of Scotland Railway's works was taking engines from all over the Region, one former employee recalls that it was a matter of logistics and the works' geographic location which meant that the bulk of the locos arriving for disposal were still of LNER origins. However, as the number of engines being sent for scrap increased, it became economically viable to transfer LMS types in convoys of five or six at a time, even to distant locations like Inverurie. However, it was not always possible to move them all the way in a single journey and as a consequence it became common to see 'dead' engines that were bound for Inverurie stored in transit. Engines being consigned from the Glasgow area were often (and one correspondent states, routinely) stored at Forfar engine shed on the route north. Yet other sheds were also used, and I recall seeing condemned engines in transit at both Perth and Kittybrewster sheds; one suspects that there would have been other locations which would probably include Dundee.

Once at Inverurie dismantling was a fairly quick process, at least compared with some works, but cutting was quite often only partial. It was not uncommon to see the works littered with boilers, frames and cabs of supposedly long dead engines. The cutters' cabin was an interesting place, for it was adorned with several name-plates from engines of Glen and Director Classes. As these types had painted names, as opposed to cast-plates, the complete splasher was burnt away and duly saved. In all, eight Directors were cut up here: Nos.62674/8-9/82/7-8/90 which had arrived ex-store from Kittybrewster, Grangemouth, Longniddry, Arbroath, Crianlarich, with No.62671 sent from St. Rollox. Other types disposed of at Inverurie included Pickersgill 3P 4-4-0s, Drummond Caledonian 0-6-0 2Fs and 3Fs, LMS 2Ps, and McIntosh 0-6-0s and 0-4-4Ts of the 431 and 439 Classes which came in large numbers. By the late 1950s the bulk of arrivals seem to have been locomotives directed from St. Rollox, since the majority of engines stored at the Bo'ness Dump were being moved to private contractors. Perhaps the most significant victims were five LNER pacifics, Class A1 Nos.60159/61-2, and the two A3s (Nos.60089 and 60098) which were reportedly cut up in March 1964. A couple of ex-LMS Black 5s ended their days at Inverurie, as did a few WD 2-8-0s but by this time private contractors were taking the bulk of the Scottish disposals.

Cowlairs Works on 11th August 1950 as withdrawn 4-4-0 No.2208 is finally stripped down to piles of scrap. Around her stand a number of engines, all similarly in their final hours. The tank engine to the right of No.2208's buffer beam has the sad distinction of being the scrapyard shunter, to it falls the onerous duty of hauling in the dead engines ear-marked for disposal.
Oliver Carter

THE SR WORKS

ASHFORD WORKS

IT HAD LONG BEEN common practice on the Southern Railway to send engines back to their works of origin for disposal and Ashford was no exception to this. However, as might be imagined, the predominance of engines traditionally disposed of at Ashford were those that had spent many years running from London out into the Kent countryside. Yet from the mid-1950s onwards strangers such as ex-LBSCR Class E1s began making an appearance. Thereafter a variety of ex-Southern engines began arriving at Ashford, with the tell-tale 'X' painted on their side. From then on Ashford, with Eastleigh, disposed of virtually the whole of that region's condemned engine fleet until 1964. Whole classes were cut up with only one or two strays going to 'foreign' works or private yards. Generally speaking, LBSCR and SECR classes went to Ashford and LSWR types went to Eastleigh, though there were exceptions to the rule and some classes were shared equally between the works; notably the Classes E3, E4, E4X, E6 and E6X. Ashford cut up all the Class C2Xs and R1s, all but 7 of the Class Cs, most of the E1s and D1 4-4-0s. In addition they took a fair percentage of Classes D1, L1, L, H and a number of Schools.

The bulk of the work began in 1955, when about a dozen engines were dispatched, but at least three more were sent to Brighton for disposal. The year 1956 seems to have been fairly quiet, whilst only a handful went in 1957. In March 1958 Nos.32493, 32502 and 31737 arrived, but the latter was strangely reprieved when it was allocated to Tweedmouth Shed. Exactly why the engine, which had spent so many years at Stewarts Lane Shed' should be sent to Scotland remains a question the authors have been unable to resolve. The following year the pattern was again a quiet one, but one peculiar disposal in 1959 was the boiler from an ex-LMS Royal Scot (No.6134) which had formerly been used for steaming boilers at the back of Ashford's erecting shop after repairs. The progress of electrification on the Southern Region began to affect the pattern, and during 1959 a steady flow of locomotives were dealt with, many being suburban tank engine types which had finally been made redundant. Around 125 engines went in 1959, the bulk being cut up after the summer holidays, including No.31755 the first of the Class L1s. At this time Ashford works were already ear-marked for closure, but at the end of the year it was given a short reprieve, and during 1960 disposal work continued apace with around six dozen being cut; additionally a large number of tenders and boilers were also handled. In 1961 around 80 engines were demolished, though many were only cut into sections that would fit in a wagon so that they could be easily shipped to private scrapyards. Finally, in 1962, some 35 engines were dealt with, but in the last year 1963, the records show that only two were fully cut up.

BRIGHTON WORKS

BRIGHTON'S FORAYS INTO THE locomotive disposal business were limited to say the least; up to the end of 1956 it had cut up large batches of locomotives, including notable classes like King Arthurs. One of these was No.30740 *Merlin*, which was sent for final cutting up after it had been partially dismembered at Longmoor Military Railway to make a 'film set prop'. In addition a number of the smaller tank engines also met their end at the seaside town, notably Classes E3, E4, M7 and 02. Yet in March of that year it was announced that the works was due to close and 260 men were issued with redundancy notices. The following month Brighton demolished No.31704, the last London, Chatham & Dover engine remaining in service. Twenty-seven more engines were disposed of that year, including No.32425 which was demolished at Slade Green Electric Shed by a group of men who travelled in motor lorries from the works. In January 1957 Nos.30570/2/4, 30747, 31574, which were awaiting cutting, were all labelled up and shipped off to Ashford for disposal. The end was already in sight. In the period up to June only three engines were handled, Nos.32422/6, 32488, thereafter it remained quiet up until February 1958 when Class T9, No.30705 became the last victim. Six engines from Nine Elms shed, Nos.31242, 31759/64/5/80/2, were pushed into the boiler shop for 'storage'. The works closed on 31st March 1958, and was later used to assemble BMW motor cars.

Out of work and waiting for the end, stored at Eastleigh Depot on 1st September 1962, stands Class S15 No.30500. The class was originally designed by Urie in 1920 for the LSWR, as a mixed traffic engine - a development of the N15. Later classified 6F, these powerful 4-6-0s still had plenty of life in them when they were withdrawn.
Gerald T. Robinson

example of steam sold for scrap - and some breaking took place in the Brading Harbour Company's engine shed at St. Helens. Number W1 was disposed of at St. Johns MPD in the summer of 1957, as the decimation of the island's railways began. Of the 19 Isle of Wight Class O2 0-4-4Ts to survive into the 1960s, only seven were cut up at Ryde Works; eleven went to Solliffe & Co. but W24 *Calbourne* escaped into preservation and now resides on the Isle of White Steam Railway with two 'Terrier' Class 0-6-0Ts.

This rare view of scrapping at Ashford Works just after the end of World War II portrays the last days of Stirling 4-4-0 No.1060, which had been built at the works in October 1891. It was rebuilt to F1 Class in 1905 and withdrawn in late-April 1946. The engine was taken in for stripping within days of this view being taken, and by the end of May it had been completely reduced to scrap. *Southern Railway Official Photograph courtesy Kent County Libraries*

Certainly the most exotic steam locomotives cut up at Brighton Works — or anywhere else, for that matter — were Bulleid's 0-6-6-0T 'Leaders' whose trials and tribulations were the source of much comment in 1949-51. Of the four engines, only Nos.36001 and 36002 were completed, only the first underwent trials and all four were cut up in the first half of 1951: No.36001 at Eastleigh, the other three at Brighton.

This is No.36003 soon after arrival at Brighton in May following store, incomplete, at Bognor Regis and New Cross Gate. She was rapidly cut up, BR preferring to invest in more conventional steam locomotives such as the Fairburn 4MT 2-6-4 tanks, the last batch of which — as this picture shows — were then being outshopped at Brighton. *Photo: Peter Hay*

EASTLEIGH WORKS

EASTLEIGH OUTSTRIPPED ALL THE other Southern works together in the quantity of locomotives cut up, eventually disposing of hundreds of engines. This included virtually all of the earlier LSWR and SR classes, specifically the Class G6s and G16s. Later the entire Class of H15s went at Eastleigh and all but three of the King Arthurs and the Class 700s. Other types which were almost virtually wiped out at Eastleigh were the M7 tanks, the mainland O2s, the U1s, and the big Class Zs. No less than 16 Schools Class met their end here, as did a fare share of Bullied Pacifics (9), Qs, Q1s, S15s, Ns, Us, and Ks. Perhaps the most illustrious engine to meet its end here being No.35020, *Bibby Line*. Worthy of note are the three BR 2-6-2Ts, Nos.82002/8/43 (from the West Country), which were the only Standard Class locomotives to be consigned to rubble by a Southern Region works. In fact Eastleigh was only one of four BR works to cut up members of the 999-strong Standard fleet, the others being Crewe, Darlington and Swindon.

In 1955 the bulk disposals began, a slow trickle at first with under a dozen being cut up. The pattern was emulated in the period 1956-8, with four, 25 and 28 engines being cut respectively. However, in 1959 the figure nearly reached 100 but in 1960 it fell back to a couple of dozen once again. In 1961 the casualty figure had had reached 85, whilst in 1962 no less than 60 engines met their end whilst many of their fellows were stored at Hove waiting a similar fate. Peak year for cutting was 1963, with 163 engines recorded as meeting their end, but the figures fell away noticeably in the first half of 1964; regular operations ceasing in June of that year when Nos.34049 and 82008 were disposed of. However, this was not the end of locomotive cutting at Eastleigh, for during 1965 and 1966 men from Cohen's dismembered at least 10 engines at the shed including departmental locomotives DS235/6 (formerly USA tank engines Nos.30066/74) and BR Standards Nos.73041 and 80132.

RYDE WORKS

AS WILL BE APPRECIATED, Ryde Works activities were strictly confined to locomotives allocated to the Isle of Wight, and therefore its operations were considerably limited. Traditionally the works handled all the engines on the island, although the scrapyard of H.B. Solliffe certainly purchased engines in the 1930s - an interesting early

The last of the Drummond Class T9 4-4-0s finally relinquished their accustomed duties on the Southern's sprawling empire west of Exeter in July 1961 when Nos.30313, 30709, 30715 and 30717 were withdrawn from Exmouth Junction shed. They were stored for a few weeks at Eastleigh before scrapping and two engines were photographed there on 8th July 1961. *Photo: Tony Copas*

LEFT: Eastleigh Running Shed on 30th April 1961: the classic profile of one of the well-recorded trio of LSWR Class 0415 4-4-2 tanks which lasted until that year on the tortuous Lyme Regis branch. No.30584 (note the odd BR emblem) was the first of the 80-year-old survivors to be condemned and departed Exmouth Junction in January, bound for Eastleigh and nearly a year on the 'Dump' before cutting up. Sister engine No.30582 arrived that July and survived in limbo until March 1962: No.30583 achieved apparent immortality on the Bluebell Railway.

BELOW: An earlier view at the back of Eastleigh Works. LSWR Class H15 4-6-0 No.30485, the first of the class to be condemned (following a collision at Bournemouth shed), is laid out like a giant Airfix kit, some three months after withdrawal in April 1955.
Photos: Tony Copas

Chapter Four

The Private Yards

9F remnant: the smokebox door of No.92101 at Buttigieg's Newport yard, summer 1968. *Photo: Rex Conway*

WHEN *STEAM FOR SCRAP* began detailing the demise and disposal of British Railways' steam locomotive fleet, the story was not then complete. Well over 40 engines remained at Woodham's Yard in Barry, and history was still in the making. The Barry legend has been well told over the years, and it has secured its unique place within the preservation story. Who would have thought, even ten years ago, that almost all of the 100 locomotives still there would eventually pass into preservation. When Class 9F 2-10-0, No.92085, was broken up in the summer of 1980, it became the very last BR locomotive to die in a private scrapyard. It must be said that Woodham's were an exceptional firm, and thereby the preservation movement was allowed a valuable breathing space in which it was able to marshal both its forces and its finances. However, elsewhere over 100 'other Barrys' mercilessly despatched their occupants to the scrap pile with clinical dispassion.

As we have seen, the traditional way of disposing of locomotives had been at a railway works, where almost every establishment had its shadowy corner in which scrapping was undertaking. Yet, the wholesale disposal of locomotives during the late-1950s and early-1960s brought about the dawn of a new era. As the 1960s began, the 'works' were no longer able to cope with the veritable flood of locomotives which were being made redundant. This brought about a vast change to the disposal scene so, thereafter, the bulk of movements were directed to the private yards. To detail them all is beyond the scope of this book, however it would be unreasonable if we did not elaborate to some degree on the activities of a number of the private breakers. In doing so, we have taken parts five and six of the original series, and supplemented these by the extensive and pain-staking research of Tony Wakefield.

The scale of the cutting work might be divided into four sections, each with self-defined boundaries, as we outlined in the original books. Firstly we have what may be termed the GRADE ONE YARDS, locations where hundreds of engines were cut up - a bizarre and formidable exercise where operations assumed 'production line' proportions and thereby almost went un-recorded. Such a situation existed at ten yards, and involved eight separate companies; Messrs. Bird of Risca, Newport, Monmouthshire; J. Buttigieg also of Newport; John Cashmore & Co, with yards at Tipton and (once again) Newport; Central Wagon Co., Ince; A. Draper Ltd, Hull; Hughes Bolckow Ltd, North Blyth; Motherwell Machinery & Scrap Ltd, Wishaw; and the Sheffield firm of Thomas W. Ward in yards at Beighton and Killamarsh.

Next we have the 21 GRADE TWO YARDS, where the number of locomotives cut could be counted in their dozens. This category includes the firm of Woodham Brothers, which would have been a Grade One Yard had they cut up all of the 213 locomotives they'd purchased. Then follow the GRADE THREE YARDS, which were of lesser importance in the disposal scene, but still contributed a significant total to the whole. Several of the 18 companies who operated the 22 locations in this grade also had yards which have been been included in the two previous categories. From this we might conclude that, whilst certain firms used specific locations to maintain their 'production line' disposals to handle their bulk acquisitions, they used their other yards for smaller lots purely for geographical expediency. Finally we have recorded 55 GRADE FOUR YARDS which purchased their victims in small quantities, often in ones and twos as required. Many of these operated for very short periods, as they found loco-breaking to be an unprofitable sport, some were parts of larger concerns which directed most of their acquisitions to other yards. The pages which follow present a detailed analysis of *some* of these yards, up-dating much of the information presented earlier.

These, then, are the major private scrapyards:

MESSRS BIRD
— Risca, Newport

J. BUTTIGIEG
— Newport, Monmouthshire

J. CASHMORE
— Great Bridge, Tipton, Staffs
— Newport, Monmouthshire

CENTRAL WAGON CO.
– Wigan

A. DRAPER
— Hull

HUGHES BOLCKOWS LTD
— Battleship Wharf, North Blyth, Northumberland

MOTHERWELL MACHINERY & SCRAP CO. LTD
— Wishaw, Motherwell

THOMAS WARD
— Beighton, Sheffield
— Killamarsh, Sheffield

TOTAL: 10

THE GRADE 2 YARDS

Also busy, each of these firms cut up dozens of engines.

ARNOTT YOUNG
— West of Scotland Shipbreaking Co, Troon Harbour, Ayrshire

BARNES & BELL LTD
— Coatbridge, Lanarks

MESSRS BIRD
— Long Marston, Warwicks
— Morriston, Swansea

G. H. CAMPBELL
— Airdrie, Lanarkshire
— Shieldhall, Renfrew

G. COHEN
— Cargo Fleet, Middlesborough
— Kettering, Northants
— Morriston, Swansea

J. N. CONNELL
— Coatbridge, Lanarks

COOPERS METALS LTD
— California Sidings, Sharpness, Glos.

R. S. HAYES
— Tremains Yard, Bridgend
Taken over by Birds c.8.65

A. KING & SONS LTD
— Hall Road, Norwich

A. LOOM (ELLIS METALS LTD)
— Spondon, Derbyshire

P. & W. McLELLAN
— Bo'Ness, West Lothian
— Langloan, Glasgow

J. McWILLIAM
— Shettleston, Glasgow

SETTLE SPEAKMAN
— Queenborough, Isle of Sheppey, Kent

SHIPBREAKING INDUSTRIES LTD
— Faslane, Helensburgh

THOMAS WARD
— Wishaw, Motherwell

WOODHAM BROTHERS
— Barry Dock, South Glamorgan

TOTAL: 21

GWR Mogul No.6370 in disarray at R. S. Hayes, Bridgend, spring 1964. Two of the nineteen Castles cut up by this yard are also visible. *Photo: H. N. James*

THE GRADE 3 YARDS

Of lesser importance, but still contributing a significant total to the whole.

ARNOTT YOUNG
— Carmyle, Glasgow
— Old Kilpatrick, Glasgow
— Parkgate & Rawmarsh, Rotherham, Yorks

M. BAUM
— Cleveland Dockyard, Middlesborough

MESSRS BIRD
— Bynea, Llanelly

CLAYTON & DAVIE
— Dunston-on-Tyne, Gateshead, Co. Durham

CENTRAL WAGON CO
– Barrow In Furnace

COX & DANKS LTD
— Wadsley Bridge, Sheffield

J. FRISWELL
— Banbury *Locos cut up on site at Banbury MPD*

GARNHAM, HARRIS & ELTON
— Steelbreaking & Dismantling Co., Chesterfield

W. GEORGE
— Station Steel, Wath-upon-Dearne, Mexborough, Yorkshire

WALTER HESELWOOD
— Attercliffe, Sheffield

HENDERSONS
— Airdrie

T. L. MUMFORD LTD
— Stratford Market, Plaistow, London

RIGLEYS WAGON WORKS
— Bulwell, Nottingham

W. & F. SMITH
— Ecclesfield East Sidings, Sheffield

STEEL SUPPLY CO.
— Briton Ferry, Glamorgan
— Jersey Marine, Swansea

T. J. THOMPSON
— Millfield, Stockton-on-Tees

THOMAS WARD
— Giants Wharf, Briton Ferry, Glamorgan
— Broughton Lane, Sheffield

P. WOOD (ROTHERHAM) LTD
— Slag Reduction Co., Rotherham, Yorkshire

TOTAL: 22

THE GRADE 4 YARDS

These purchased locomotives in small quantities, often in ones and twos as required. Many operated for very short periods.

ARDMORE STEELS, Craigendoran, Helensburgh — ARMITAGE, Sheepbridge, Derbyshire — ARNOTT YOUNG, Bilston, Staffs; Dinsdale, Co. Durham; Dudley Hill, Bradford — BARLBOROUGH METALS, Briton Ferry, Swansea — T. BURTON LTD, Middleton, Lancs — BUSH & SON, Birchwood Sidings, Pye Bridge, Derbyshire — G. W. BUTLER, Bowling Ironworks, Bradford; Otley, Yorkshire — CARREX METALS, Rochdale — G. COHEN, Coburn Works, Tinsley, Sheffield; Kingsbury, Warwicks — COX & DANKS LTD, Barry, Glamorgan; Brindle Heath, Manchester; Park Royal, North Acton, London; Oldbury, Warley, Worcs — CRUMP, Dentith Sidings, Connahs Quay, Flint — ELLIS METALS LTD, Swalwell, Blaydon, Gateshead — HAYES METALS LTD, Abbey Works, Gloucester — HOLINTER, Co-operative Sidings, Grays, Essex — T. JENKINS, Port Talbot — T. H. JONES (IRON & STEEL), Newport, Monmouthshire — MADEN & McKEE, Stanley Station, Bootle, Liverpool — J. MAHONEY, Portland Street, Newport, Glamorgan — MARPLE & GILLOTT, Attercliffe, Sheffield — I. & R. MORKOT, Cylla, Ystrad Mynach, Caerphilly; Energlen, Caerphilly — C. MURPHY, Dale Lane Siding, Liverpool — NORTH WALES WAGON CO, Chester — J. S. PARKER, Altrincham, Cheshire — ROUND OAK STEELWORKS, Brierley Hill, Staffs — J. ROUTLEDGE, Muspratt Estate, Bootle, Liverpool — SLAG REDUCTION CO LTD, Briton Ferry, Swansea; Hindpool, Barrow-in-Furness — H. B. SOLLIFFE, Newport, Isle of Wight — SLATER BROS, Beighton, Sheffield — TAYLOR BROS, Trafford Park, Manchester — R. S. TYLEY, Barry, Glamorgan — D. WARD, Woodville, Burton-on-Trent, Staffs — THOMAS WARD, Brindle Heath, Manchester; Bolton-on-Dearne, Mexborough, Yorkshire; Ramsden Dock, Barrow-in-Furness; Columbia Wharf, Grays, Essex; Inverkeithing, Dunfermline; Preston Docks, Preston; Ringwood, Hants; South Bank, near Middlesborough; Mostyn Ironworks, Flint — W. WILLOUGHBY, Choppington Station Yard, near Morpeth, Northumberland — P. WOOD, Glasson Dock, Lancaster — I. C. WOODFIELD, Town Dock, Newport, Monmouthshire; Cadoxton, Barry, Glamorgan (taken over by Buttigieg 7.66) — WOODFIELD & WAY, Peterston, near Cardiff; Bridgend, Glamorgan

TOTAL: 55

ABOVE: A possibly unique photograph of the very limited operations at Marple & Gillott's Sheffield yard: LNER B1 No.61153 was recorded in May 1965. *Photo: Tony Wakefield*

BELOW: In marked contrast to the 'big business' of the Cashmores and Drapers, the smallest yards often had a 'home-spun' atmosphere. This is well conveyed in this view of GWR 0-4-2T No.1469 being despatched at the Caerphilly site of I & R Morkot on 4th April 1959. *Photo: E. R. Mountford*

Notes

A small number of very minor or doubtful locations have been omitted from the above lists. Reference should be made, however, to the following:

1) BUTTIGIEGS at Pontnewydd, where this important firm's loco-breaking operations may have started.
2) COX & DANKS may have cut up locomotives at Cardiff.
3) COHENS also cut up a small number at Rotherwas, Hereford.
4) BARLBOROUGH METALS had a small operation at Llanelly.
5) A firm named L. C. HUGHES is believed to have purchased a small number of engines but no further information is available.
6) MAYER, NEWMAN & CO of Blackwall made an unknown number of purchases.
7) STEEL SUPPLY CO are believed to have had a small yard at West Drayton.

It must be stressed that written records covering the operations of these private yards were often incomplete or inaccurate and most have now long since been destroyed. The above information is believed to be the most accurate and complete available but amendments or additions are welcome.

YARD BY YARD

TO DETAIL THE FULL activities of *all* the major scrapyards would be a mammoth task in its own right, without even giving consideration to the minor ones. Though it might be possible to recount the basic details, this in itself would create an extensive tome, which at best would be repetitive. As a consequence, the authors decided to present an overview on a couple of dozen yards, so as to present a more detailed picture of what happened therein. Though acquisitions and disposals varied greatly from yard to yard, the overall pattern does appear to have certain unifying threads. The slow trickle of locally-based engines beginning to appear, followed by the purchases from the various works and shed dumps. Then came the onslaught into displaced express locos and the relatively new Standard Classes, culminating in the final massacre as steam was ousted from its last stronghold in the North-west. The march of 'progress' continued, as many of the larger yards continued their cutting work by scrapping some of the early diesel classes which had proved to be failures.
known, for example books on Woodham's have become almost a cottage industry, whilst Draper's yard has been covered in a recent work. Atlantic has also played a part in the information process, not only by *Steam For Scrap,* but in the magazine **Back-Track** with articles such as *'Carnage At Cashmore's'* in Volume One. Yet, even so, the work of many of the yards is still sketchy. In determining where to start our story, we felt that it might be prudent to once again begin with the activities of John Cashmore Ltd. who, by far, led the field in this venture.

JOHN CASHMORE LTD, NEWPORT

THE FIRM OF JOHN CASHMORE Ltd. were the singularly most important company involved in the disposal of steam. One of their major centres of operation was situated in the heartland of locomotive disposal - Newport, Monmouthshire. This yard was located on the site of the old Western Dry Dock, and it started the destruction around April 1959. The volume of locomotives it handled never quite matched Great Bridge, but when it finished with steam engines early in 1969 over 1,000 had been consigned to oblivion. In that period, it too broke a number of records, including the lion's share of the Bullied Pacifics - 42 engines. Thirty-seven GWR Castles met their end here, more than at Swindon where only 32 of the elegant 4-6-0s died. A large percentage of the yard's victims were of GWR origin, and it is significant that

Awaiting scrapping at Cashmore's Newport yard on 19th November 1967 Standard Class 2-6-2Ts, Nos.82003/31/4 stand in line with Class 8F No.48249 and Standard Class 5 No.73002.
Alan Sommerfield

the first arrivals were probably the four Churchward 2-6-2T 45xx Class (Nos.4545/76/79, 5502) which arrived from Swindon on 9th April 1959. Swindon consigned two further batches in late-November, these were comprised of Nos.2808/10/24/26, 4358, 5378, and 6308/59. In February 1960 Nos.4212/60, and 5163 came ex-store from Barry, followed in June by three more engines (Nos.4547/77, 5559) hauled in from the same location. However, these were just the prelude to what was to follow as the serious business of clearing the Swindon dump began. Throughout the next 12 months batches of pannier tanks of the 57xx, 67xx, 77xx, 84xx, 94xx Classes began drifting in but it wasn't until late in 1962 that the Castles and Kings were purchased. On 4th December, No.4037 *South Wales Borderer* arrived from Exeter and it was completely reduced to assorted piles of metal within just ten days. Other Castles arrived during the same period, including Nos.4077/85/86, 5003/7/12/16/17/24/35/53/61/64/75/90/4, though Nos.5011/36/66 were diverted to Great Bridge. Four Kings, Nos.6009/19/21/29, turned up from Old Oak Common during the same months.

Members of the Hall Class came in strength at the start of 1964, and three County Class engines arrived on 22nd January; these were Nos.1003-4/15 which had travelled through the night from Laira in convoy with No.7316. A second batch of the 1000 Class 4-6-0s, Nos.1000-1/10/12-4 were purchased in December. About this time the first bulk purchases from the Southern Region were also beginning to appear, predominantly Classes 'U' and 'N'; though Z Class No.30952 purchased in September 1964 may be credited as the first. Cashmore's were also very busy receiving former S&DR stock from Bath, Standard Classes from Eastleigh and Feltham, and GWR types from South Wales, Swindon and Southall to name but a few. The first West Country Class engine, was No.34031 *Torrington* which was purchased ex-Eastleigh in April 1965. About the same time the Class 9Fs started appearing, and though barely run in (so to speak) Nos.92003, 92222/42/8 were the yard's first Standard 2-10-0s. So many classes arrived between 1965 and the end of 1968 that is almost impossible to even generalise and a complete list would be impractical, however interesting examples were Grange Class Nos.6819/29/38/48-9/56/72/76 and Merchant Navy Class No.35019 in April 1966. The latter arrived from Salisbury, and was the first of this Class to appear.

The fabled mountain of scrap at Cashmore's - no engine lies beneath it, but dozens of dissected locomotives do. Alongside No.45417 waits its turn., but note how carefully the tubes have been bundled and stored to one side.
Rex Conway

Sales from the London Midland Region, particularly sheds in the North-west, were now being directed to Newport. The bulk of these acquisitions reflected the traditional allocations of the industrial north, 2-6-4Ts, Black 5s, WD and 8F 2-8-0s. However, as time went on, the proportion of BR standard Classes shot up as they too were ousted by the newly arrived diesels. Britannia No.70017 *Arrow* came from Carlisle, which seemed odd considering the number of nearer Scottish yards, yet this was not an isolated purchase as No.70026 appeared from Stockport in April 1967. Throughout 1967, and well into 1968, Cashmore's were fully occupied in clearing out stock from Bournemouth, Weymouth, Salisbury and Eastleigh. This meant that a fair proportion of the engines which the yard was handling were large locomotives, and West Country and Standard Class engines stood in the disposal rows alongside 2-8-0s and 4-6-0s from the Liverpool and Manchester districts. The last steam engines obtained were those from Patricroft, which were reputed to have been in very good condition. The last purchase was No.73069, in January 1969, but by this time their voracious appetite had turned onto diesels. The story is more fully told in our companion book, *Diesels & Electrics For Scrap*, but Cashmore's, Newport entered into the slaughter by purchasing a number of the North British Class D63XX from the Western Region and Nos.20001/2 from Brighton.

ABOVE: Another extraordinary photograph taken at Cashmore's Newport yard, this time in August 1968. Backed by the mortal remains of steam locomotives she had helped make redundant, Class D60XX diesel hydraulic D604 *Cossack*, one of the original Warships, has been unceremoniously stripped to her frames, the scrap merchants — accustomed to the heavy work involved in despatching a steam locomotive — no doubt appreciating the comparative ease of cutting up diesels.

At that date, BR planned a major revision of its main line diesel fleet, from 2,976 engines of 28 types to 2,240 of 15 types, with particular emphasis on the elimination of those classes which had been costly or troublesome (or both) to operate. This particular locomotive had a service life of less than ten years.

RIGHT: Taken on the same day, this general view shows the yard to the left of the view above. The crane is used to load hoppers of conveniently sized pieces of locomotive into lorries. Lurking behind the cars, as if anxious to avoid attention and their inevitable fate, are two more Warships: Nos.D602 *Bulldog* and D603 *Conquest*. They will survive two more months. *Photos: John Bird*

Cashmore's other yard was at Great Bridge, Tipton, Staffordshire — seen here in two views.

LEFT: The unmistakable profile of an ex-LNWR Class G2 7F 0-8-0, awaiting the torch on 13th March 1965. Behind No.49430 is Class G2a 0-8-0 No.49361. The LNWR 0-8-0s were remarkably long-lived, outlasting the later LMS 0-8-0s and these examples were the last of their classes, a distinction commemorated by their use on a SLS Special over West Midlands metals on 12th December 1964. Both were withdrawn from Bescot shed that Christmas Eve, the last engines of LNWR origin in service.

BELOW: Under the yard's gantry a few months earlier on 16th August 1964 was LMS Jubilee 4-6-0 No.45709. Formerly *Implacable*, she has a new name chalked on her cab side — 'Duane Eddy': a rock'n'roll star of the period; a comment, perhaps, on her riding qualities? No fewer than 37 Jubilees were cut up at this yard and the 190-strong class was disposed of at a wide variety of sites: the BR works at Crewe, Horwich, Darlington and Cowlairs and a large number of private yards at locations ranging from Swansea to Airdrie. Also visible is Fowler 2-6-4T No.42419 and both engines had been sold to Cashmore's after some eight months in store at Saltley shed. *Photos: Michael Hale*

JOHN CASHMORE LTD, TIPTON

IT MAY BE ARGUED that Great Bridge (Tipton, Staffordshire) was perhaps the most significant private scrapyard, by virtue of sheer number and variety of locomotives cut there. For here Cashmore's cut up more ex-LMS Black 5s than anyone else, no fewer than 152 of the class. Apparently, not content with this, the yard bought and broke up one third of all the ex-LMS 8F 2-8-0s, a quite astonishing proportion which defies easy explanation. No less than 219 of these big freight engines went to Great Bridge, totalling, the student of useless information will be pleased to learn, 27,539 tons of Scrap Metal!

The Cashmore group had been in business a long time before the demise of steam, demolishing factories and disposing of old machinery during the depressed years of the twenties and thirties. Much of the redundant machinery that was purchased had many years of life left so, rather than scrap it all, the company found it profitable to recondition many of the items for resale. Over the years, experience in loco-breaking had been gained on a number of industrial engines, both in Cashmore's yards and on site. Yet, the firm's first major incursion into BR stock came in the latter part of 1959 when they began cutting up electric motor coaches after the closure of Wolverton Works. Initial purchases of BR locomotives appear to have commenced in December 1959, when six ex-LMS engines; Class 2P, Nos.40553/87/675, and the 3-cylinder compounds, Nos.41083, 41113/22 arrived from a store near Derby. The following February, the 18 LNWR 0-8-0s and the LT&SR tank engines arrived from the dump at Winsford. They were followed in the early summer by the 12 ex-MR locos from Badnall's Wharf, whilst on 24th August Nos.43878, 43965, 44108 arrived from Saltley. The first Western Region purchase was noted in May, No.2237, though it would appear that only former LMS types arrived throughout the remainder of the year. Operations during 1961 centred on redundant stock taken in locally from Saltley and Bescot depots, which included another five LNWR G2a 0-8-0s, Nos.49021/77, 49275, 49343, 49411 and Stanier 2-6-4T No.42552. In June three 4Fs, Nos.44064/93, 44513, arrived following a protracted period in store at Uttoxeter, though the majority of the purchases in this period were 3Fs with a sprinkling of Class 2Ps.

Activities during 1962 eased slightly, possibly due to the volume of purchases that were being directed to Cashmore's Newport yard which, by this time, was taking in Castle and King Classes from Swindon. In March, two Stanier 0-4-4 2Ps, Nos.41902/09, were hauled from store at Coventry to Great Bridge by No.42940. Passengers travelling through Water Orton during April may have been surprised to see Cashmore's men cutting one of the old Johnson 2Ps, No.40396 in the goods yard - presumably because the locomotive was in a poor mechanical condition and unfit to travel! During November, four ex-GER Class J15 0-6-0s arrived from Stratford, these being Nos.65420/53/60/76. This was the first batch of ex-LNER types, but in the years which followed Classes K3s, B1s, O4s and finally V2s were all disposed of by the yard. After the J15s the next acquisition was a major one, as ten Castles were purchased from Old Oak Common and Swindon. These were Nos.5008/11/32-34/36/66/68/82/84, which began arriving about mid-December and were cut up in January.

With the yard disposing of over 100 locos in 1963, Cashmore's enjoyed a busy year. Four K3s, Nos.61807/21/31/89 arrived during February followed by a consignment of B1s from the Doncaster, Mexborough and Staveley areas, including No.61027 *Madoqua*. Castle Class, No.5027 *Farleigh Castle*, arrived, with ex-GWR colleagues Nos.4906, 5910/26/30/59 - all Hall Class 4-6-0s. Yet the year's highlight (or blackest moment depending on your viewpoint) must have been in October, when No.6005 *King George* II arrived and was totally destroyed by the 26th of the month. To round off the year, standard bearer of the Western Region, No.7007 *Great Western* arrived despite the fact that some would have said it was a candidate for preservation. The following year saw a host of once-important engines, including; Castle Class Nos.4098, 5001/22/25/41/74/91, 7000/2/18/21/31/33/36, Manor Class No.7800, Hall Class Nos.4905/54/66/91, 5942/51/98, 6940/48. An interesting arrival was No.46112 *Sherwood Forester* which (officially) turned up from Annesley with front-end accident damage. However, for some time the 'Scot' had sat in a small dump at Rigley's Wagon Repair sidings, and it seems probable that it came directly from that location to Tipton. Other ex-LMS inmates were mostly Jubilee Class 4-6-0s, with Nos.45557/61/4/79/99, 45611/20/22/31/41/84 45709/23 all meeting their end. The solitary LNER type in 1964 was a Class B1 No.61006, *Blackbuck*.

A real coup was experienced in November with the purchase of nine LMS Pacifics, Nos.46228/39/40/41/45/48/51/54/56. They should have been joined by another member of the class, No.46243, but the deal fell through and *City of Lancaster* went to Central Wagon, Ince. *City of Leeds* was the first to arrive on the 17th, and with astonishing speed it was despatched into wagon loads of scrap and condemned to the history books within four days. On 8th December, Nos.46245/51/54 were sent from Crewe, and these were finally destroyed just six days before Christmas. Of the remainder, Nos.46228/39/56 were all cut up in the first week of the New Year; *City of Coventry* appears to have been the last, as it was seen in Oxley sidings on January 17th. Further Jubilees were purchased in 1965 including No.45552, *Silver Jubilee* the doyen of the Class and Nos.45556/63/67/95, 45604/32/76, 45705/21, which all went towards the staggering 37 members of this type which were disposed of by Cashmore's. More Castle and Hall Class locomotives were dealt with, along with *Bodicote Grange* towards the end of the year. The last two members of the once numerous LNWR G1 Class, Nos.48895 and 49361, came from Bescot to face extinction. Interestingly, No.49361, and G2 No.49430 which also came in about the same time, had worked an SLS special as their last duty. A Class K3, No.61912, which had latterly been used as a stationary boiler at New England depot arrived in May, and in September the yard was host to an A1 *Holyrood*. Three Class V2s came in from York, including No.60847 *St. Peter's School York A.D.627*, followed by Nos.60828/43/95/923 in December.

Throughout the remaining few years hundreds of locos were dealt with, and by 1966 the yard was employing six teams of men (two in each). Their sport was not entirely confined to steam, for during 1967 some older diesels including No. 15001 were cut. In January 1968, the pioneer locomotives Nos. 10000, 10201-3 arriving from Derby, despite their obvious candidacy for preservation. By this date locomotives were arriving from the last steam strongholds, Speke, Patricroft, Trafford Park and Normanton. The last batch arrived during September 1968, all Standard Class 5s from Patricroft. The last of these, Nos.73133/5/42, met the torch during the week ending 24th November and were finally cut up by the end of January 1969. However, this was not the yard's final incursion into steam, as Nos.1502 & 1509 came in October 1970 from Coventry Colliery. According to Cashmore's records over 1,500 locos went through Great Bridge, but figures around 1,250 seem nearer the mark. However, it is interesting to note that no ex-SR examples were dealt with.

At the Great Bridge Yard of John Cashmore on 27th January 1969, BR Standard Class 5 4-6-0s still await disposal, five months on from the end of main-line steam. The two engines concerned are Nos.73135/42.
H. L. Holland

73142

ARNOTT & YOUNG LTD.

WE BEGIN OUR ROUND up of the other private yards with a look at the firm of Arnott & Young, whose contribution to the disposal of steam was on par with such other large concerns such as T.W. Wards in the number of yards they had up and down the British Isles. To document them all would be impossible, but we might begin with the firm's Parkgate & Rawmarsh Yard. Details of what happened here are extremely scarce, as it was tucked away in a small quarry on the northern side of the Rotherham-Leeds main line, but it was probably established because of the close proximity to the local steel industry. In fact it was on the doorstep of the Aldwalke steel plant, where a wide variety of free-cutting steels were produced by a process which alleviated the traditional problems caused by a high sulphur charge in reclaimed scrap. Due to the Parkgate & Rawmarsh yard's cramped location, only one or two locomotives were taken at a time. The problem of space was compounded because only one track was available for cutting, and consequently many of the locomotives had their tenders removed. Work on cutting these was deferred and a small dump was established on a siding further along the tracks. Several of these 'reprieved' tenders were to postpone the inevitable even longer, when their under-frames were re-sold to the Parkgate Iron & Steel Co. (later British Steel, Rotherham) for use as ingot carriers. One of these tenders, probably from an A4, was regularly used at the Aldwalke Soaking Pits until about 1978 when it was cut up because of repeated derailments in the ingot stock yard. From around 1963 onwards, over 70 engines were disposed of at the yard, mostly WDs, 9Fs, 84XXX tank engines, O4s,

At the yard of Arnott & Young in Rotherham, a travesty is about to take place as Standard Class 9F 2-10-0 No.92223 awaits the cutters' torch on 24th September 1968. Even today, in the 1990s, this engine could have been still expected to have been in service had steam not been withdraw - in 1968 it was barely run in.
A. Coleman

The scrap metal business had no sentiments about what it was doing, and to them this was good business - British Railways' loss was their gain, so Arnott & Young had a variety of operational centres all over Britain. This one at Old Kilpatrick has a nice mix of ex-WD, LNER and BR Standard classes waiting to be demolished.
J. L. Stephenson

and the occasional 4F. The most interesting classes were perhaps the former Staveley Works shunters which had been in store at Canklow (Nos.41528/33, 41734/63, 41804, and 47001/5) and two named B1s, Nos.61237/40 from Wakefield. Towards the end the yard was predominantly preoccupied with diesel shunters, but it did find time to chop up the remaining loco tenders and some DMUs before closing in the early 1970s.

Additionally, Arnott & Young had a good foothold in Scotland, where its cutting operations were largely concentrated at Old Kilpatrick and Tollcross, Glasgow, though it is also reputed to be the parent company for West of Scotland Shipbreakers at Troon harbour. The Old Kilpatrick yard at Greenock was served by a siding from the station and had a 'Pug' of it's own (Peckett 0-4-0T No.5 *Avon*) to handle the arrivals. These began late in 1959 and included Caledonian engines Nos.54468/79/97 from Princess Pier, Class D11 No.62675 and Glen Class No.62477. Consignments continued in small batches right up to March 1967 and consisted mainly of former Caledonian locos and J36/J38 types from Fife. The Carmyle yard saw a mix of slightly larger locomotives but in the early years noteworthy celebrities had included Class D30 No.62418 *The Pirate*. Although the shed staff at Thornton had tried their best to hide this old favourite inside the depot, only to be towed out occasionally for photographic purposes, the powers that be finally had their way! Class K2 No.61790 *Loch Lomond* also finished it's days here as did four Class D11s, Nos.62676/84/92/94. By 1964 Bathgate shed finally yielded and sent a large number of A3 Class locos, Nos.60037/42/57/77/87/99/101 whilst No.60096 arrived from store at Parkhead. A further A3 No.60041 arrived in October 1966 from Cowlairs, but by this time it was Black 5 and Standard Class disposals that were the order of the day.

'Jinty' 0-6-0T No.47305 at the yard of Arnott & Young Ltd, Troon on 5th June 1967. At the time the Tri-ang/Hornby model of this class was the mainstay of most basic train sets, what a pity the real thing could not have been as popular with the bigger boys at British Railways' headquarters.
C. Richards

Though Arnott & Young's yard at Bilston may not have been as busy as some of the firms other operational sites, it still took in and demolished some very large engines. On 4th May 1963, two such examples, ex-WD 2-8-0s Nos.90028 and 90414 stand silent, whilst new gas cylinders lay alongside.
Michael Hale

BIRDS GROUP

THE BIRDS GROUP WERE long established in the scrap metal industry, but their yard at Long Marston in Warwickshire was a late starter in the disposal of steam. It had originally been part of the Royal Engineers army base, and was initially acquired by the company for breaking up motor cars. Steam engines were first purchased in June 1965, with Nos.6995, 43918, 47442, 73044/9 being in among the earliest batches. Around a 130 purchases were made, the majority coming from Birmingham, Liverpool, Crewe and Nottingham districts. Perhaps the most worthy of note are the ex-GWR passenger types handled here which included Hall Class Nos.6911/18/22/63/95, Grange Class Nos.6803/13/16/23/27/51/54 and Manor No.7814. Other interesting victims were the first Class 9F, No.92000 and a named B1, No.61024 *Addax*. Standard Class 4s were disposed of in some quantity, most of which came from the Stoke district; Nos.75002/6/13/24/36/45/6/7/52/6/63/71. After April 1968 diesels intermittently appeared including a batch from Polmadie Nos. D8547/56/60/4/70/2/6-7. Railway work had gradually diminished by late 1969, with what was probably the last engine, D8572, being cut in August that year.

The yard at Llanelly commenced much earlier and probably began its work in the early summer of 1964 with 0-6-0 pannier tank engines of the 57xx Class of which Nos.3613/92,3701/31/57/61/8 were the first examples, though it is known that members of the 56XX Class were also being handled simultaneously. Towards the end of that year three GWR railcars, Nos.W21W, W24W and W32W were cut, along with more members of the 57xx Class. Early in the New Year the yard was heavily into ex-SR types; particularly West Country Class Nos.34030/96 and Battle of Britain Class Nos.34054/65. In the spring it was again the turn of ex-GWR types with Nos.5673, 5686 and 6655 coming from a small dump at Radyr. In June another batch of ex-GWR engines came along, this time made up from Classes 2251, 42xx, 43xx, 72xx, 74xx, 94xx and named engines *Little Wyreley Hall* and *Longworth Manor*. It was also around this time that the first Standard Class engines arrived, in the form of Nos.75007 and 80035. The year drew on

A study in decimation, as 'Jinty' No.47272 is carved to pieces at Long Marston on 27th November 1966. Bird's men have removed the cab and cut away the side tank, yet the fireman's shovel still adorns the foot-plate, but this boiler will never feel the warmth of live steam again.
N. E. Preedy

with a continual flow of locomotives as the dumps around the Welsh sheds disgorged their unwanted inhabitants, but as the yard's work drew to an end it was LMS types that were to be its last victims, including Nos.42844, 42961, 44169, 43967, 44489, 44536, 48389, 48607, 48716.

Quite why the work ended at the Bynea site is not defined, conflicting reports about the reason for its demise only leave uncertainty behind - perhaps the decline in available stock made it more logical for more distant purchases to be sent to Long Marston. The remaining purchases from the western side of the country were transferred to Birds at Morriston near Swansea. This yard had begun its incursion into steam in March 1964 when 57xx Class No.4661 was vanquished. In June a profusion of ex-SR locos were acquired, these being Nos.31913/7 and 33010 from Feltham and Nos.33024/34 and 31819 from Fratton. In July more engines arrived from Feltham, Nos.31407, 31837/70 and 33022, coming via the store at Swansea East Dock. More Southern and Western engines arrived in June, as well as the first batch of ex-LMS locos. Nos.47368, 48172, 48420, 48524 and Jubilee Class 4-6-0 *Trafalgar*. Between September and the end of the year only three engines were purchased, these being Southern Region N Class Nos.31812/49/56, and one must conclude that there must have been a bit of a backlog in the tendering process because what happened next is quite staggering. In December Birds' purchases included at least 51 GWR locos and 27 SR types - an amazing figure when you consider it. Of course they did not all arrive at once but, considering the variety in the classes and the places where the engines were laying in store, this is not surprising. Some of the better known examples that had been acquired were *Hutton Hall, Levens Hall, Sudeley Castle, Seaton, Watersmeet, Hurricane, 74 Squadron, 222 Squadron, Sir Trafford Leigh Mallory, Blanford Forum, Lydford, and Calstock.* In February and March just seven engines were acquired, but this included no lesser names than No.5000 *Launceston Castle,* No.34099 *Lynmouth* and No.35001 *Channel Packet.* April saw Nos.30542, and 33004/12, with Nos.4679, 5613/89, 6628/50, 6826, 7813 and 9426/46/61/75 being obtained in June. October was the next busy month for the firm's buyer, as Birds successfully tendered for 23 engines including Standard Class Nos.80048, 80101 and 82032. November and December witnessed the firm laying its hands on No.5235, Hughes 'Crabs' Nos.42753, 42814/27 and Black 5 No.45429. But after this things went decidedly quiet with the only recorded purchases in 1966 being Nos.41305, 41325, 75005, 78001/6 and 80147. In 1967, when most other yards were brimming with work, Morriston only purchased Black 5 No.44685, and Standard Class 4 2-6-0s Nos.76005-7/11/31/64.

The same dramatic fall off was noted at Birds' other yard at Risca near Newport during the period 1966-7, and from this we must conclude that the firm were indeed directing its remaining efforts to Long Marston and to the yard of R.S. Hayes at Bridgend which Birds had purchased in 1965. However, between 1964 and 1966 they certainly had a time with steam at Risca. By virtue of the numbers of locomotives disposed of - at least 172 steam engines, one diesel locomotive and two GWR railcars - it may classified as a GRADE ONE YARD. The carnage began at the Pontymister Works in or around May 1964 with Nos.1028, 1421, 2204/51/77, 3206/16, 3720, 4916/24, 5410, 6769, 6943, 9770 and 41245/76 being bought for the scrap line. In July 18 locos were purchased including Jubilee Class *Barfleur*. August evidenced 13 more acquisitions including the two railcars and the first Southern Region victim - N Class No.31821 which, after languishing in store for some considerable time, arrived in an appalling condition - complete with a bird's nest in the smokebox. The next loco to come in was another SR class, Q1 No.33036, which arrived in November before it again went quiet until the end of the year. In December Birds tendered for and began receiving no less than 61 locomotives - all of Great Western pedigree, including Grange, Hall, Manor, 16xx, 2251, 28xx, 42xx, 43xx, 45xx, 51xx, 56xx, 57xx, 61xx, 72xx, and 94xx Classes. In January 1965 named engines *Lady Margaret Hall, Swansea Castle, Blackwell Hall, Civil Service Rifleman* and a pannier tank No.9707 were consigned to Birds, to be followed in March and April by a further 10 GWR locomotives and No.44102. June was again a busy month with 31 more engines being purchased all of which were ex-GWR types (with the exception of an ex-LMS 4F No.44135). The yards' last purchases of the year were Nos.6163/7 in November. January 1966 saw four Hall Class 4-6-0s being obtained, No.4962 *Ragley Hall,* No.6910 *Gossington Hall,* No.6927 *Liford Hall,* and No.6931 *Aldborough Hall.* The following month two 2-6-2 tank engines were obtained, these being of the 61xx and Standard Classes. It was October 1967 before the next purchase was made, and this was the yards' only known diesel; D2757. In the final bout of slaughter, it was all BR Standard Classes that were purchased in November of 1967 and January 1968, with Nos.75068/76, 76007/31, 77014, 80011/16/85/134/40/52 being the unlucky casualties.

General scene at Bird's Yard at Morriston on August 7th 1965, with standard tank No. 82017 standing at the head of a rake of steel mineral wagons. Though this may shadow the familiar sights of the Welsh coal trains, this Standard Class 2-6-2T has no future left. This class had some 45 members, all of which were condemned – making the type extinct.
Atlantic Collection

J. BUTTIGIEG, NEWPORT, MONMOUTHSHIRE

THE FIRM OF J. BUTTIGIEG were also located in that great locomotive disposal area, Newport. Accordingly the firm were to play a major role in the demise of steam, thus becoming one of the GRADE ONE YARDS. A significant role of Buttigieg's was their part in the demise of the Bullied Pacifics - 24 engines; six Merchant Navy Class locos and 18 members of the West Country/Battle of Britain Class. Yet, like so many of their contemporaries, the firm began by cutting up humble 0-6-0 tank engines of which No.5745 is reputed to be the first in May 1960. After an initial batch of 8 locomotives things seem to have been quiet for a time, but in 1962 the firm were noted cutting up No.9469 in a siding near Lower Pontnewydd Station. Operations in the earlier part of the 1960s seem to have been a bit hit and miss, with some work also being carried on at Pillgwelly Wharf. Late in 1964 a few purchases were made, including ex-LMS Class 8F No.48306. As the new year arrived, so did more locomotives including Standard Class Nos.73024 and 92210. The tally had risen to 15 by the end of the first quarter, including two more Standard types, then the first arrival in April turned out to be No.31799 from Eastleigh. During the rest of 1965 a regular procession of engines turned up at Buttigieg's, so that by the end of the year around 40 locomotives had been cut up. In 1966 the carnage was slightly higher with 42, a large percentage of which were Standard Classes. In 1966 well over 120 were cut up, with big engines such as Battle of Britain, West Country, Merchant Navy, Black 5, Standard 5, 8F and 9F classes being included. The last year saw around 83 engines being dismembered for their scrap value, of which no less than half were Stanier 2-8-0 8Fs. The

The death of West Country Class No.34032 *Camelford* at Buttigieg's yard on 19th November 1967. This engine had taken a year to die, having been withdrawn from Salisbury MPD as early as October 1966.
Alan Sommerfield

Like some giant jig-saw puzzle, the dismembered remains of Stanier 8F No.48675 litters Buttigieg's Newport yard. Note the tenders to the rear, like a number of firms Buttigieg initially concentrated on engines, tenders were quite often not cut up until some considerable time after the demise of their engine.
Rex Conway

final victim appears to have been No.34017 *Ilfracombe* which was cut up at the end of the year, but only after it had been laying around the yard for about 18 months.

Photographs of operations in Butler's yard are virtually nonexistent, so this one has to be included if only for posterity. The men have begun the arduous task of recovering the inner firebox - a particularly valuable prize because of the copper. Work on WD 2-8-0 No. 90639 is well underway on 4th August 1964; next the outer shell of the boiler will be sliced, then the crown stays removed, the operation then being repeated on the side stays, one of the most time-consuming aspects of the job.
Keith Preston

G. W. BUTLER, OTLEY, YORKS.

BASED AT BOWLING IRON Works, Butler's venture into the locomotive business was rather short-lived. On page 157 we present a view of No.43072 following an accident at Adolphus Street, Bradford. As it was impossible to retrieve it, the Ivatt 2-6-0 was cut-up where it fell by this firm. However, in volume 2 of the original series, we erroneously stated that it was the firm's sole purchase. Actually Butler's cut up a small number of BR locomotives, including Jubilee Class *Sanspareil* which arrived ex-store from Stockport and a Class B1 No.61080 in July 1964. During the following month an Austerity 2-8-0, No.90639 (ex-Wakefield 56A), was also despatched with speed. Further activities of this firm have still to be discovered, but it is known that several industrial tank engines were cut, including at least three on a site near Shipley station. In later years the firm also undertook the demolition of several wagons and at least one steam crane from the Rodley crane works in Leeds, whilst a visit to the yard in 1976 revealed a partially dismembered Midland Railway (Cowans Sheldon) 60' turntable awaiting attention.

G. H. CAMPBELL LTD.

THE FIRM OF G.H. CAMPBELL had two main sites, the first being the Atlas Works in Airdrie, Lanarkshire, the other at Bognor Road, Shieldhall, Renfrewshire. The majority of the early occupants of these yards had been towed north from the Manchester area presumably via Hellifield and the Settle & Carlisle route to avoid the busy West Coast main line. Class 3F Nos.43400/ 43763 from Gorton definitely went via this route, the former taking over a month to complete the journey. Such a move was surely something of a farce, when so many other yards were almost on the doorstep. In terms of variety,

The yards of G. H. Campbell were hard places to get into, so this is yet another pleasing picture to add to the collection. Taken on 3rd June 1963 it shows Class 3F 0-6-0 No.43721 being cut up, its tender stripped down to the frames. However, note the inscription on the cab-side which reads 'Have Steam Will Travel?'.
J. L. Stevenson

Campbell's had some interesting types during 1963, the following being recorded,:- L&YR locos Nos.52275 ex-Lees and Nos.52345/523 from Bolton as well as No.52456; two LNWR 0-8-0s Nos.49382/426 and an LMS 2P No.40453 all came to Shieldhall from Patricroft, whilst Nos.52275 and 49335 went to the Atlas Works together with a batch of Stanier 2-6-2Ts from Heaton Mersey. Towards the end of 1963 a batch of Jubilees were cleared from stores at Corkerhill and Lugton with Nos.45640/87/92/3, 45707/11/27 being sold to Atlas Works and Nos.45621/65/73/77, 45720 destined for Shieldhall although ultimately some of these may have switched yards

Two A4 Class Nos.60027/31 were purchased for the Shieldhall yard early in 1966, but by the middle of that year the yard closed and operations were concentrated on Airdrie. The policy adopted was that one engine would arrive on a given date and would be cut immediately, the proof being the demise of a 2-6-4T No.42264 which arrived on 16th September 1966 at 10am and was completely cut up by 4.15pm! How many men were employed on this task is not recorded but one would say quite a lot! Whether this system continued or not is unknown but it seems unlikely considering the influx during the period 1967-8. Some choice locomotives finished their days at Campbell's. Worthy of note are the A4 No.60005 *Sir Charles Newton;* two Class A2s, Nos.60529/34; V2 Class No.60835, the Patriot *Illustrious* No.45532; No.72007 *Clan Mackintosh,* and no less than ten Britannia Class 4-6-2s, Nos.70002/3/5/8/25/33/46/47/50/2. Numerous Class 9Fs arrived during 1968, many travelling from Speke Junction. However, by then Campbell's operations had drifted into the diesel field with many of the early Barclay, Hunslet and Drewry shunters that had failed to perform anything like satisfactorily on the Scottish Region coming under the torch at an early stage.

CENTRAL WAGON CO. LTD.

THE ACTIVITIES OF THE Central Wagon Company are not well recorded, and we are unsure about why this should be, because locomotive disposal in the Wigan area seems to have been a thriving industry. Three yards around Ince were taking withdrawn stock, these being principally the Central Wagon Co. Lower Ince, and what are reported as two subsidiary companies Ince Wagon and Iron Works Co., and Thompson's. Quite a 'mixed bag' of information has been presented on these yards, as well as on the dead engines which were stored/dumped(?) on the Springs Branch Shed. It would appear from the comments of a former shed-master, that all these engines were destined for the local yards, but 'an odd one or two' might have ended up elsewhere. Ince Wagon Works were located between Springs Branch and Lower Ince station, just to the north of the bridge where the Springs Branch crosses the former Great Central line. Thompson's was situated past the L&YR Wallgate line and was visible from Central Wagon.

As time went on, however, all locomotive sales were classified as being to Central Wagon Co., Wigan which was a trifle misleading. Why this should be, is still unknown, but no doubt an authority on the subject will explain it all. Similarly, it is difficult to understand why early activity went unrecorded, so many questions remain unanswered. However, the same may be said of the other yards, and only information from those who were involved will resolve the issues. For the time being, we can only surmise that so much was taking place at this time that it became difficult to keep detailed records. The earliest purchases seem to have been in August 1960, when 'dumped' engines (Nos.40068, 43660, 49160, and 51546) came from Heapley along with No.43623 from Badnall's Wharf; however, there remains a suspicion that these were not necessarily the first. By 1961 scores of engines were being sent to Thompson's Yard. Many of these had also been residents of the Heapley and Badnall's Wharf dumps, whilst others came from Crewe and Horwich. The bulk of these were ex-LMS types: Fowler 2-6-2 tanks, 'Jinties', 3Fs, 4Fs, LNWR. 0-8-0s and various L&YR classes. This remained the pattern through the period from 1960 to 1962, though as time went on, some GWR specimens started appearing. Of particular note were the 57xx Pannier tanks, Nos.3723, 5744/61/66/79/89/93, 8715/27/50/88/97, and 7753/62. These came from as far away as Neath, Taunton, Westbury, Southall and North Wales. One would have thought that Cashmore's at Newport would have been more suitable recipients, particularly when transportation costs are considered. Yet these acquisitions were not confined to the smaller classes, as testified to by the unusual purchase of *Patshull Hall* and *Warfield Hall* during 1964-5.

The sight of such 'foreigners' must have caused quite a stir in this neck of the woods, but more 'treats' were to be experienced by local enthusiasts. For example, ten Class B1s, Nos.61052/4/66/96, 61149/71, 61254/80/6 and 61363, had arrived from March by 2nd July 1963. They were accompanied by four K3s from the same depot, Nos.61817, 61915/42/63, and followed by two ex-GNR 02s, Nos.63961/71 from Doncaster a month later. At the end of the year, four more members of the same class, Nos.63923/30/33/48, had appeared from Grantham, whilst No.63966 found its way from Mexborough in March 1964. More B1 locos were received during 1964; never, in all its years had Wigan seen so many ex-LNER types. As 1964 progressed, the yard's bread and butter work consisted of WD 2-8-0s, 4Fs and

Crabs and perhaps the only other real locomotives of note to arrive that year was No.45710 *Irresistible* which could resist 'progress' no more, and No.46129 *The Scottish Horse*. The former turned up at Springs Branch from Gorton in September, whilst the Royal Scot came from another Manchester shed (Longsight) on 14th November. The real 'cream' started appearing during 1965, as Coronation Class *City Of Lancaster* and four Jubilee Class locos (Nos.45592, 45601/57/81) were purchased in January. Surprisingly, all the 4-6-0s were still intact as late as mid-April, and No.46243 survived until August. Patriot Class No.45522 *Prestatyn* had been purchased from Buxton shed where it had languished in store for some time, until it took its last journey in April. Two more Jubilees, *Assam* and *Palestine* were received in mid-1965, but now the yard's regular consignments were locomotives of the Hughes 2-6-0 'Crab' and WD 2-8-0 types.

Towards the end of that operation, BR Standard Classes, 8Fs, and Stanier Black 5s were coming in from the last bastions of steam - the North-west sheds. However, Central Wagon's carnage did not out-last steam itself and as 1966 progressed, they saw a gradual fall-off in the numbers of engines being received. The last purchases would seem to have been No.47416 from Edgehill, and No.78002 from Lostock Hall in September - both of which were completely cut by early October. Although the earlier volumes of *Steam For Scrap* reported that Central Wagon's yard at Barrow-in-Furnace was a Grade One Yard, it was never in the same league as Wigan, though it did play a small part in the disposal of steam.

Number 46243 *City Of Lancaster* stands face to face with ex-LNER No.61056 in the arrival sidings of the Central Wagon Co. at Ince on 15th March 1965. Other locos in this line up included Nos.61144, 90157 and 42077, whilst Jubilee Class No.45681 *Aboukir* is just out of this picture. The Coronation remained intact for another five months until it was cut up on 17th August 1965, meanwhile the two B1s had been disposed of by late July. On the left, the branch from Springs Branch Junction passes underneath the former L&YR line from Wigan to Hindley just before reaching it's truncated terminus at Ince.
H. L. Holland

G. COHEN LTD - 600 GROUP

THE COHEN'S GROUP WERE well established as locomotive breakers by the mid-1960s especially in South Wales and the North East, but they disposed of hundreds of locomotives from all regions at their sites up and down the country. The company's only yard in central England was at Sheffield, but it was small and congested. The first clear signs that Cohen's had started cutting steam locos there occurred in September 1962, however from local intelligence it would appear as though the work had begun at an earlier date. Yet, it was during that month that the remains of No.65773 were noted in the yard after the Class J27 had arrived in pieces after being partially cut at Darlington works. During the next five years locos continued to trickle in - but never in appreciable numbers. The yard seemed to concentrate on the smaller, more manageable types, mainly Classes 4F, 1F and B1. The most notable engine cut up here was named B1, No.61249 *Fitzherbert Wright*, but the LMS Kitson 0-4-0STs Nos.47002/8-9 and Fowler 0-6-0 dock tank No.47164 are worthy of note. The last engine recorded as being cut here was No.47534 in November 1967.

It may have been the increase in engines being acquired from depots and stores in the Midlands that prompted the utilisation of the Coburn Works at Kettering. The yard was situated on the site of the old Cransley Iron Works and was initially used for the disposal of coach, tube and LTE stock. The site was ideal in that it was close to the Birmingham and Nottingham districts where much of the redundant stock was then being purchased. In addition there was a good main line connection to the London area. The first purchase was a consignment of former Southern Region classes during March 1964. This was comprised of four S15s Nos.30497/507/9/14, five Q1s Nos.33002/8/13/16/24 and three Schools Nos.30902/21/35 together with the odd member of the H16, Q and W Classes; most of which came from the Feltham and Nine Elms. Three more W Class Nos.31912/14/24 arrived later that year, during November, together with a batch of five 82XXX 3MTs Nos.82011/2/3/4/5 which had been displaced from Nine Elms. The most common class to arrive in any number was the LMS 4F but occasionally a surprise turned up, in particular two Grange Class locos Nos.6808/39. By the end of 1964 50 locomotives had been disposed of, but in contrast the following year saw very little activity. The first Class 9Fs arrived at Kettering in the form of Nos.92036, 92142/3/81, all from New England, whilst No.6928 *Underley Hall* appeared from Reading. But it wasn't until February 1966 that the yard returned to normal when a batch of Grange Class 4-6-0s arrived from the Birmingham area, Nos.6831/33/71 from Oxley and Nos.6853/5/61/79 from Tysley. These were cut during March/April and were followed by batches of Class B1 and O4 locos from Doncaster and Colwick respectively. For the record these consisted of:- Nos.61042, 61121/58, 61250, 61329/60, 61406, 63644/74-5 and 63816/73. From then onwards a mixed bag of ex-LMS 'Jinties', 8Fs, Black 5s and Standard Classes continuously converged there and by 1967-8 the Standard Class 5 had become the predominant type, with the inmates having mostly come from the Lancashire sheds or storage dumps such as Speke Junction.

An amusing incident befell one convoy of LMS Black 5s en-route to Kettering on 27th September 1968, when Nos.45104/290/312 were abandoned at New Mills near Gowholes Sidings. After the driver decided that his eight hours were up and refused to go any further, the locos were shunted into the up goods loop and left for over a month. Consequently the vandals descended on them and they were declared unfit to travel until the C&W Dept. had inspected

Cohen's yard at Morriston, pictured with 49xx Class No.6915 *Mursley Hall* in the last stages of life. The picture was taken on 20th May 1965, but within the week the 4-6-0 had ceased to exist.
Keith Preston

TOP: An interesting general view of Cohen's yard at Kettering: a reminder that not all scrap merchants are situated in industrial conurbations. The cutting up roads are to the left with one or two locomotive hulks visible among the neatly stacked scrap. A little 0-4-0 diesel shunter, used to marshal the dead locomotives, is at rest. The two intact steam locomotives are strangers from the Southern: Class S15 4-6-0 No. 30507 and Schools 4-4-0 No. 30935 *Sevenoaks*, but perhaps the most interesting feature is the large quantity of LT underground stock. A May 1964 picture. *Photo: G. G. King.*

BOTTOM: Two months later and No. 30507 has virtually ceased to exist, the design of her firebox throatplate clearly visible. The scrapmen appear to be enjoying their work. Sister engine No. 30506 made it to Barry, was purchased by the Urie S15 Preservation Group and her restoration has been partly financed by the sales of that Bible of the Barry connoisseur: The Barry List. *Photo: G. D. King.*

them. It wasn't until 6th December that Nos.45104/290 were allowed to proceed, then in company with 8F No.48467 they departed for Kettering. Number 45312 was left there and it wasn't until 10th January 1969 that it was eventually pulled out of the sidings, and then only after considerable attention to it's moving parts. The last steam locos dealt with were Nos.44708/816 and 45134 during March 1969, and of these No.44816 had the distinction of being the last to survive until April. By this time the yard was busy disposing of substantial numbers of diesels displaced from the Eastern Region, from Stratford in particular. It may be pertinent to note that diesels were continually broken throughout the end of the 1960s and into the early 1970s, Baby Deltics D5900/3-4 being of particular note. Approaching 250 engines were purchased including two industrial locos, and up to late 1969 around 63 diesels had been similarly dealt with at Kettering.

Cohen's yard at Middlesbrough was adjacent to Cargo Fleet Station on the south bank of the River Tees, and therefore did not command as much publicity as Kettering but it still made heavy inroads into steam. Initial purchases comprised Class J72 Nos.69003/11/19 and 4F No.44197 in 1964, followed by a batch of J94s from Darlington in August 1965; these were as follows:- Nos.68010/11/23/37/43/47/53/60/62, along with Class Q6 Nos.63378/91. The next purchases of any consequence were 11 Black 5s, mainly from Carnforth during 1968, these were in order of purchase:- Nos.44780, 44818/45, 45200, 44963, 44758, 45394, 45268, 45206, 45310/30. In all probability No.45310 was the yard's last BR steam engine, though unconfirmed reports detail the destruction of various industrial locomotives in the early 1970s.

Inside the main gate of Cohen's works at Cargo Fleet, Middlesbrough on 11th July 1965. Not the easiest of location to gain access to, as the sign clearly portrays. Situated in the heart of an industrial complex on the south bank of the River Tees, this yard had an appetite for the heavy freight engines developed by the NER and LNER, of which Class Q6 No.63378 is a specific example.
A. Brown

Four years later, and still not savaged by the guard dogs, our correspondents returned to the site and took this view in April 1969. It shows Black 5 No.45310 waiting to be cut, along with No.45330, these were the last of the 11 Stanier 4-6-0s disposed of at Cargo Fleet.
Martin L. Brown

J. N. CONNELL LTD. COATBRIDGE

JAMES CONNELL WAS ONE of the fore runners in the railway scrap business and his Union Works site, near Calder Goods Yard, was certainly busy early in 1959. Two of the earliest purchases were 8Fs Nos.WD508 and WD511 purchased from the Ministry of Defence in April that year. The first major bulk purchase from BR came in December consisting of a variety of classes including K2 Nos.61758/70/8, D30 No.62436, D34 Glen Class Nos.62470/2/5/87/92 and two Pickersgill 3Ps Nos.54472/3. By February 1960 operations were in full swing and things continued that way until the end of 1964. In the main it was ex-Caledonian locomotives of the McIntosh and Drummond types that formed the backbone of the work, with many being sent from the Carnbrae sidings or Bo'ness dump. By 1963 however, former ex-MR Class 2Ps, 4Fs and even Stanier 3MTs were being demolished, many coming from Hurlford, Ardrossan and Ayr depots. During October 1964 the yard was host to Nos.45545/71, 46118/62 and 46200 The Princess Royal all ex-store Carlisle Upperby, No.45696 being one of the final purchases.

At the yard of Connell's of Calder a semi-aerial view presents the end of two pre-Grouping 0-6-0s. These being an ex-Caledonian Pickersgill No.57659 (on the left) and an ex-Midland Railway loco No.43884 as they are cut up on 9th June 1962. *J. L. Stevenson*

COOPER METALS [CALIFORNIA SIDINGS], SHARPNESS, GLOUCESTERSHIRE.

THIS COMPANY HAD A rather chequered career, but it's relatively short sojourn into the locomotive business is worthy of note since it highlights the fact that it wasn't a bed of roses for all scrap merchants. In July 1959 the company's Swindon office purchased three locomotives, 14xx Class No.5810 and 64xx Class Nos.6409/28. No photographic evidence has surfaced but it seems likely that these first three were cut in the firm's own yard at Highworth Junction, Swindon. That seems to have been the end of things until September 1963 when 28xx Class No.3858 was purchased, however the sale was cancelled and the engine eventually went to Cashmore's. It may have been that the firm had no site suitable for larger hulks and not just a question of being outbid. The inference is that a more convenient site was being sought for operations. By February 1964, No.1409 was purchased from Gloucester shed and reputedly directed straight to Sharpness by the Swindon office. During May two more consignments were directed to this location, comprising Nos.2245, 3633, 6319/65 and 7335 from Gloucester and Nos.5978, 4087, 5040/50/71, 5420 from St. Phillip's Marsh. July 1964 saw the bulk purchase of 26 GWR locos including Nos.1066/27, 4701, 4908/24/64/75/81/96, 5908/19/35/43/54/77, 7009/15/37.

What happened next is a bit of a mystery but by all accounts BR discovered a weight restriction on the Sharpness Branch and movements of large locomotives had to stop, presumably because of the restriction red category; but in the event many of the Hall and Castle Class locos were down at Sharpness already. Coupled to this fact it is evident that some sales were falling through, and we may ask with confidence, had someone done a miscalculation with the costs? Perhaps we will never know, but the County, Hall and Castle Class locos purchased that July were said to have been re-sold to Cashmore's Newport though some reports indicate Nos.4924/64/96, 5943/54 and 7015 being cut at Cooper's, so what was the truth? Stranger still, No.5986 was purchased in December 1964 and reported as being sold to Cashmore's the following July, which was about the time that operations at Cooper's suddenly appeared to cease. The whole situation remains a 'grey area', but some observers must still hold the answers!

In deepest Gloucestershire, a row of ex-GWR express types wait the chop, with 2-8-0 No.4701 at the forefront. Behind the engines are believed to be Nos.7037, 7009 and 5071. *B. G. Staddon*

At the Park Royal works of Cox & Danks Ltd. on 7th April 1965, 45xx 2-6-2T No.5564 sits at the end of a weed-covered yard. Its future has already been determined, a consignment tag on its handrail tells the story 'sold for scrap'. Its bunker still retains a full load of coal; just one more example of how BR squandered tax-payers' money.
Atlantic Collection

COX & DANKS. WADSLEY BRIDGE, SHEFFIELD

THE SIGHT OF DEAD locomotives in transit to, or stored at local sheds would always command great interest amongst enthusiasts but by 1963 it was apparent that locos were beginning to disappear as fast as they arrived. For example, turning up at depots such as Darnall in Sheffield, they would then vanish within days; creating something of a mystery as they were not arriving at the 'known' local yards. This prompted the 'Big Search' which eventually revealed that other 'unknown' breakers were at work, including the firm of Cox & Danks whose yard was adjacent to the Woodhead line near Wadsley Bridge station. A visit to the site in March 1963 confirmed that activity was well under way, with the complete front end Class B1 No.61060 being one of the first pieces of evidence to be witnessed. Inside were Class K3s Nos.61950/1/70/81 and the cab of No.43760 which had been cut up at Derby in April 1962. Operations had apparently been in full swing for quite a while, but regretfully the records of the firm's activity were scant.

Thereafter a variety of engines are recorded as arriving, many of which came from the West Riding, the most notable being Class A1 pacifics Nos.60119/25 in October 1964. Class V2 No.60837 was dealt with in January 1966, but the bulk of engines round this period were WD 2-8-0s and LNER Class 04s from the North Derbyshire sheds. The last recorded arrivals were Nos.90345 and 90654/78 in October 1967, but there are reports of other engines meeting their end there after that date and these probably include a Class 17 diesel seen in pieces at the yard late in 1969. The firm also had other yards around the country, including Barry, South Wales, Oldbury in the West Midlands, Park Royal and North Acton in London and Brindle Heath near Manchester, but none matched the activity of the Sheffield yard.

A. DRAPER LTD.

AS MENTIONED EARLIER, A separate work has already been published on the work of this Hull scrapyard, and it is not intended to cover the same ground here. However, it is worth noting that the Dairycoates Yard cut up dozens of members of many notable classes. They held the record for the BR Standard 9Fs (38 engines totalling 5,320 tons) and for the ex-LNER B1s (37 engines = 4,556 tons). They also ran Cashmore's, Great Bridge, a good second on the LMS 8Fs (156 engines) and the Black 5s (111 engines). To detail all the disposals at Sculcoates would be impossible within the pages of this book, but a year by year tally may give an impression of the vastness of the undertaking.

The firm were late starters into the demolition of steam, and the first engine seems to have been Class B16 No.61420 in September 1964, quickly followed by six of her sisters. By the end of the year another 14 engines, all ex-LNER classes had been handled. The year 1965 began with Jubilee Class No.45568 and ended with No.90629, a mere 124 engines came in between. The pattern was continued in 1966, as 153 locomotive met their end at Hull, 110 of these being ex-WD types. Two hundred and sixteen steam and two diesel engines were despatched at the yard in 1967, and if that was not enough around a score more were cut up in Neptune Street. The following year they commenced with Nos.42141 and 42269/87 and then swallowed a further 182 locos as a chaser. The last year was 1969, steam was now dead on BR, but Drapers were swallowing up the residue, with 25 more engines still to go; the last of which appears to have been Black 5 No.45444.

Number 90688 stands outside the Hull yard on 4th May 1966. Just one of the many ex-WD 2-8-0s that met their end at the yards of Alfred Draper Ltd.
A. Wakefield Collection

AS WITH ALL labour-intensive industries, in the scrapyard it is important to keep the men occupied. To this end, locomotives bought from BR by a merchant were frequently privately re-sold to another yard with a lighter work load, simply to keep the torches burning: a practice which has since caused considerable confusion to those enthusiasts intent on keeping the historical record straight. And since scrap metal is sold by weight it was clearly desirable to have method and efficiency in the demolition process to ensure that the maximum amount of scrap could be processed and despatched in the shortest possible time.

These two views taken at Draper's yard, Hull, give a good impression of an efficient scrap line.

TOP: Workmen take a break for a smoke while stripping the tubes from LNER Class A1 Pacific No.60157 *Great Eastern* on 8th March 1965. To the rear, others use an identical method on a sister A1. Ten of this class were sold to Drapers, along with eight A3's. Note the floodlights for the late shifts and the row of mineral wagons standing ready to take scrap to the steel works. *Photo: D. Hardy, via Ken Hoole*

ABOVE: The impression of almost clinical efficiency at this yard is heightened by this 18th December 1964 view of LNER Class A3 Pacific No.60071 *Tranquil*, looking anything but .... she is in a later stage of demolition than No.60157 and the cutter's torch has been turned onto her smokebox and buffer beam. *Photo: Ken Hoole*

J. FRISWELL, BANBURY

DURING NOVEMBER 1964 FRISWELL'S cut up 43xx No.6309, ex-store Didcot, this being the first loco purchased by this firm since two ex-LBSCR terriers from the Edge Hill Light Railway had been disposed of ten years earlier. One of their next incursions into locomotive disposal was the cutting of 2-8-2 No.7207 in January 1965 outside Banbury MPD, from where the 72xx Class locomotive was considered unfit to be moved. Other locomotives cut by the firm were Nos.2221, 7221, 7900, 73164, 6904, 5990, 6916, 6917, 6930, 6868, 6921, 6957, 6980 roughly in that order. It is interesting to note that No.7900 *St. Peter's Hall* and the Standard Class 5 were cut in the shed, with the work being completed by 26th March 1965.

Outside Banbury MPD, 72xx class 2-8-2T No.7207 is seen in the process of demolition by employees of J. Friswell Ltd. Work is well under way, in this January 1965 view, though the operation way have been a repeat performance of the scrapping of No.6309 (ex-store Didcot) two months earlier.
Keith Romig.

A rare candidate for demolition pictured in the East Midlands in October 1967, as ex NER Class Q6 0-8-0 No.63455 is pictured at the Chesterfield yard of Garnham, Harris & Elton. These engines were often seen in Yorkshire, some working as far south as Normanton, but Chesterfield was well off their beaten track. The locomotive was completely cut up by the end of January 1967, though there is no clue as to the fate of its chimney - despite the chalked legends 'save chimney' seen on No.63455's side.
Graham Wignall

GARNHAM, HARRIS & ELTON (STEEL-BREAKING & DISMANTLING CO.) CHESTERFIELD.

THE FIRST LOCOMOTIVE CUT by this firm was probably WD236 (Hudswell No.845) which was delivered to the yard from Shoeburyness in January 1947. Furthermore, it is suspected that Derby was directing scrap there during the 1950s; for example, the boiler of No.43513 was in the yard for a long time during this period. Meanwhile ex-London Transport loco L50 was also cut up there 1959. Whether this firm had previously owned premises just next to Chesterfield Station, where the cab from ex-GER Class J15 No.65565 was seen, is not known - but it remains a possibility. They did, however, cut up a fair number of locomotives from the B1, 4F and WD 2-8-0 classes, mostly those taken in from sheds in the South Yorkshire and North Nottinghamshire areas. Notable arrivals were No.50705 from Heapley Dump, No.41068 from Derby, Q6 class No.63426 and Nos.61002-3. During the last week of January 1970, the firm carried on with the carnage of British steam, but this time its victims were two London Transport 0-6-0Ts L97 and L98 (formerly Nos.7749 and 7739) which were delivered by road from Neasden.

R. S. HAYES LTD, BRIDGEND, GLAMORGAN

THE FIRST ARRIVALS AT Hayes' Tremains Yard appear to have been a batch of 28xx Class 2-8-0s from Swindon, with Nos.2812/7/25/30/3 being at the forefront. These came in during August 1959, closely followed by Nos.4377, 4540/53/84, 5315/86/8/90, 5566, and 6318/22/28/54. This must have kept the Welshmen busy for a while, because the next recorded arrival is No.40332 from Derby which did not arrive until December. In the New Year, 1960, a spate of ex-LMS engines were sent for disposal from Crewe with no less than 7 Whitelegg 0-6-2Ts and one ex-LNWR G2A arriving. The following month it was the turn of Barry Works, who consigned 8 0-6-0 pannier tank engines. The next block arrival came, once again, from Swindon with 8 tank engines arriving late that summer. The pattern of 0-6-0PT disposals carried on through 1961, but the records for 1962 seems to show no new acquisitions. In 1963 the work resumed, albeit spasmodically, with a variety of ex-GWR types being decimated - some in Bridgend Goods Yard. In 1964 the sport really began, with the yard handling at least 66 engines, almost all of which were ex-GWR types; but there were notable exceptions, such as No.41213 in September, No.34075 in October and Nos.34014/62/75/83 in December. The following year the ex-GWR types continued to come in, with 28xx Class No.2891 being the first, but in February Standard Class 4 No.76054 from Eastleigh met its end. The same month Nos.41300/10 broke the run of ex-GWR types which remained the yard's principle victims that spring. In May No.80042 was obliterated, whilst in June more Western Region disposals came in from Radyr and Cardiff Canton. Towards the end of June Hayes began to get very ambitious, with 9F No.92236, Heaton Mersey's No.42787 and taper-boilered 2-6-0 No.42972, Jubilee Class 4-6-0s *Keith* and *Cornwallis,* Stanier 2-6-4T No.42558, Lostock Hall's Nos.42716 and 90268 all being acquired.

Then it came to an end, with work still in progress on Nos.1632, 3635, 7803 *Barcote Manor,* 42558, 42716 and 90268 the yard was suddenly sold to the Birds' Group. So the story must be followed from the records of that company and, whilst it is continued, under the section dealing with R.S. Hayes, it must be remembered that purchases and acquisitions reflected the policy of the new owners. It was another of the common-place 0-6-0PTs, No.7734 from Leamington, which started the ball rolling, but this was quickly followed by named engines *Winchester Castle* and *Corndean Hall.* An 0-6-0PT No.3772, came next but again this was followed by express engines *Hereford Castle,* and *Ince Castle* towards the end of August. A batch of engines acquired in late September remained unreported at the time, but it transpires this contained no less than *Wyke Hall* and also included a cluster of ex-LMS types; Class 4F No.44139 and three 0-6-0Ts Nos.47286/432/499. During 1965 it is recorded that Birds demolished at least 40 engines, mostly from Wales but with long-distance acquisitions being noted from Carlisle, Barrow and Carnforth. In 1966 only 7 steam engines and two diesel locomotives were reported cut up, as the yard's loco disposal operation went into rapid decline. However, included in this tally was Bournemouth's No.34063 *229 Squadron* and D1671 *Thor.*

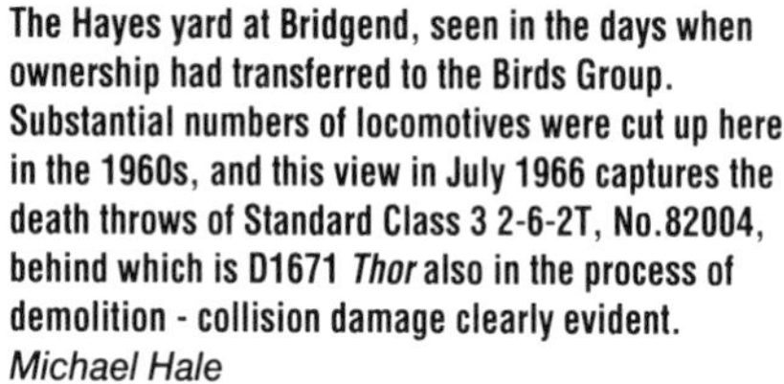

The Hayes yard at Bridgend, seen in the days when ownership had transferred to the Birds Group. Substantial numbers of locomotives were cut up here in the 1960s, and this view in July 1966 captures the death throws of Standard Class 3 2-6-2T, No.82004, behind which is D1671 *Thor* also in the process of demolition - collision damage clearly evident.
Michael Hale

Laying in the rubble alongside 1000 Class 4-6-0 No.1021 *County of Montgomery* in the Bridgend yard of R.S. Hayes, is a can of Regent lubricating oil. The sad fact is that no more lubricants will be used on this once attractive engine, it has but a couple of weeks left to live.
Gerald T. Robinson

Number 61188, Class B1 4-6-0 still looks to command awesome power as it sits quietly at Battleship Wharf, North Blyth. The class was a particular favourite of Hughes Bolckow, and a number of these fine 'maids of all work' met their end here.
D. Tithebridge

HUGHES BOLCKOW LTD.

BY THE MID 1960s about a dozen yards in the North East were busy cutting locomotives, but other than Draper's at Hull, the majority of these firms were small ones. Many just took around a dozen engines, the only other exception being Hughes Bolckow at Battleship Wharf, North Blyth, Northumberland. Whether the firm entered the field of loco-breaking due to a shortage of marine work at the time is not known, but events at the Darlington works may have been significant. The scrap yard there closed on 14th March 1964 and thereafter engines were cut-up in the stripping shop when they were deemed beyond economic repair. As the works were due to close during April 1966, their contribution towards the disposal of steam diminished as more and more locos were put to outside tender. Bolckow's first purchase was a Class Q6 No.63401 during July 1964, which came from Tyne Dock. Thereafter, the activity in steam disposal was continuous until October 1967 when the last victim, No.63395, was finally reduced to piles of saleable scrap. Despite its late involvement, the yard made 151 purchases and will probably be remembered for the former LNER types. These acquisitions included several Pacifics ex-store from Heaton Shed, of which Class A3, Nos.60040/83 were the first to arrive during September 1964. They were followed in January 1965 by Nos.60051/84, all of which had also been stored at Heaton shed. A further A4, No.60001, *Sir Ronald Matthews* arrived from Heaton at a price of £2,913; a peppercorn amount these days but nevertheless a tidy sum in December 1964.

Six A1 Pacifics arrived in 1965, Nos.60114/58 from Doncaster and Nos.60116/27/32/42 from Gateshead, these costing between £2,823 and £3,000, the price based on the total weight involved. Two more A4s, Nos.60024/34 were consigned from Ferryhill and Perth in 1966. A strange arrival from Crewe Works was No.60026 *Miles Beevor,* minus tender, which had arrived in a greatly disfigured state after parts had been removed to refurbish No.60010 prior to its move to the Canadian Railroad Historical Museum. Another surprise arrival was a solitary Class J37, No.64595 ex-Thornton Junction in May 1966, why it travelled so far south is a bit of mystery, as it surely can not have been economical to send it Northumberland when there so many active yards in Scotland. In the main, former NER types were the commonest casualties of the yard, mostly coming from sheds in the Blyth, Sunderland and West Hartlepool districts. As might be expected, Classes Q6 and J27 formed the bulk of these acquisitions, but in addition there were some 19 K1s. Twenty-seven Class B1s, also met their end at Battleship Wharf, including named engines Nos.61012/16/21/23/37, and 61238/48. Towards the end ex-WD 2-8-0s constituted the final bulk purchase and by 1968 operations had declined sharply with only the odd diesel shunter making an appearance.

Hughes Bolckow ended up with several surprise acquisitions, perhaps none as perplexing as a pair of Jubilee Class 4-6-0s, Nos.45584 and 45736, from Carlisle Kingmoor. This shed sent the majority of its larger engines to the Scottish breakers, so why Hughes Bolckow finished up with them is a bit of a mystery. In this view No.45584 *North West Frontier* (appropriately named from engine that came from the last stronghold of steam) stands alongside 'Jinty' No.47345.

A. KING & SON, NORWICH.

EAST ANGLIA SEEMED A somewhat unlikely location for breakers yards, the nearest steel making plants being situated in North Lincolnshire around Scunthorpe. As these works were of the integrated types, they mainly took bulk iron ore for the blast furnaces and it was unlikely that Kings were doing any business there. In fact it seems as though most of their scrap was being exported, which is logical when you recognise that they were located near the coast. Several readers have reported that the vast percentage was sent to Japan via Great Yarmouth; might this equate to Class B1s being converted into Datsun cars?

Whether or not King's had purchased steam locomotives before 1963 goes unrecorded, so the first sightings were of two Class B1 locos Nos.61282 and 61364 (ex New England) plus a solitary Class K3 No.61864. All three were in the process of being cut by 8th February 1963, but it wasn't until August that engines began to appear in significant numbers. This period saw ex-GWR types arriving from Old Oak Common, Oxford and Southall which came by way of Willesden, Bletchley, Sandy, and Cambridge in batches of three or four at a time, then stored at Trowse Lower Junction. Number 5099 *Crompton Castle* arrived towards the end of August, followed in October by two Hawksworth County Class locos Nos.1007/18 from Didcot. The following month two members of the Castle Class, Nos.5065 and 7030 arrived from Oxford, followed by Hall Class 4-6-0s, Nos.5917-8/60/6. Number 7013 *Bristol Castle* was reported as being consigned to King's, but in the end it finished up at the Park Royal yard of Cox & Danks Ltd., though sister engine No.7017 *G.J. Churchward* did arrive at the Norwich firm in December. As the year rounded out, many of the stored 57xx Class tank engines were cleared from Old Oak Common and duly consigned to the firm. A surprise arrival was Churchward 7F No.4705 which came in from Southall, but as the year progressed Nos.4703-4/7 also met their end at King's. As will be noted from the above, the vast majority of locos being cut here were of GWR origin, but named B1 No.61006 *Blackbuck* and a rake of Oerlikon carriages broke the sequence.

Most of the ex-GWR engines were of the 2251 Class, but 2-8-2T No.7203 had been received from Severn Tunnel Junction along with No.4910 *Blaisdon Hall* which had latterly been at Didcot. Then the monotony of breaking GWR types was relieved as the firm began taking in engines from the Southern Region. The first arrivals were noted in April 1964 as Stewarts Lane shed began sending pairs of Class K, N, and U1 locomotives to Norwich, including Nos.31822/51/93-4/6, 32337/40/3. The next class to come in were the Qs and Q1s, with Nos.33016/24 and 30546/9 arriving during the summer, followed by Nos.33003/23/30/3/5/9 from Eastleigh, Feltham and Nine Elms in September. Class M7 No.30111 from Eastleigh, and Three Bridges' H Class No.31518 were also noted. It seems unlikely that so many GWR and SR types had ever been seen in East Anglia, but the sad fact is that their journeys were all strictly 'one way'. Although not a major yard, King's was an interesting one, and by the beginning of 1968 around 100 locos had been dismembered there and their mortal remains sold for reprocessing. Notable purchase include *Birchwood Grange* from Worcester, Class A3s *Minoru* and *Flying Fox* from Peterborough and the A1 *Guy Mannering*. In contrast, no true LMS engines were seen, and only the taper boiler Ivatt Class 4MTs from the ex-Midland & Great Northern sheds were represented. By 1966-7 the purchases were trailing off, as King's found it less profitable to bid for engines from more distant locations. East Anglia by this time had been largely dieselised, and few depots in the Great Eastern section had any steam locos left. Some of the last arrivals were a batch of BR Standard types and No.41319 from distant Salisbury. In August 1968 diesel pioneer No.15000 was purchased from Crewe, and so a new era began.

Much of King's initial business in the railway field was concentrated in the disposal of coaching stock, as their acquisitions were sent down the old line from Wymondham to Forncett. This line consisted of about two miles of double track ideal for storage, and about one mile along it a large clearing was utilised for the removal of coach bodies from the wheel sets and frames. All the wooden parts were burnt away and the remaining metal subsequently sent to King's yard at Hall Road, Norwich for disposal. This view of mostly ex-LNER stock dates from 1963, showing two rakes waiting to be scrapped.
Dr. Ian C. Allen

A. LOOM (ELLIS METALS LTD), SPONDON

THIS WAS AN INTERESTING establishment, and it must be said a very cooperative one. Once they became aware of the *Steam For Scrap* series, the company duly made their records available for inspection to help with the compilation of the book. From the details we have a fairly precise idea of what went on there, starting back in June 1959 when a batch of 'Lanky' 2-4-2 tanks were despatched to the yard from Badnall's Wharf. Many of these had been employed at sheds around the West Riding, so several of these engines were known to me - a good few had provided illicitly obtained cab rides as well. The engines involved were Nos.50646, 50725/57/77, and 50818/31/55/65. By August they were joined by a couple of Johnson 2F 0-6-0s, Nos.58167/308, five 3Fs and No.47216. The next consignment came in September, with eleven engines that were to keep the firm busy for some time to come. In October 1960 five of the engines from the small dump at the Turntable Sidings arrived, Nos.43253, 43355, 43506, 43930 and 58178, whilst bits of No.43926 were seen littering the yard. On 17th November four engines came from store at Burton shed, Nos.43327, 43839, 44316 and 58130. By now the dump at Derby was beginning to yield its inhabitants, and in January 1961 10 more engines were consigned to Loom's. June saw five engines arrive ex-Hasland, whilst August witnessed the acquisition of a dozen engines, 75% of which were 4-4-0s. Five engines from Toton and Westhouses on the 3rd and 4th October rounded out the purchases for the year.

As the dumps began to vanish, Loom's activities were markedly less noticeable, with only four engines, Nos.40054/142 and 43250/77 being obtained in 1962. The following year 14 engines were purchased, including 11 ex-LNER locos from the Staveley area. Number 61163 was the first of the B1s to be demolished by this firm, whilst No.61166 had the distinction of being cut straight away when it entered the yard on 7th November. The mixture of ex-LMS and ex-LNER types continued through 1964, the firm's busiest year with 35 engines coming to an end there. This tally included Jubilee Class *Eire,* three ex-WD 2-8-0s and Standard Class 2-6-2T No.84007. Then, as the larger firms took the lion's share of disposals, it suddenly became unprofitable to bid for engines from more distant locations. So after dismantling No.90408 early in 1965, the firm turned its attention to other avenues of business.

Robinson Class 04/8 2-8-0, a type introduced by the LNER in 1939, but one which still retained the GCR pattern smokebox. As it stands in the yard of A. Loom at Spondon in May 1964 it is already a thing of the past - no longer will it haul the huge, sloth-like coal trains on former Great Central metals as it once had done - evolution had passed it by.
H. N. James

J. McWILLIAMS SHETTLESTONE GLASGOW.

THIS FIRM WAS YET another late starter in the loco-bashing business, so it wasn't until October 1963 that Shettlestone Yard began buying engines. Out of 32 initial purchases, 30 consisted of former LMS 2-6-0 Hughes 'Crabs' mainly from Carlisle and Ayr, the exceptions being No.42876 from Stoke, No.42804 from Crewe and No.42746 from Barrassie Wagon Works. Many of the Glasgow-based Royal Scots stored at Parkhead finished up at McWilliams in the period June/August 1964 these being Nos.46102/4/5/7/21 with Nos.46110 and 46140 following during 1965. Two Clan Class locos, Nos.72006/8 came mid-way through 1966, but by far the most celebrated class to come in a significant quantity were the Britannias. No fewer than 22 were dealt with during 1967/68 and all came from Carlisle's Kingmoor depot. For the record these were:- Nos.70006/9/10/11/5/6/20/8/9/31/2/4/7/8/9/40/1/2/8/9/51/3 - a figure approaching half the class. Like many of the other local yards numerous Black 5s, WDs, 9Fs and B1s came and went, but even after the end of steam large numbers of troublesome diesels were cut up. The North British Class D61xx and Metropolitan-Vickers being the most abundant, but by early 1969 even the Clayton Class 17s were receiving attention!

Polmadie depot's Black 5 4-6-0 No.44796 at the Shettleston Yard of J. McWilliams, a solitary steam engine in a line of condemned mineral wagons. The diesel shunter is being used to move victims around the yard, and is not yet a candidate for the scrap.
J. L. Stevenson

One of the most useful little tank engines north of the Border, this Holmes North British 0-4-0ST was a member of class designed in 1882. Several of the class were permanently attached to a wooden tender, but No.68095 pictured here was one of those provided with coal bunkers - although not of a very high capacity. Thankfully this little engine, now 80 years old has not lost its fight for survival at McWilliams in Glasgow, being later purchased for preservation by Helical Springs, Lytham.
D. Huntriss

MOTHERWELL MACHINERY AND SCRAP Co.

BY FAR THE LARGEST concern in Scotland's role in the disposal of steam was the Inshaw Works of the Motherwell Machinery & Scrap Co., Wishaw. Exactly when this yard started goes unrecorded, but way back in 1949 this firm had cut up Manning Wardle No.1394/98 *Bamburgh* from the North Sunderland Railway for which they paid £71. In Easter 1953 they were the contractors for the complete demolition of the North Sunderland line, using their own Ruston & Hornsby 48HP diesel mechanical loco. The arrival of three ex-LT&SR tank engines, Nos. 41991-3, from Winsford on 23rd February 1960 was the next event of significance. Shortly afterwards, bulk purchases began to become the order of the day. Practically all the remaining Class D30s left in service were despatched there early in 1960, these being:- Nos.62422/5/8/31-2/9/40-2. As well as locally directed J83 and N15 Classes from the Edinburgh districts, a large number of locomotives were being hauled there from far and wide; K2s such as Nos.61723/31/53 arrived from Colwick after arduous journeys via Wakefield over the Settle - Carlisle and even old L&YR veterans such as Nos.50647, 52237/68 turned up. On reflection it seems uncanny that we have seen few photographic reminders of this period - in a reversed situation, Scottish locos in England, it would have unquestionably been a magnet to the enthusiasts.

After a lull during 1961 the firm started receiving boilers from engines cut up at various works, though Inverurie and Kilmarnock were the likely candidates. Boilers noted with number plates still intact, were from Nos.40647/93, 55220/61. It may be pertinent to note that the firm of Maden & McKees at Liverpool were also preoccupied with the same work, taking boilers from both Crewe and Doncaster works. From September 1962 right through to early 1968 this yard saw an unending procession of condemned locomotives practically every class in service during that period being represented. Of particular note were Nos.55204 and 57258 the last two former Caledonian engines in service. Additionally, No.54398 *Ben Alder* came ex-store from Kipps, even though it had supposedly been ear-marked for preservation! Four A4 Class Nos.60004/6/12/23, six A2 Class engines Nos.60512/22/4/27/30/35 and Clan No.72009 were also dealt with. Patriots, Royal Scots, Jubilees and Britannias also turned up but the bread and butter types were Black 5s and various Standard Classes. Exact figures are not available but it would seem that well over 500 engines saw their end at Wishaw during the sixties.

As will be appreciated, firms like Motherwell Machinery & Scrap Ltd. made appreciable in-roads in to the large Scottish-based classes, with many of the pre-Grouping types finding their way there for disposal in the 1950s and 60s. Of these, Class J35s and 37s were often taken in abundance, as seen on 4th September 1967.
Keith Romig

It may seem difficult to believe, but this dismembered hulk was once a Stanier Black 5, though all traces of its identity have been obscured as the men's torches strip it down to the frames. Usually they worked in groups of four per loco at Motherwell Machinery & Scrap, so we must assume the missing man has either gone to make a 'brew' or is working round the other side.
Trevor Rees

SETTLE-SPEAKMAN LTD. QUEENSBOROUGH

THIS YARD, SITUATED ON the Isle Of Sheppey, was often referred to as Peter Wood's and may have been part of, or at least associated with the Slag Reduction group of companies. The railway line at Queensborough was a single track affair, which left the main line at Sittingbourne for Sheerness and Leysdown on Sea. Access to the sidings at Queensborough was by a junction just to the south of the road bridge by the station. The double tracked siding was reduced to a single line leading to the 'Washer', which was, to quote one correspondent, 'In such a state of decrepitude as had to be seen to be believed and even then it was incredible! The sidings serving Settle-Speakman's also carried traffic for nearby fertilizer, glass, glue and sulphuric acid factories and were quite busy, but the whole area was quite dreadful in appearance. The actual process of cutting was done at the 'Washer' down by the River Swale on the Chetney Marshes, so that the scrap metal could be loaded directly into ships. The company owned a few industrial locomotives of it's own, including 0-4-0 saddle tanks Stafford and Hussar plus a Dick Kerr named Maybury; in addition there were two Planet types Nos.3944 and 3986. For a long time the bread and butter work of the yard had been coaching stock. of which over 300 examples had been broken up there since October 1963. However, as more and more engines became available, the firm began in-roads into this work disposing with three M7 Class tanks from Feltham during March 1964; these were Nos.30035, 30249, 30320, all of which had lost their chimneys and side rods. Activity lasted just over a year and saw the arrival of another M7 No.30032 in April together with 'H' Class No.31005. During July three Q Class locomotives s arrived Nos.30534/7/40, as well as Standard Class 4MT No.76034. All the locomotives came from either Feltham or Nine Elms depots. In 1965 a notable acquisition by the firm were four Southern Pacifics, Nos.34003/29/61/91. During 1967, the firm purchased D2726 for it's own use, but by this time over 20 engines had been destroyed and the work had already come to an end.

A West Country Class locomotive sent to die on the Isle of Sheppey; No.34091 *Weymouth* stands with No.41260 on the siding leading to the 'Washer' at Queensborough on 17th February 1965. The 4-6-0s main connecting rod has come to grief and lies on the floor somewhat bent, while the casing shows where the nameplate and crest were once affixed.
Arthur G Wells

SLAG REDUCTION GROUP (PETER WOODS)

IN ANY STEEL-MAKING area, the Slag Reduction Group will be well known, its activities centring on the reclamation of waste steel from the dumps and slag heaps around the steel works. However, the firm was also involved in a variety of other enterprises connected with the steel and construction industries, so it was not surprising that it also ventured into the railway disposal business. As early as the 1950s Slag Reduction were disposing of wagon under-frames at Corby, whilst at Consett a railway steam crane was cut up in 1953. Exactly when the carnage commenced in earnest remains unrecorded, but in February 1964 a consignment of semi-cut locomotives arrived at the Steel Peach & Tozer works in Rotherham, consigned for the Slag Reduction Co. A quick search revealed that the remains included pieces of such locos as Nos.42228, 43969, 67617/23/30, 68034/40, 90751/62, and even the front end of an unidentified A4. It was soon discovered that these remains were being directed from BR works at Darlington, Derby and Swindon, so the actual scrapping process was not being carried out by Slag Reduction; however, they were soon to move into that area in their own right as a new site was to be opened at Orgreave Tip.

Operations commenced at Orgreave about March 1964, but they were short lived and full of curious anomalies. An early visit registered Nos.42491 and 44750 in pieces, and the firm's log showed pioneer diesel DP2, but it was never seen. A Castle Class 4-6-0 was reported as being purchased, and indeed the number 7028 appeared in the log but there is no evidence to say whether it ever arrived here. What did arrive were two Royal Scots, Nos.46101/14 which came from Willesden - with somebox number plates still intact. Yet, the powers that be had already decided the yard's future was limited - presumably due to the high transportation costs to Rotherham. Accordingly, the new firm of Peter Wood Ltd was created as an offshoot of Barlborough Metals, which in turn was an amalgamation of British Steel and Slag Reduction. A new site was built alongside the GCR line at the Ickles (named after a nearby country house), with a redundant Pullman car being acquired to serve as the main office. Activities started in earnest in August 1964 with the arrival of 24 locomotives of the LMS 4F and WD 2-8-0 Classes. These were soon followed by ex-SR engines from Nine Elms, with the early arrivals being U Class No.31793 and the first two members of the Merchant Navy Class to be withdrawn Nos.35002/15. Cutting up continued until the following April, but higher than envisaged sulphur melts were causing costly problems for the electric furnaces and considerably extending the refining periods. As a result the firm suddenly began taking in coaching stock for disposal, until the Templeborough Steel Works were reduced to just two furnaces. Thereafter, with a surfeit of scrap metal plants in the area, the Ickles site closed.

TOP: Ward's, Killamarsh, in November 1965. Cutting up will soon start on 9F No.92200 but first she is set alight to burn off oil and grease deposits. Smoke pouring from her cab windows shows that her floorboards are well alight. Sister engine No.92183 is also present.
ABOVE: The same yard on 10th March 1967. Fairburn 2-6-4T No.42161 waits its turn for the torch. *Photos: R. Turner*

THOMAS W. WARD LTD.

THE NAME OF THOMAS W. Ward has long been associated with the demolition of both main line and industrial railways and, by implication, locomotives as well. For example, when the LNER abandoned the Rosedale Railway on the North Yorkshire Moors in 1926 it made little effort to recover what it left behind. It sat there over two years, but when the firm of T.W. Ward were given the job of recovery in January 1929, they began work at once and the task was fully accomplished in just five months. This is typical of the operations undertaken by Ward's men throughout the first half of the 20th century, and just a foretaste of what was to come when steam neared the end of its working life on British Railways. By the 1960s the company had a number of yards engaged in the sport and, while most were in our grade 4 category, several were much larger.

Their yard at Attercliffe was one of the first in Britain to begin the carnage of BR steam locomotives, and significant numbers of condemned engines began arriving in May 1959. However, a former works manager informs us that part cut locomotives had been acquired from Doncaster, Gorton and Wolverhampton works as early as 1948 and the work was completed by Wards before the bits were sent on for smelting. Among the early locomotives purchased complete were LMS 4-4-0 compounds and a number of ex-L&YR engines, but as time went by a variety of other classes appeared including B1s, 'Crabs', 4Fs and WD 2-8-0s. Perhaps the most unusual engines to arrive were GWR County Class Nos.1017/22/26 in December 1963 and Large Prairie No.5152 the following April. Locomotives were initially stored at Broughton Lane goods shed and coal yard but were eventually towed into the main yard at the top of Weedon Street, the very place where dozens of Sheffield's trams had met their end a few years earlier. The last steam engine was despatched in 1971, this being an industrial 0-4-0ST from a nearby steel works.

As a consequence of overcrowding at the firm's Broughton Lane site in Sheffield, Wards began directing new acquisitions out to the former wagon works at Beighton where there was considerably more room to work. Cutting complete locomotives probably began in 1963, but for some strange reason it did not appear to catch the attention of those enthusiasts interested in such things until the spring of 1965. It had long been known that the cutting of wagons and coaches was going on at Beighton, so it may have been this fact that obscured the truth that engines were dying here as well. Some of the earlier casualties were ex-GWR Class 57xx, along with several L&YR, GCR and MR tank engines. By the time people were aware of what was happening at Beighton, Wards were into the big time, with Jubilee Class Nos.45554/80, 45617/63/72 and 9F Class Nos 92198-9 being noteworthy examples. By now the cutters at Beighton had become proficient in their trade, and the time taken to demolish a locomotive had been reduced to the bare minimum. Accordingly they despatched their victims with clinical efficiency, including J50 Classes from Doncaster, A1 Pacifics Nos.60118/31/34/54 and Britannia Class Nos.70030/43-4 and even a Hall Class 4-6-0 No.6964 *Thornbridge Hall*. The full list ran into hundreds of engines and lasted until 27th March 1969 (eight months after the end of BR steam), when LMS 8F No.48493 met its end. Even so railway work did not cease immediately, as rails, wagons, coaches, industrial locos and even the odd DMU were handled through into the early 1970s before the yard went on to other areas of business.

Ivatt 2-6-2T No.41204 at Ward's, Killamarsh, in April 1967. *Photo: Tony Wakefield*

Finally, we might consider the Killamarsh site where cutting operations began in a small way in November 1959 when the first of a long line of the redundant LMS 4-4-0s came in from Derby. Soon types such as 3F and 2-6-4Ts were being handled, along with the occasional GWR engines like No.2880 noted on 25th August 1960. The yard was in a difficult place for enthusiasts to reach, hidden in a rail complex south east of Sheffield and operations were rather shadowy, though this was more by circumstance than intent. By 1962 dozens of engines from the Manchester area were arriving each month, mostly from Gorton, Trafford Park and other locations where ex-CLC engines had been stored or dumped. Stockport was another area sending regular consignments, but more distant acquisitions were arriving such as ex-Metropolitan electric locos LTE Nos.4/6/8/9/10-1/14. In 1965 locomotives arrived from the store at Rigley's Sidings in Nottinghamshire, but whether this included Jubilee Class Nos.45598,45626, and 45726 which were cut at Killamarsh around that time is unrecorded. Other noted casualties were the premature deaths of 9F 2-10-0s Nos.92178 and 92200. In February 1966 an A1 Pacific No.60146 *Peregrine* was another notable victim. In 1967 engines of the 8F, 9F, 04, B1 and Standard Classes arrived for disposal. As soon as one line of engines had been dissected and dumped into the scrap wagons another was ready to take its place, and the carnage went on into 1969. Like Beighton, Killamarsh continued into the early 1970s with coaches, DMU and diesel stock.

WEST OF SCOTLAND SHIPBREAKERS, TROON HARBOUR

THIS SITE WAS NOT utilised until late 1962 and one suspects that the yard may have been short of work with shipping; indeed the Arnott & Young's yards at both Carmyle and Old Kilpatrick were certainly not under any great pressure during this period, which might otherwise have suggested a need for a shift of workload. Throughout 1963 former Caledonian locomotives, mainly from the Ayrshire district, were despatched to Troon and it was not until late 1964 that the pattern altered when larger tender engines started arriving. Perhaps Troon will always be remembered for the appearance of the Duchess Pacifics, which were sent from Carlisle Kingmoor. The first batch had originally been invoiced to the Slag Reduction Co. at Barrow but the sale was cancelled on 15th December 1964 due to route restrictions, over the Maryport and Carlisle line. As a consequence the full consignment was offered to Arnott & Young's, these were:- Nos.46225/26/37/38/44/50/55/57. The Pacifics were hauled to Troon in three lots on 30th November and 1st/2nd December, causing quite an emotional stir as they left the 'Border City'.

Other notable engines despatched from Carlisle around this period were Patriot Class No.45527, Jubilees Class Nos.45613/35, Royal Scots Nos.46132/55/66 and Standard Class Nos.70019 and 72005. In addition one of the few named Black 5s No.45158 *Glasgow Yeomanry* was cut up in October 1964. The yard continued to take stock from the Glasgow, Carlisle and Ayrshire districts until the bitter end. One Black 5 No.45460 was still intact there in June 1968 making it the very last Scottish member of the class to exist. Jinty 0-6-0 No.47305 was another engine left to rot, both these engines were abandoned for over two years, standing on the quayside along with Nos.45486, 46450, 42702, 76001, 76100.

On 2nd December 1964 a batch of four LMS Pacific 4-6-2s arrived at Troon from Carlisle for breaking up by the West of Scotland Shipbreaking Co. Ltd. The sad end for No.46250 *City of Lichfield*, No.46237 *City of Bristol*, No.46225 *Duchess of Gloucester* and No.46257 *City of Salford* is now assured - there will be no reprieve.
J. L. Stevenson

WOODHAM BROS. BARRY.

SO, AS OUR ACCOUNT of the private yards comes to an end, it is perhaps fitting that the last entry should be Woodham Bros. of Barry. Though Woodham's did not occupy the role of sole supplier to the preservation movement, it is an inescapable fact that this firm played a remarkable part and so deserve their inclusion in this, the final part of the *Steam For Scrap* story. It would be an easy task for us to list the engines that Woodham Bros. disposed of, the figures are well quoted - but such a course seems ungrateful to a firm who saved more engines than anyone else. However, for those who want to know more about the activities of Woodham's Yard, the book *'The Barry Scrapyard: The Preservation Miracle'* by Alan Warren (David & Charles) is highly recommended.

Interestingly, the first locomotive to leave the yard, No.43924, had also gone to Keighley, as early as September 1968. It had been in the yard for just 35 months, and was in such a relatively good condition that it was quickly restored and steamed in 1970. Around this time the yard was taking in its last batch of acquisitions, Nos.48151, 48305, 61264, 76077/9/84 and 92212, all of which were later to be preserved. Perversely, as steam died on the main line, and whilst other yards engaged in the last round of the wholesale slaughter, Woodham's eased off in their loco-cutting. Apart from a handful of diesel locomotives, the only engines cut up at Barry after September 1968 were Nos.3817, 4156, 76080 and 92085. The last to go was the Standard class 9F, which went in July 1980, though by this time it had been cannibalised of every conceivable part which might be re-used to keep its nine remaining sisters alive. One of my last visits to Barry revealed that almost all of the locomotives had the names of preserved railways or individual groups painted on their sides, but I wondered whether or not these rusted hulks were actually beyond redemption. To date, around 64 of the locomotives which escaped from Barry have been steamed, and others are nearing restoration. Yet, for the vast majority, it will take millions of pounds and many man-hours to get them to anything like an acceptable standard - some may even be beyond redemption, but it would take a brave man to make such a categoric statement!

GWR 2-8-0 No.3862, November 1942 – February 1965, pushes up the daisies at Woodham's scrapyard, Barry, on 7th June 1975. ***Photo: Nigel Trevena***

Chapter Five

myths and legends

AS WITH ANY SUBJECT rich in emotional appeal and so lacking in quotable statistics, a smoke-screen of myths, legends and tall-tales developed. For the past quarter of a century these elements have obscured exactly what went on in the process of disposing of British steam. Yet, strange to say, some of these stories continue despite the fact that *Steam For Scrap* has long endeavoured to set the record straight. Even so, dozens of different stories have arisen - few of which had any real substance, but they still persist by sheer doggedness. Though the advent of the great steam preservation movement has ensured that there were survivors (thereby removing the sting out of the scrapping of BR steam), some of the erroneous stories of the scrapping era continue and are almost in danger of becoming 'recognised history'. Every one seems to have their own personal favourite, ranging from the story of the engine buried below a mountain of scrap in Cashmore's yard, to the fabulous account of the 'strategic reserve'. As it would take far to long to explore all the stories we hope that the rest of the book will give the statistical information which provide the answers; meanwhile we will once again take a detailed examination of the 'strategic reserve'.

THE STRATEGIC RESERVE

THE EXISTENCE OF A large dump of mothballed locomotives stored at secret military establishments, perhaps even hidden away in some large underground bunker is a lovely idea. Indeed, the popular railway press has made a meal of such stories and the topic was repeatedly discussed, until the *'Steam For Scrap'* series laid this particular ghost to rest - by proving conclusively that NO such dumps ever existed. In theory, of course, it is a good idea to hang on to some steam locomotives: mothballed, lubricated and stored out of sight ready for a national emergency, foreign unpleasantness, or the simple geophysical exhaustion that, presumably, will sooner or later drain the last drop of oil. Then, so the story goes, the reserve fleet would be triumphantly resurrected, steaming proudly from a secure depot to become the saviours of an oil-less British Rail. However, in our desire to perpetuate appealing romances, we have endowed the planners with more foresight than they actually have. As a theory, the 'Strategic Reserve' has always had its detractors, and many would point out that it was illogical to retain steam locomotives once their service infrastructure of sheds, water columns and coaling stages had been dismantled. Others have sought to demolish the theory by citing the greater logic of storing fuel oil - as loco coal used to be stored, or of mothballing earlier internal combustion locomotives. Both are viable arguments - as would be the expansion

Graveyard of the Pacifics: Newport cut up exactly half of the 140 Bulleids – Buttigieg's yard, seen here in October 1968, accounting for twenty-five.
Photo: Rex Conway

This photograph is probably unique, for it answers one of the great myths of the scrapping of steam - might this be the mystical Strategic Reserve. Sadly no, the location is Sutton Bridge on, appropriately enough, April Fools Day 1968. The main line to Hereford is straight ahead, beyond that South Wales and the great scrapyards such as Buttigieg's, Cashmore's and Woodham's. The line to the right goes to Welshpool, not some secret MoD installation. As best we know it this line-up came from the Merseyside area, and contained only two engines which still remain today Nos.76077/9, both of which were salvaged from Barry.
A. J. Sommerfield

of the electrified system.

However, the main reason that the 'Strategic Reserve' theory can be dismissed is not based on such arguments; it is purely a matter of statistics. Simply, with the exception of all but a tiny handful - perhaps 10 engines, the fate of every BR locomotive has been firmly established. The only uncertainties lie in the exact location and precise date of the cutting up of a few engines, and even the most cursory examination of the records proves beyond any doubt that a reserve could not exist. If BR had been maintaining one, to make any sense at all it would have had to comprise a minimum of 200 engines, preferably more - while most enthusiasts would cite their favourite class (including one correspondent who insisted that the entire class of Castles should have been stored pending emergency use), logic and practicality would dictate that something simple, rugged and, above all, modern was chosen. The most logical choice would have been a batch of 9Fs, or Standard Class 5s, and yet the records for these classes reveals no gaps, no mysterious absences: the tiny hotch-potch of locomotives with uncertain fates constitutes no national asset at all. Peter Hands series *What Happened To Steam* confirms this finding, with the disposal of all the likely contenders for a reserve being accounted for.

Why then did such tales arise, and why were they perpetuated? The answer is as easy as it is complex - a belief that steam hadn't ended, and a lack of comprehension that a major national asset could just be thrown away! There was also a feeling that no-one in their right mind would dispose of so many relatively new engines, some asked did BR have an ulterior motive? Surely they were not being scrapped, just being mothballed for a time when steam once more came into its own - being saved for a rainy day! Sentiments ran high, and feelings were emotive, so from this clouded perspective a legend arose. Just imagine travelling on the former Shrewsbury & Hereford Joint line late in 1968 and then, in the middle of nowhere, the view from the carriage window revealed dozens of silent locomotives silhouetted against the night sky. To all intent and purpose steam had finished, so why were they there? To the romantics and the uninitiated it was easy to speculate...... and come to the wrong conclusion!

The scene described above was at Sutton Bridge near Shrewsbury on the main line to Hereford, where the sidings became a useful storage point for locomotives from the Merseyside area. Due to operating considerations, by early 1968 it had become particularly important to clear the dumped locomotives from the storage sites around Liverpool. A prime example being Speke Junction where, in December 1967, over 100 locos were gathered: this included 44 engines which were either dead or stored at the MPD, as well as a large dump of 57 redundant locomotives silently waiting their fate in the sidings opposite the airport entrance in Speke Road. In order to clear these large concentrations of condemned engines, including 32 relatively new 9Fs, a number of little-used sidings were pressed into service. The three principle locations for the final 'dumps' were at Sutton Bridge, and the goods yards at Coton Hill and Shrewsbury. However, the proximity of these sidings to a number of military installations in the Welsh Marches led to the unjustified speculation mentioned above. Slowly and surely the engines moved south, not to a secret store, but to the ignominious fate of the cutters' torch. With their departure, the Loch Ness Monster of the British steam age, the mysterious mothballed 9F of the 'Strategic Reserve' can safely - if a little regretfully - be consigned to the scrap-heap where, in fact, she had been all the time!

Demand For Scrap

'BUT WHERE DID THEY all go', one reader wrote, 'surely they couldn't have needed so much scrap metal?' True the statistics were staggering, for example the numerically small BR 'Clan' Class produced no less than 875 tons of scrap without even taking into consideration the tenders - calculate what 666 8Fs weighing around 72 tons each would amount to. Yet in the post-World War reconstruction of western Europe, there was a voracious demand for steel and other metals, and the British steel industry was in the front line when it came to supplies. Both for markets at home and overseas, our steel mills produced millions of tons of metal. This was a process that could consume almost incalcuable amounts of scrap metal from railway sources. If this seems amazing, we must then consider the large numbers of obsolete aircraft, the 'surplus to requirement' naval ships, redundant merchant vessels, and a whole host of military hardware. If we add to this all the civilian scrap produce which became available between 1945 and 1965, the quantities of surplus metal then go beyond comprehension.

A national scrap drive was started during the war years, and the fervour with which this was accepted led to parks and cemeteries being denuded of fences, houses losing their gateways, and industrial properties being thoroughly searched for any old iron. Every bit of available metal was scoured out, and metal reclamation moved from the age of the rag and bone man to a multi-million pound industry. Even the railways got in on the act for, as a member of the BR Board said in 1964, 'The plan for the re-shaping and modernisation of British Railways, which is part of the great movement for the modernisation of Britain, involves a huge scrap drive.' This was at a time when thousands of steam engines, coaches and wagons were already being cut up in the name of progress! Waste reclamation has long been an important part in the cycle of industry, so it therefore should come as no surprise that there was a ready demand for the ferreous and non-ferreous metals which went in to making up a steam locomotive. As an advertisement for scrap merchants, Thomas W. Ward stated in 1946 'The Recovery and Conversion of Scrap Metal is an integral part of the country's industrial economy.' Every redundant locomotive coach or wagon which became available had a ready buyer, there was no reprieve, no miraculous escape - only the cutter's torch and the smelting furnace.

RIGHT: One minor but interesting facet of the great scrappings of the 1950s and 60s was the survival of numerous life-expired locomotives, deemed superfluous by the Operating Departments, which assumed retirement jobs as stationary boilers, the source of steam heating for a surprising variety of establishments from engine sheds to factories, including at least one hotel and even a laundry!

During the period 1950-68 some 150 ex-BR locomotives were recorded on such duties. Noteworthy and faintly bizarre examples — all recorded in February 1963 — were SR USA 0-6-0 tank No.30068 supplying steam to the SS *Canterbury* in dry dock at Southampton; and two very humble duties for LNER Pacifics: A3 No.60109 *Hermit* at Wood Green carriage sidings and A2 No.60514 *Chamossaire* which performed a similar duty at Hitchin for one month until her tender was empty.

Many other such engines were of ancient origin. For many years, two L&Y Barton Wright 0-4-4 tanks, Nos.903 and 925, were retained as stationary boilers at Newton Heath MPD, Manchester. By the date of this picture, 11th August 1967, their scrapping on site appears to be well under way.
Photo: A. Wyn Hobson

LEFT: As we are considering a period of railway history not short in ironies and incongruities it should come as no surprise to find two Bulleid Pacifics proudly displayed by BR at Bristol Bath Road Open Day while actually on their way to the scrapyard. Perhaps the shedmaster saw the chance to gain two extra exhibits at his public relations exercise with the minimum of effort or expense; perhaps BR had its tongue firmly in its cheek. Whatever the reason, here are WC No.34100 *Appledore* and No.34013 *Okehampton*, only weeks from the torch, enjoying this strange interruption to their journey to South Wales from store at Salisbury. The date is 21st October 1967. *Photo: John Bird*

Peculiar things sometimes happened to parts of the scrapped engines. Certain instances were recorded in the first series: an LNER Pacific tender in use at Aldwalke Soaking Pits until 1978, for example. Tenders were, in fact, useful simple vehicles worth retaining and a number survived their parent engines by several decades: some thirty tender chassis still existing at Duport Steel Works at Briton Ferry in 1978. Smaller components, often useful to the preservationists, occasionally turn up at scrapyards which continued to trade and as for those yards which have been cleared – such as Cohen's at Kettering, would not a little archaeology, a little judicious pick and shovel work, be rewarding? Photographs taken at the height of cutting operations show a sea of engine bits extending in all directions: it surely could not all have been recovered – could it have been bulldozed into the earth where, perhaps, fragments of Granges, Halls and Standards linger on?

And what happened to the scrap metal? Melted down and reforged into new steel, a couple of million tons of steam locomotives were transformed into all manner of artifacts, from pins to bridges. But some went back to the railway: in the period 1964-5 it was a condition of sale that the copper firebox of a

Mention the name of the Motherwell Machinery & Scrap Company to most railway enthusiasts and they will look blank. Yet, hundreds of BR steam locomotives passed through the firm's premises at Wishaw, Motherwell, arriving in full running order — sometimes barely cold — and leaving in small pieces. It was, moreover, only one of dozens of such yards whose important role in the history of British steam passed almost unrecorded.

These two photographs convey something of the unique and compelling atmosphere of these great scrapyards and form part of a comprehensive photographic record by *Keith Romig.*

TOP: 18th October 1966: demolition of this unidentified 'Black Five' is almost complete.

BELOW: A few weeks later, on 16th November, centre engine is North British built 0-6-0 No.64608 (LNER Class J37), late of Dundee Tay Bridge shed. The great bulk of the LNER 0-6-0s of Classes J6, J11 and J35 were cut up by BR works but the J37s survived later than most of their type — the last engine going as late as April 1967 — and MM&S took no fewer than 42 — or over 40% of the class, surely something worth recording? Also visible here is LNER Class B1 No.61349, one of 18 of the class purchased by this yard from Scottish Region sheds.

locomotive sold for scrap to a private yard was removed and returned to BR. Most went to Derby where, stripped of all 'foreign' metal, they were melted down and reforged as copper wire to be strung from the catenaries along the West Coast main line. Thus, part of the Duchesses, part of the Jubilees, was hoisted high above the rails they once knew so well and in a weird metamorphosis continued to work the trains.

So, the scrapping of steam presents an intriguing story, rich in statistic, wide in scope and with just the right touches of pathos and irony. It needs no artificial edifice of myth and legend to sustain it, the serious enthusiast will find stimulation enough in the truth.

Before we move on to examine the fate of some of the best loved locomotives ever to run in this country, let us leave this compendium of stories true and false with one that is indisputably true.

A line up of dismembered fireboxes ready for salvage and return to BR at the Bridgend yard of R. S. Hayes on 5th July 1964. *Photo: H. N. James*

No.71000 *Duke of Gloucester* outside Cashmore's yard during its unscheduled call at Newport. On the right is the tender of a second engine purchased by Woodham Bros but also delivered to Cashmore's by mistake: BR Class 4 4-6-0 No.75014. Once the error was pointed out to Cashmore's, this engine also went on to Woodham's and was moved to the North York Moors Railway in February 1981. It would seem that the preservationists have a lot to thank Maurice Sheppard for. *Photo: M. Sheppard*

The torch denied

When No. 71000 *Duke of Gloucester* was steamed in May 1986, the solitary BR 4-6-2 Pacific repaid the efforts and finance expended on her in the 12 years since she had been rescued from Barry. As she breathed life again, she momentarily rested the title of Britain's most celebrated preserved locomotive from *King George V Flying Scotsman* and *Mallard*. Those present that day may have reflected on the vagaries of the scrapping years in general, and one incident in particular, nearly saw her vanish for ever, unrecorded and *by mistake*.

It occurred in South Wales one morning in October 1967. Maurice Sheppard, ex-BR fireman who still retained an interest in steam and whose parcels round took him via the docks at Newport, arrived at Cashmore's scrapyard to check on the new arrivals. Locomotives sold for scrap were dumped by BR in the long storage sidings outside the yard gates and Sheppard, camera in hand, spent many hours recording them. On this particular morning a very singular engine had just arrived: No. 71000 from Crewe Works, without both cylinders, smoke deflectors and chimney but otherwise intact and still an immensely impressive machine. Engines left in the reception sidings outside the yard were regularly subjected to pilfering, accessible brass and other non-ferrous fittings disappearing overnight, and it had become Cashmore's practice to strip engines of these parts immediately upon their arrival. This was already occurring on *The Duke,* the cab fittings being partially removed.

Sheppard approached the engine to speak to the cutters and examined the destination tag attached, as was BR practice, to the cab handrail, and was surprised to note that the purchaser's name inscribed on the tag was Woodham, Barry. He drew this fact to the cutters' attention and their disbelief finally gave way to acceptance in the face of incontrovertible proof. Nevertheless, the big Pacific was next in line for the yard, Cashmore's was cutting at least one engine a day at that stage, and Sheppard – not expecting to see her again – took No. 71000's photograph, believing it to be the last record of the unique and historic Standard, and departed.

However, when he returned later that same day, the Pacific had gone. To Sheppard's relief and to the later benefit of thousands of enthusiasts, *Duke of Gloucester* had recommended her royal progress to Woodham's yard at Barry from where she moved again in April 1974 – to Loughborough and restoration, safe at last and bound for glory.

Chapter Six

A detailed look at the disposal of eight famous express classes

Scrapping the giants of the steam age

Locomotive	Disposal		Yard record	Scrap tonnage	Engines in stock at year's end†								
	BR Works	Private Yard			1960	1961	1962	1963	1964	1965	1966	1967	
GWR KING	10 (33%)	17 (57%)	Cox & Danks, Oldbury (37%)	3,664	30	30	—	—	—	—	—	—	(3)
SR MERCHANT NAVY	1 (3%)	18*(60%)	Buttigieg's, Newport (20%)	2,696	30	30	30	30	23	16	10	—	(11)
SR LIGHT PACIFIC	9 (8%)	81 (74%)	Cashmore's, Newport (34%)	11,574	110	110	110	100	70	54	36	—	(20)
LMS PRINCESS ROYAL	9 (75%)	1 (8%)	Crewe Works (75%)	1,340	12	6	—	—	—	—	—	—	(2)
LMS DUCHESS	17 (45%)	18 (47%)	Crewe Works (45%)	5,658	38	38	35	22	—	—	—	—	(3)
LNER A4	15 (44%)	13 (38%)	Doncaster Works (38%)	4,630	34	34	29	19	12	6	—	—	(6)
BR BRITANNIA	1 (2%)	52 (95%)	McWilliams, Shettleston (40%)	7,632	55	55	55	55	55	53	42	1	(2)

*Includes one loco cut up on site at Eastleigh MPD

Percentages are calculated on percentage of class, not percentage of scrapped locomotives (some being preserved)

†Courtesy RCTS

One of Stafford Road's Kings, No.6027 *King Richard I*, was stored for nearly a year at Banbury MPD but she escaped the attentions of Friswell's scrapyard adjacent to the shed and her final movement was to Cox & Danks at Oldbury. This photograph was taken at Banbury on 19th May 1963 by which time the King had been derelict for nine months: also visible is Class 41XX 2-6-2T No.4112, destined for Cashmore's, Great Bridge. *Photo: Michael Hale*

Killing the Kings

AS THE YEAR 1962 opened, British steam was in full retreat. Of the 16,000 steam locomotives in traffic only four years before, one quarter had been withdrawn and, already, a pattern was emerging which was to alarm and dismay many enthusiasts. For while a full 84 per cent of freight train mileage was still worked by steam, the figure for steam hauled passenger traffic had been shattered by the influx of main line diesels and stood at just 31 per cent. More than anything else, this stark statistic signalled the imminent demise of the classic express passenger flagships of the old 'Big Four'.

And the Kings were the first to suffer. On paper, their withdrawal dates — all in 1962 — indicate summary execution: Swindon devotees will tell you their destruction was hasty and premature. Yet the demise of the Kings commenced a full four years earlier with the advent of the main line diesel hydraulic — itself the product of that same pioneering, independent spirit traditionally associated with the Great Western and which, to some degree, still fired BR's Western Region.

With the advent of the Warships the Kings fell into decline, but it was two years before the real turning point: February 1960, when the last of Laira's Kings, No.6002, was transferred to Old Oak, ending the class' thirty year sojourn on the Plymouth shed and emasculating its work in the West Country. During that summer, the big 4-6-0s became increasingly rare sights on the West of England main line: instead, it suffered under the onslaught of a not particularly reliable fleet of Warships. It seemed a poor exchange.

The transfer of eight Kings to Cardiff Canton to work the Paddington expresses and the Shrewsbury line was the first such allocation for the class and probably postponed withdrawals: throughout 1961 the class remained intact and at the commencement of withdrawals the engines were shedded at Old Oak (11), Wolverhampton Stafford Road (11) and Cardiff Canton (8).

First to go was Old Oak's No.6006 in February 1962, followed in June by Nos.6003, 6004, 6010, 6023, 6024 from Cardiff and Nos.6008, 6013 from Old Oak. July marked the end for the first Stafford Road engines: Nos.6017 and 6020, plus No.6029 from Old Oak, while September saw the virtual destruction of the class: Nos.6001, 6002, 6007 (the lowest mileage King, rebuilt after the 1936 Shrivenham crash), 6009, 6012, 6014, 6015, 6016, 6019, 6021, 6022, 6026, 6027 — thirteen engines discarded at a stroke. Of the six survivors, Nos.6005, 6028 were condemned at Old Oak in November and Nos.6000, 6011, 6018, 6025 at the year's end.

During the last week in April 1963, however, No.6018 *King Henry VI* was steamed again at Tyseley, working local trains between Snow Hill and Leamington Spa in preparation for an SLS Special from Birmingham to Swindon Works on 28th April. It was the Kings' swan song and No.6018 lived up to the occasion, achieving 91 mph at Denham and topping Hatton Bank at 42 mph. This engine very nearly achieved immortality for later that year No.6000 *King George V* was examined at Swindon Works and found to have badly cracked frames, a discovery which threw into doubt the plan to preserve her and gave rise to the suggestion that her name and number plates be transferred to No.6018, then still at Old Oak shed where her future use had not yet been ruled out.

Several Kings lingered on. Exact cutting up dates have, in several cases, been unreliably recorded but of the 27 engines now just a memory, certainly Nos.6011, 6025 were not cut up at Swindon until the first half of 1964 and Birds, Risca, finally despatched No.6028 in August of that year. Amazingly, No.6010 clung to life at Swindon until September 1965 when she finally gave up the ghost. Amongst Swindon cutters and management alike there was, reportedly, great reluctance to cut up the Kings.

Those enthusiasts still mourning the end of the Kings will draw no comfort whatever from the fact that each of the 17 engines sold — complete and in working order — to a private scrapyard in the 1960s changed hands for less than just their nameplates would fetch today.

ABOVE: End of the Stafford Road Kings. Still fully coaled, complete with plates and protective chimney sacking — but destined never to steam again — are Nos.6014 *King Henry VII* (the only King streamlined, in March 1935) and 6012 *King Edward VI* make a sad sight at 84A on 8th September 1962, their official month of withdrawal. Behind them is No.6017 *King Edward IV*, her lack of chimney covering testifying to her earlier withdrawal two months previously. *Photo: Michael Hale*

TOP: Cashmore's, Newport, took four Kings. This line up at the yard's reception sidings shows No.6019 *King Henry V* in company with No.5021 *Whittington Castle* and No.5064 *Bishop's Castle.* After withdrawal from Cardiff Canton the former Castle had been stored at Swindon and then journeyed back to South Wales for cutting – a somewhat pointless exercise not uncommon at the time. Later, as the rate of withdrawals increased and sales to private scrapyards became more established the practice of passing condemned engines through Swindon was abolished, direct movement from running shed to scrapyard becoming normal procedure. Just discernible, extreme right, is a second King, No.6009 *King Charles II*. Taken on 15th April 1963, this photograph disproves earlier published scrapping dates for these engines.

BOTTOM: No.6005 *King George II* only hours from complete extinction at Cashmore's, Great Bridge, on 26th October 1963: a disturbing photograph which appeals directly to the emotions.

Photos: Michael Hale

Disposal of the GWR Kings

COX & DANKS, Langley Green, Oldbury, Warley, Worcs.

6001	6002	6007	6012
6014	6015	6016	6017
6020	6022	6027	

11 engines

SWINDON WORKS

6003	6004	6006	6008
6010	6011	6013	6018
6025	6026		

10 engines

CASHMORE'S, Newport, Mon.

6009	6019	6021	6029

4 engines

CASHMORE'S, Great Bridge, Tipton, Staffs.

6005

1 engine

BIRD'S, Risca, Newport, Mon.

6028

1 engine

PRESERVED

6000	6023	6024

3 engines

ABOVE: Of the nine Kings to end their days at Old Oak Common, one was preserved, five went to private yards and three were cut up at Swindon. Two of this latter trio, Nos.6025 *King Henry III* and 6026 *King John*, are seen here outside 'A' Shop at Swindon on 25th August 1963. No.6025 had been stored at 81A for four months after withdrawal, No.6026 for about a month: both were to present a mournful sight at Swindon Works for many months pending possible resurrection for the summer service. It never happened, and final disposal came in November 1963 (No.6026) and April 1964. *Photo: T. W. Nicholls*

TOP: 26th April 1964 and No.6025's time is up. Inside 'C' Shop her destruction has commenced.

BOTTOM: Two more of the Swindon-cut Kings are visible in this earlier view (9th September 1962) of the works dump. Nearest camera is No.6013 *King Henry VIII* only weeks from scrapping and bearing two chalked inscriptions: a terse 'C Shop' on her cab side and an affectionate 'Farewell' on her centre splasher. She was the highest mileage King (1.9504m miles). Between Class 57XX 2-6-2T No.5180 and Class 42XX 2-8-0T No.4293 is No.6008 *King James II*, late of Stafford Road and still – incredibly – wearing her full set of name and number plates. *Photos: Michael Hale*

ABOVE: 23rd September 1962 and Nos.6023 *King Edward II* and 6024 *King Edward I* have arrived at Swindon from Cardiff. This photograph will be of particular interest to those hundreds of people who have contributed time, effort or money towards the continued existence of these very lucky engines for, of course, they were not cut up at Swindon, moving two months later to Severn Tunnel Junction, purchased for scrap by Ward's of Briton Ferry.

Fate, however, was to take a hand and BR refused to allow the Kings to be towed to Ward's over lines for which the class was not cleared. Woodham Bros of Barry bought them from Ward's and the rest is history.

Notice that the pair are not only complete with name, number and smokebox plates but also have their rods still in situ. They will be re-united with their tenders before leaving Swindon but were later to become the only engines to arrive at Woodham's without rods — a factor which would later cost their respective preservation groups around £10,000 a set. All non-ferrous parts are also still intact, years of dereliction at Barry (10½ for No.6024, and no fewer than 22 for 6023) will allow ample time to strip injectors, whistles, safety valve bonnets, cab fittings, axlebox brasses, brass beading *at al*, before funds were raised for the engines' purchase.
Photo: G. T. Robinson

BELOW: Ample evidence of mutilation is provided in this comparatively early scene at Woodham's: No.6023 is seen on 13th April 1971.
Photo: Tim Edmonds

Breaking the Bulleids

DEVOTEES OF THE EXPRESS passenger flagships of the GWR, LMS and LNER, mortified at the scrappings of the Kings, Duchesses and A4s, could gain some small consolation that those engines, with an average working life of around thirty years, had at least had a career of respectable length. Nothing of the sort could be said about the Southern Pacifics and the argument that electrification can now be seen clearly to provide the most efficient, economical and environmentally acceptable modern railway will cut little ice with Bulleid enthusiasts, incensed at the destruction of locomotives — particularly the rebuilds — with such pitifully short careers.

The Merchant Navies

BY JUNE 1959 THE great days of the 'Golden Arrow' and 'Night Ferry' were over for the MNs, Stewarts Lane losing its last allocation that month, but it was nearly five years before the first of the class were condemned — Nos.35002, 35015 from Nine Elms in February 1964, which achieved considerable celebrity by travelling all the way to Rotherham for breaking.

Four more engines went at the end of the summer — Nos.35006, 35018 in August and Nos.35009, 35025 in September — the latter engines the last of the Exmouth Junction MNs, withdrawn following the commencement of WR Warship diesel working on the Exeter-Waterloo main line. This quartet went to Woodham's, Barry, (and all still exist) and Nos.35001 (November), 35024 (January 1965) continued an unbroken run of the class sold to private scrapyards, No.35020 (February 1965) was the only MN to be cut up by BR, at Eastleigh Works.

There followed a brief respite until August when Nos.35016 and 35021 were condemned with Nos.35019, 35004, 35005 succumbing the following month to complete the year's withdrawals. Thus, sixteen MNs soldiered on into 1966, during which year only six were withdrawn: Nos.35011 (February), 35022 (May), 35017 (July) and 35010, 35027, 35029 (September). Five of these still exist, No.35029 sectioned in the NRM, York.

Nos.35014 and 35026 went in March 1967 — Weymouth engines destined for Cashmore's, Newport, they were followed by No.35012 the following month. Up to this date, the usual story of steam heating and mechanical problems with the new Brush diesel electrics had ensured a reasonably strong steam profile on the Southern's SW Division: indeed, it was probably the steam workings which were the most reliable in a rapidly evolving diesel and electric regime. However, the introduction of partial electric working to Bournemouth on 3rd April 1967 marked the culmination of many months of electrification work and signed the death warrant for Southern steam, and by June there had been a substantial reduction in the number and scope of steam diagrams. But seven MNs clung to life, and on Sunday 2nd July the SR's official 'Farewell to Steam' tours saw Nos.35007, 35008 and 35028 at work on the two specials. Even this was not the end and the big Pacifics, grimy and running without nameplates, were not giving in without a fight: No.35003 being noted active on the 5th July and on the same day No.35023 arrived at Waterloo 18 minutes early on the 17.30 Weymouth. On the 6th No.35007, in a two-fingered salute to the BR planners, hauling the same train, blasted through Bramshot at a shade below 100 mph: two days later it was No.35023 again — 94 mph down Winchester Bank and 7¾ minutes early at Bournemouth despite signal checks and a special stop at Woking — and back to Waterloo with the up Channel Islands boat train, arriving — predictably — well before time.

At 1st January 1967 the last surviving Merchant Navies were shedded at Weymouth, a short-term allocation during Bournemouth electrification work, and eight re-allocated to Nine Elms in March. When, on 9th July that year, both sheds closed to steam, Weymouth saw a continued flicker of life as a diesel stabling point although the usurpers had to fight for space among dozens of dead steam locomotives. Foreground in this view of Weymouth MPD, dated 31st July 1967, is No.35003 *Royal Mail*, one of the last seven MN's withdrawn that month. Nos.35014/35026 are discernible in the background and five light Pacifics were also present. *Photo: John Bird*

Next day, 9th July 1967, saw the last Southern Pacific steam working of all and, fittingly, it was MN No.35030 *Elder Dempster Lines* which had the honour of the final Pacific steam entry into Waterloo when she arrived with the 14.11 Weymouth. Then, as the faceless, depressing, electrics took over six of the last seven MNs — Nos.35003, 35007, 35008, 35013, 35023, 35030 — were prepared to meet the torch.

Handsome, erratic, underused, problematical but capable of astonishing feats, the Merchant Navies are sorely missed.

ABOVE: From July 1967 the former steam shed at Salisbury was used as a storage and dispersal point for SR engines destined for the big private scrap yards in South Wales, which were then buying in large numbers from the Southern and London Midland Regions. It was at Salisbury that tenders were emptied of coal and motions partly dismantled in preparation for the final journeys: the silent machines, already patched with rust, made a sombre sight as they stood in long lines on the weed-choked sidings. This view shows MN Pacifics Nos.35007 *Aberdeen Commonwealth* and 35013 *Blue Funnel* already prepared for departure to the waiting cutters at Buttigieg's. Sister engines Nos.35008, 35023 and 35030 were in store there at the same time, the last MN departing Salisbury in March 1968. Also visible in this 30th September 1967 view are BR Standards and USA tanks. *Photo: N. E. Preedy*

October 1968 and No.35008 has arrived at Buttigieg's and is next in line for the torch. One of her rods has been unceremoniously thrust into her firebox. At left are the remains of an LMS tender, inscribed with part of Buttigieg's address and the words 'From Bolton 9K', and at right is MN No.35030. *Photo: Rex Conway*

Disposal of the SR Merchant Navies

BUTTIGIEG'S, Newport, Mon.

35007	35008	35013	35017
35023	35030		

6 engines

CASHMORE'S, Newport, Mon.

35003	35012	35014	35019
35026			

5 engines

BIRD'S, Bridgend, Glam.

35016	35021

2 engines

SLAG REDUCTION CO, Rotherham, Yorks.

35002	35015

2 engines

EASTLEIGH WORKS

35020

1 engine

BIRD'S, Morriston, Swansea, Glam.

35001

1 engine

COHEN'S, cut up on site at Eastleigh MPD

35004

1 engine

WOODFIELD'S, Town Dock, Newport, Mon.

35024

1 engine

PRESERVED

35005	35006	35009	35010
35011	35018	35022	35025
35027	35028	35029	

11 engines

The SR Light Pacifics

THE RANKS OF THE West Country and Battle of Britain Light Pacifics were intact until June 1963. In that month Nos.34035, 34043, 34055, 34074 were condemned, followed by six more engines before the year was out. Apart from No.34067, which went to Woodham's and is now on the Mid Hants Railway, all these early withdrawals went to Eastleigh Works for disposal.

Further batches followed in 1964: two engines in April, one in May, four in June, one in July, five in August and a full dozen in September at the end of the summer service. Five more engines had gone by year's end, making thirty withdrawals that year — all sold to private yards and including a dozen to Woodham's (two of which were cut up) and the only four to be disposed of in Kent. Predictably, it was the unrebuilt engines which were suffering most — thirty of the 1963-4 condemnations being unmodified.

1965-66 saw withdrawals slowing to a trickle: 16 in 1965, 18 in 1966, one or two every few weeks with small peaks in both Octobers. Cutting up of Pacifics at Eastleigh had ceased in June 1964 and the great South Wales yards now held sway, dozens of Bulleids, dead, rusty and forlorn, flowing north and west, through Gloucester and down to Cashmore's, Buttigieg's, Bird's and Woodham's.

By the start of 1967 only three dozen engines were left, shedded at Bournemouth, Eastleigh, Nine Elms and Salisbury. None was condemned in either January or February but fifteen went in March-June. The end of Southern steam in July saw withdrawals *en masse*: twenty-one engines of which only two — Nos.34023 (preserved) and 34102 — were unrebuilt.

Among the last engines at work in July 1967 were Nos.34025, 34021, 34001, 34095, and on the evening of 7th July No.34093 headed the final 17.23 Waterloo-Bournemouth; No.34025 the 18.54 Basingstoke and the same day the 17.30 Weymouth arrived 9½ minutes early at Waterloo behind No.34013. Nos.34037 and 34095 worked out of Waterloo on the 8th on Portsmouth and Bournemouth trains respectively and on the final day of SR Pacific steam at Waterloo (9th) the Light Bulleids were represented by No.34021 which headed the 11.00 boat special from Southampton Docks.

That same day, down on the largely WR Weymouth-Westbury route, Nos.34052 and 34095 were hard at work on 'perishables', after which they ran disconsolately, light engine, back to Weymouth for store, stripping and disposal.

Thus, Southern fires died for good.

LEFT:
Buttigieg's again: WC No. 34102 Lapford, famous as one of the last two unrebuilt engines in service, had a long, painful demise: nearly eight months in store at Eastleigh and Salisbury and then several more languishing in Newport, South Wales before moving into the scrapyard. This picture was taken on 9th September 1968, one year after the engine's withdrawal: she had been partially cut up for several weeks, the piles of scrap in the foreground suggesting that s periodic 'log jam' is occurring. *Photo: M. Sheppard*

ABOVE:
The 'standard' view of Cashmore's yard at Newport. Understandably, most scrap merchants did not welcome visitors, but Cashmore's could do little about this vantage point on Octopus Bridge where the enthusiast's camera could be poked through railings. Each locomotive appears to have been cut up on the same spot, seen here occupied by long-time Salisbury engine No. 34052 *Lord Dowding* – just one of no fewer than 43 Bulleid Pacifics sold to this yard. A large crane to the right handled the loaded hoppers of scrap and added inexorably to the awesome mountain of engine bits towering in the background: it was there for years and exerted a powerful fascination on many who saw it.

Just visible on the extreme right of this 26th March 1968 picture is one of the three Sherman army tanks mentioned in this book. Interestingly, they were of the type equipped during WW2 with rotating flails for exploding mines, and military enthusiasts will no doubt be intrigued as to how and when they had ended up at Cashmore's. What else was buried under the scrap mountain? *Photo: N. E. Preedy.*

Bound for Gloucester and thence Cashmore's, Newport, are (leading) Bulleid WC Pacific No.34048 *Crediton*, BB Pacific No.34079 *141 Squadron* and SR Class U Mogul No.31803, while the Standard 4MT tank, No.80142, will end up at Bird's, Bridgend. In view of steam's defeat at the hands of the diesel it is entirely appropriate that the train engine is Warship diesel-hydraulic No.D860 *Victorious.*

While in store at Eastleigh these engines would have been prepared for their last journey in keeping with standard procedures for dead engine movements, the fundamentals of which were common to all the Regions. Rods were removed to free the motion, tenders and bunkers emptied and, meanwhile, the Operating Department was preparing a Special Notice, a particularly vital document which governed every aspect of the special train's operation. It would specify passing times, where and when stops were to be made to inspect the engines (typically every 25 miles) and maximum running speed (usually 25 mph).

Ancillary requirements of the Notice included, if no brake van was available, the provision of a 'rider' for one or two of the dead engines: his job, an unenviably cold and uncomfortable one, was to operate the locomotive handbrake and to inspect his mount regularly with particular vigilance for hot boxes, to which dead engines were particularly susceptible. The Notice stressed the importance of warning the 'rider' about overhead wires if his engine was not fitted with warning flashes, and carried instructions covering the removal of each engine's stock of detonators — a very necessary task before it was subjected to the cutters' torches. The train carried a class 8 headcode and was signalled 'out of gauge load' or OGLO. Virtually all dead engine movements were special workings but it is believed that at the height of the 1960s scrappings one or two regular turns were rostered.

Notice, on this particular working, the six vans ahead of the leading Pacific: they are not condemned stock but vacuum fitted vehicles added to increase the braking effectiveness of the train. Four engines were the maximum permitted on a dead engine movement and it looks as if restricted bridges do not feature in the specified route as 'spacer' wagons to spread the load have not been incorporated in the train.

Tied to each dead engine's cab handrail will be a small tag on which its purchaser and destination were recorded. Thus, a once proud, breathing steam locomotive was reduced, almost, to the status of a parcel. *Photo: Ivo Peters*

Disposal of the SR Light Pacifics

CASHMORE'S, Newport, Mon.

34001	34002	34004	34006
34012	34013	34015	34018
34019	34021	34024	34025
34031	34034	34036	34037
34038	34040	34041	34044
34048	34052	34056	34057
34060	34071	34076	34077
34079	34082	34087	34088
34089	34090	34093	34095
34097	34100		

38 engines

BUTTIGIEG, Newport, Mon.

34005	34008	34009	34017
34026	34032	34033	34042
34047	34066	34084	34085
34086	34098	34102	34103
34104	34108		

18 engines

EASTLEIGH WORKS

34011	34035	34043	34049
34055	34068	34069	34074
34110			

9 engines

BIRD'S, Bynea, Llanelly

34020	34030	34054	34065
34078	34080	34096	34106
34107			

9 engines

BIRD'S, Bridgend, Glam.

34014	34062	34063	34064
34075	34083		

6 engines

WOOD'S, Queenborough, Kent

34003	34029	34061	34091

4 engines

BIRD'S, Morriston, Swansea, Glam.

34050	34099	34109

3 engines

WOODHAM BROS, Barry, Glam.

34045	34094

2 engines

WOODFIELD'S, Town Dock, Newport, Mon.

34022

1 engine

PRESERVED

34007	34010	34016	34023
34027	34028	34029	34046
34051	34053	34058	34059
34067	34071	34072	34073
34081	34092	34101	34105

20 engines

Two more views at Buttigieg's, chillingly emphasising just what the South Wales yards did to Bulleid's masterpieces.

TOP: Framed by what appears to be a pair of 5ft drivers from a 9F 2-10-0, two Bulleid Pacifics, cab-to-cab, await their fate.

RIGHT: Work is almost complete on this unidentified engine, standing amid the carcasses of her sisters. Both views were taken in October 1967, towards the end of a busy few months of cutting at the yard during which four light Bulleids were cut up: Nos.34005, 34009, 34026, 34066.
Photos: John Bird

Scrapping the Stanier Pacifics

The Princess Royals

AT THE BEGINNING OF 1961, the brand new English Electric Type 4 diesels were arriving in force on the Midland and Western sections of the LMR. Predictably, they played havoc in the ranks of the earlier Stanier Pacifics and by mid-March only one of the Princesses, No.46209, was active, the other eleven engines being in store. Nos.46210/46212 were unserviceable but several of the others were re-allocated away from their strongholds at Crewe (North) and Liverpool (Edge Hill). Nos.46203/46211 went to Carnforth for store — the first time the class had been allocated there — but were back at Crewe for the summer service, the former engine returning to Carnforth in September. No.46206 spent a brief spell at, of all places, Rugby, while Nos.46201/46210 went north of the border to Polmadie. Nos.46205/46207 went to Willesden.

But re-allocation could not long stave off the inevitable and, with the summer service over, six engines were condemned: Nos.46204, 46205, 46207, 46210, 46211, 46212, all for disposal at Crewe Works.

To the delight of enthusiasts, however, the Type 4s were soon to disgrace themselves with a spate of train heating boiler failures and persistent mechanical defects and in January 1962 the Princesses steamed again, Nos.46200, 46201, 46203 at Upperby, 46208 at Edge Hill and 46206, 46209 at Camden. Even better, they worked the top link: No.46208 and 46206 spitting fire on February 10th on the 'Ulster Express' and down 'Mid-day Scot' respectively. Such workings continued through that summer but in September five of the survivors retired again to store at Carlisle and Camden, No.46209 being immediately condemned at the latter shed. The following month, with the commencement of the winter timetable, Nos.46201, 46203, 46206 were withdrawn leaving pioneer engine No.46200 to soldier on a few more weeks, finally succumbing in November.

Disposal of the LMS Princess Royals

CREWE WORKS

46204	46205	46206	46207
46208	46209	46210	46211
46212			

9 engines

CONNELL'S, Coatbridge, Lanarks.

46200

1 engine

PRESERVED

46201 46203

2 engines

Pioneer engine of the 'Lizzies', the last to be withdrawn and the only member of the class to be cut up by a private yard, No.46200 *The Princess Royal* is seen here at Carlisle (Kingmoor) on 6th April 1963, some four months after withdrawal. Her heavily greased motion and protected chimney suggest that her reinstatement in traffic had not been entirely ruled out and, indeed, a protracted period in store at Carlisle Upperby and Kingmoor followed withdrawal and it was not until October 1964 that Connell's of Coatbridge finally got their hands on this important and timelessly elegant engine. Behind the 'Crab' in this view is a much more fortunate engine: No.46201 *Princess Elizabeth* which will leave Kingmoor in August for a suitably celebrated retirement in preservation. *Photo: Gavin Morrison*

The last day of Duchess steam: Carlisle Upperby on 26th September 1964. Foreground are four withdrawn engines from the last batch in service: Nos.46250 *City of Lichfield* and 46238 *City of Carlisle* – complete with plates – with Nos.46225 and 46237 beyond. Visible above the tender of No.46238 is No.46256 *Sir William Stanier FRS* which that day performed the very last Stanier Pacific duty – the RCTS 'Scottish Lowlander' railtour.
Photo: E. Lowden

The Duchesses

THE YOUNGER DUCHESSES LASTED a little longer. Continuing mechanical problems were seriously affecting the availability of the Type 4 diesels and ensured that the Duchesses were still very much part of the Midland scene until the late summer of 1964.

It was a trio of Polmadie engines which held the doubtful honour of being the first to go, Nos.46227, 46231, 46232 being condemned in December 1962, eventually being cut up at Crewe after almost a year in store. Interestingly, the two latter engines had both been severely damaged during their careers, No.46232 by bombing at Berkhamsted in 1940, No.46231 in a collision at Ecclefechan in 1945 — a factor which may have contributed to early withdrawal.

Among the engines still in traffic, there was considerable re-allocation and a number were periodically in store. While still active on express passenger — regularly delayed by water stops necessitated by the removal of water troughs following partial dieselisation — the Pacifics also worked a variety of more menial turns such as parcels and freight, often displacing Class 5 motive power, and started to appear at a variety of locations where the class was previously unknown.

Three engines died very early in 1963: Nos.46234, 46246, 46253, followed in April by the pioneer engine No.46220. May saw the end for No.46221, June Nos.46247, 46252 and October Nos.46222, 46223, 46224, 46242 (the engine involved in the horrific double collision at Harrow in 1952) and November saw the last of Polmadie's engines condemned: Nos.46230, 46249.

And so, twenty-two Duchesses worked on into 1964, allocated at Crewe (North), Liverpool (Edge Hill), Carlisle (Kingmoor and Upperby). Many, kept as standby engines, were worked only intermittently but most were kept in excellent condition, notably Edge Hill's Nos.46229, 46233, 46241, 46243. Some of the Carlisle engines were put back into traffic at the beginning of February, once again to cover for the unfortunate Type 4s. On 9th March Upperby's No.46225 was noted on the up 'Caledonian' and on 21st March four Willesden Pacifics worked Grand National Specials out of Euston.

Early 1964 casualties were Nos.46229 and 46233, both Edge Hill engines destined for preservation. Kingmoor lost No.46236 in March but, surprisingly, sister 12A engine No.46226 which had been lying derelict on shed with a cracked cylinder since the summer of 1963 and which most observers considered to be not long for this world, was in April suddenly moved into the roundhouse for repairs and reinstated in traffic.

Even at this late date, the Duchesses could still put on a show of strength, shouldering the shiny and unreliable newcomers into the wings and delighting their legions of fans. On 5th July no fewer than seven of the class were noted on Willesden shed and the same month an observer at Bletchley recorded, over several hours, the same number in traffic. Nos.46240 and 46245, Willesden's pride and joy, were running in virtually ex-works condition and it was difficult to accept that they were soon to become just a memory.

For time was fast running out. As summer died, sightings of Duchesses on passenger workings became rare. On 2nd September the 'Caledonian' — so long a Stanier Pacific turn — ceased to run but fittingly, and movingly, the very last down working came thundering through behind Edge Hill's No.46243. As from 7th September, when electric working on a trial basis reached Rugby, the Duchesses were barred from working south of Crewe, but it was a mere formality for Stanier's masterpieces had at last disappeared from the West Coast main line.

Nos.46241 and 46248 were condemned in September, the first of the class to be sold to a private scrapyard, and those few engines still in steam worked out their last turns in the first two weeks of the month. Officially, their last day was the 12th, but one or two engines over-ran their death warrant by a few days and No.46256 headed a RCTS Special on the 26th. The last batch condemned comprised Nos.46225, 46226, 46228, 46235, 46237, 46238, 46239, 46240, 46243, 46244, 46245, 46250, 46251, 46254, 46255, 46256, 46257: every one went to a private scrapyard, so it would seem the privilege of staying in service longest cost these engines their chance of a dignified end, 'at home' at Crewe. And then that was that. Stanier's Pacifics had gone and, for many, the London Midland died with them.

BELOW:

A dead engine movement *par excellence.* Her massive purposeful lines accentuated by a low sun, No. 46226 *Duchess of Norfolk* arrives at the Troon Harbour scrapyard of the West of Scotland Shipbreaking Company on 27th January 1965. This engine had been sold previously to Slag Reduction Co at Barrow, a notice for movement there on 15th December 1964 having been issued. This sale was cancelled for route restriction reasons. In charge here is Caprotti Standard Class 5 No. 73143, an engine which went on to become one of the very last BR steam locomotives in service, leaving Patricroft shed for Cashmore's, Great Bridge, in October 1968. *Photo: The late Derek Cross, courtesy D. M. Cross.*

RIGHT:

Her last moment of glory on the final down 'Caledonian' over, No. 46243 *City of Lancaster* became the most celebrated engine to be cut up at Wigan by the Central Wagon Company. Photographed at their yard on 20th May 1965. *Photo: P. J. Wood.*

Disposal of the LMS Duchesses

CREWE WORKS

46220	46221	46222	46223
46224	46227	46230	46231
46232	46234	46236	46242
46246	46247	46249	46252
46253			

17 engines

CASHMORE'S, Great Bridge, Tipton, Staffs.

46228	46239	46240	46241
46245	46248	46251	46254
46256			

9 engines

WEST OF SCOTLAND SHIPBREAKING CO. (ARNOTT YOUNG), Troon Harbour, Ayrshire

46225	46226	46237	46238
46244	46250	46255	46257

8 engines

CENTRAL WAGON CO, Ince, Wigan

46243

1 engine

PRESERVED

46229	46233	46235

3 engines

Photographs of Duchesses being cut up are exceptionally rare and many enthusiasts, understandably, will think it's just as well. Nevertheless, these two views, taken by *Michael Hale* on 27th March 1965 at Cashmore's, Great Bridge, are historically very important.

TOP: No.46240 *City of Coventry* stands under the yard's gantry. She ran the highest mileage of all the Stanier Pacifics – 1.685m miles – and was in the last batch to be condemned. Notice that she carries the yellow restriction stripes on her cabsides; painted on only days before her withdrawal. The Pacific has Jubilee No.45586 *Mysore* for company.

ABOVE: An interesting view of No.46240's tender in process of cutting, showing design features normally hidden from view. Prominent is the cylindrical coal pusher mounted on the sloping bunker floor; fitted to all Duchess tenders this was a useful aid to the firemen on the West Coast expresses, its steam operated piston connected to twin rams forcing coal down the slope towards the footplate. The pusher's operating handle is visible, top left of the tender front. Note, too, the cross bracing and baffle plates of the water tank, essential for structural rigidity and to reduce surging and illuminating to those enthusiasts under the mistaken impression that a locomotive's water tank comprised a simple steel box.

End of the A4s

ABOVE: Last hours of the A4s. By August 1966 steam was virtually extinct on Scottish Region and at Perth MPD, seen here on the 17th, almost every engine on shed was dead or stored. At right are A4 Nos.60026 *Miles Beevor* (rear), *sans* nameplates and in decrepit condition after nine months in store here and at Ferryhill, and No.60024 *Kingfisher*, the last active non-preserved A4 and then just coming to the end of an exuberant period of railtours. Here she appears to be awaiting pairing with the tender of No.60034 *Lord Faringdon* (just withdrawn and in store at Perth en route to Hughes Bolckow's at North Blyth), after which No.60024 will return to traffic for the last time. One of her last turns was the 07.15 Perth-Aberdeen in early September and on the 14th she headed the 08.25 Glasgow-Aberdeen — the very last time a BR-owned A4 turned a revenue-earning wheel. *Photo: A. Wyn Hobson*

WHILE TO THE WEST LMS enthusiasts were following the decline of the Stanier Pacifics, Gresley afficienados on the East Coast were sadly recording the last days of the A4s.

The 'Streaks' remained intact until December 1962 when five of Kings Cross' A4s were withdrawn: Nos.60003, 60014, 60028, 60030, 60033 — all, predictably, bound for Doncaster for scrapping — particularly regrettable in the case of *Silver Link*. By the following April, Top Shed's long and illustrious association with the class was drawing to a close: Nos.60013, 60015, and — most famous of all, No.60022 *Mallard* — were condemned at 34A that month, the depleted Pacific stock at the shed causing problems as summer workings commenced. The honour of hauling the final through Tyneside working, the down 'Car Sleeper Limited', fell to 34A's No.60026 on 15th June.

The same month marked the end for Nos.60018 from Gateshead, No.60008 following in July. Eleven of the Kings Cross A4s had transferred to New England from where more withdrawals soon inevitably followed at the end of the summer service: Nos.60017, 60021, 60025, 60029 and 60032 died in October. No.60021 had worked the last normal A4 turn out of Kings Cross — the 6.40 pm Leeds on 29th October 1963.

Nineteen A4s, then, were left as 1963 drew to a close. The five ER survivors were transferred to the Scottish Region together with four from Gateshead, a fifth 52A engine, No.60020, being withdrawn in March 1964. No.60005, a Ferryhill engine for nearly eighteen months, was condemned there that same month and she became the first of the class to be sold to a private scrapyard: Campbell's of Airdrie. May saw the end for Nos.60002 (Gateshead) and

Ferryhill's 60011; August was the last month for No.60012, October for Nos.60001 and 60023 and that month also saw the very last A4 working from Kings Cross when No.60009 worked the RCTS/SLS 'Jubilee Requiem' special on the 24th.

A dozen left now — two at St Margarets (Edinburgh), one at St Rollox, and nine at Ferryhill were they worked out a well remembered Indian Summer on the tightly timed three-hour Aberdeen-Glasgow expresses. The 1965 casualties were Nos.60016 (March); 60010 (May); 60006 and 60027 (September); 60031 (November) and 60026 (December). In February 1966 No.60007 was withdrawn and by May the last five A4s were concentrated at Ferryhill but were now confined to just three diagrams. June marked the end for No.60009 (destined for preservation and a final fling railtour on 25th March 1967), No.60004 following in July 1966, No.60034 in August.

And so it fell to Nos.60019 *Bittern* and 60024 *Kingfisher* to carry the A4 banner into the autumn of 1966, the last A4s in traffic, condemned in September.

To most enthusiasts, six preserved A4s will seem enough, but two are lost abroad and the others are becoming depressingly familiar. Where is *Kingfisher?* And, especially, where are the 'Silver' engines?

ABOVE: 26th November and *Kingfisher* keeps her appointment with Hughes Bolckow. Surrounded by sombre enthusiasts and lit by an evening sun she is slowly propelled into the scrapyard by D2312/2104. Sister No.60034 was also present, newly arrived from Perth via Heaton and arriving with the A4 are LNER Q6 No.63379 and J27 No.65819.
Photo: Peter W. Robinson

LEFT: Inside Hughes Bolckow's yard on New Year's Day 1965 is No.60001 *Sir Ronald Matthews*, long-time Gateshead stalwart. Of the four 52A A4s to travel to scrapyards direct from their running shed, this was the only engine to end up at North Blyth.
Photo: E. Lowden

Disposal of the LNER A4s

DONCASTER WORKS

60003	60013	60014	60015
60017	60018	60021	60025
60028	60029	60030	60032
60033			

13 engines

MOTHERWELL MACHINERY & SCRAP CO, Wishaw, Motherwell

60004	60006	60012	60016
60023			

5 engines

HUGHES BOLCKOW'S, North Blyth, Northumberland

60001	60024	60026	60034

4 engines

DARLINGTON WORKS

60011 60020

2 engines

CAMPBELL'S, Shieldhall, Renfrew

60027 60031

2 engines

CAMPBELL'S, Airdrie, Lanarks.

60005

1 engine

COHEN'S, Cargo Fleet, Middlesborough

60002

1 engine

PRESERVED

60007	60008	60009	60010
60019	60022		

6 engines

BELOW: Another Gateshead engine, pictured on 9th October 1964 at Cohen's Middlesborough yard: No.60002 *Sir Murrough Wilson* is newly arrived from store at Heaton MPD and already the cutter's torch has nibbled tentatively at her bogie and driving wheels, presumably so that the 71ft locomotive could more easily negotiate the tight radius curves in the scrapyard. *Photo: N. Skinner, via Ken Hoole*

ABOVE: 6th April 1967 and *Miles Beevor* clings to life, continuing her curiously protracted period in store which included three different locations and which will not be mercifully concluded until August 1967 when she will leave Crewe for Hughes Bolckow's. Lurking behind her, disfigured after surgery to remove her valve gear for display in the Science Museum, is BR Standard Pacific No.71000 *Duke of Gloucester.*
Photo: A. Wyn Hobson

RIGHT: Headless at Darlington MPD on 21st August 1965 is No.60010 *Dominion of Canada,* last recorded in steam on 11th May. She had been sent down to Darlington Works from Ferryhill for repairs but the condition of her boiler did not warrant them and her death warrant was duly signed. She lost her chimney soon after, possibly to No.60024 or 60004, both at Works that July: other visiting A4s were Nos.60019 (heavy repair, February) and 60034 (heavy repair, March), while the frames and wheels of No.60011 were noted dumped at Works on 27th March – one of the pair of A4s cut up at Darlington.

Darlington MPD closed to steam on 26th March 1966 and No.60010 was still there, quietly rusting at the back of the shed. But salvation was to come: she moved to Crewe Works that May and restored to BR green – on 10th April she took to the waters aboard MV *Beaveroak* at Royal Victoria Dock and sailed for the Canadian Railroad Associations's museum at Montreal, where she still resides.
Photo: P. J. Wood

Britannia twilight

ABOVE: Despite the daubed slogan 'Return to Crewe Works for repair' No.70030 *William Wordsworth* will never steam again. The location is the large Beighton, Sheffield, yard of T. W. Ward and the date 14th October 1966.
Photo: Tony Wakefield

RIGHT: A last glimpse of one of two Britannias to be scrapped in South Wales. No.70026 *Polar Star* was cut up immediately after this photograph was taken in May 1967. Cashmore's other Britannia No.70017 *Arrow*, arrived that January with substantial front end collision damage. *Photo: M. Sheppard*

ONCE COMMON TO ALL the Regions, the 55 'Brits' fought a long rearguard action with the diesels. The Southern was first to bid the class farewell, in June 1957, followed by the Western in September 1961, North Eastern August 1962, Scottish October 1962, and the Eastern by the end of 1963.

As 1964 dawned the Britannias — still intact as a class — were all on the London Midland: as more and more diesels came into stock they re-allocated repeatedly, grew dirtier and dirtier, were reduced to plain unlined green livery and became increasingly anonymous as BR removed their nameplates for safekeeping. The Pacifics also put in some of the best running of their short lives.

The first engines fell in June 1965 — Nos.70007 and 70043, the former engine being the sole Britannia to be cut up by BR. 1966 saw another nine engines condemned, most in the latter months and including pioneer engine No.70000 which commenced many years in store prior to eventual salvation. By December 1966, with the exception of five engines at Stockport and two at Carlisle (Upperby) the Britannias had become Carlisle (Kingmoor) engines and there the class was to end its days, playing a significant and well recorded role in British steam's death throes in the north west. The Pacifics fought an unwinnable battle for survival in rapidly deteriorating conditions, handling every imaginable type of traffic and fully vindicating Riddles' twin design essentials: ease of maintenance and full route availability.

Nearly every month in 1967 the numbers dwindled: January six engines condemned; March one; April four; May three; June one; July four; August three; September four; October one; November one and a body blow of thirteen engines slaughtered at year's end, rendering the class virtually extinct. Only No.70013 *Oliver Cromwell*, the last steam engine to receive a general overhaul at Crewe Works, soldiered on to become the last active non-preserved Pacific in BR service, her final triumph before preservation coming on the very last day of steam, 11th August 1968, when she hauled the last special of all.

Scrapping of the Britannias makes depressing reading for those who would have preferred dignified disposal at a BR Works, but their late withdrawal dates prevented that. No fewer than 43 of the class were cut up in Scotland, an odd fact considering that Scottish Region had lost its allocation of Britannias five years before.

ABOVE: The sorry remains of No.70001 *Lord Hurcomb* at Motherwell Machinery & Scrap, Wishaw, in December 1966, the first of five Britannias cut up at the yard, the others following in February, June and November 1967.
Photo: Keith Romig

Disposal of the BR Britannias

McWILLIAM'S, Shettleston, Glasgow

70006 70009 70010 70011
70015 70016 70020 70028
70029 70031 70032 70034
70037 70038 70039 70040
70041 70042 70048 70049
70051 70053

22 engines

CAMPBELL'S, Airdrie, Lanarks.

70002 70003 70005 70008
70025 70033 70046 70047
70050 70052

10 engines

MOTHERWELL MACHINERY & SCRAP CO, Wishaw, Motherwell

70001 70018 70027 70036
70054

5 engines

WARD'S, Inverkeithing

70004 70014 70021 70022
70035

5 engines

WARD'S, Beighton, Sheffield

70012 70030 70043 70044
70045

5 engines

CASHMORE'S, Newport, Mon.

70017 70026

2 engines

WARD'S, Killamarsh, Sheffield

70023 70024

2 engines

CREWE WORKS

70007

1 engine

WEST OF SCOTLAND SHIPBREAKING CO. (ARNOTT YOUNG) Troon Harbour, Ayrshire

70019

1 engine

PRESERVED

70000 70013

2 engines

Major Great Western classes

On 11th April 1964 at California Sidings, Sharpners, where Cooper's Metals have made their mark on Castle No. 5071 Spitfire. *Photo: W. Potter.*

SWINDON WORKS HAD A virtual monopoly (not quite 100% as we shall see) in the scrapping of GWR engines up until March 1959 when BR's policy of selling redundant locomotives to scrap metal merchants was implemented. Even after that date Swindon's C shop was very fully employed, particularly in the period 1963-4 (when so many of the modern standard engines became redundant) but its contribution to the total then became proportionately less. Nevertheless, over the period 1958-65, BR cut up almost exactly 1 in 3 of condemned GWR locomotives, approximately 98% of these at Swindon, with Wolverhampton, Caerphilly and Barry works picking up the crumbs.

As on all the regions, the earlier the engine was withdrawn the more chance it had of being cut up by BR. Thus, Swindon cut up some 66% of the Churchward Moguls and 56% of the 45XX 2-6-2Ts (both classes suffered withdrawals throughout the 1950s) but very few of the Modified Halls (11%), Granges (19%), 56XX tanks (17%) and Manors (just 3%), all of which were condemned primarily in the period 1963-5.

Of those GWR engines sold for scrap, the vast majority went to contractors in South Wales where the local steel industry had spawned a thriving scrap metal industry centred on an almost wholly ex-GWR railway. Cashmore's yard at Newport took the lion's share — about 1 in 6 of all GWR engines sold, nearly twice as many as its nearest rival, R. S. Hayes at Bridgend. Of those yards sited outside South Wales, only Cashmore's at Great Bridge achieved a large GWR total but three minor but most interesting tributeries to the main flow should be noted. Cohen's yard at Kettering took 24 major GWR engines including 10 Granges; Central Wagon at Ince, Wigan, took 20, including 16 57XX tanks, and King's of Norwich some 48, including a few real gems as recorded later. Friswell's, whose yard was adjacent to Banbury MPD but lacked rail access, cut up 15 major GWR engines on that shed.

The top ten private contractors purchasing GWR engines were (classes which follow *only*):

1. Cashmore's, Newport	490
2. Hayes, Bridgend*	233
3. Cashmore's, Great Bridge	207
4. Bird's, Risca	162
5. Ward's, Briton Ferry	102
6. Cohen's, Morriston	98
7. Bird's, Morriston	83
8. King's, Norwich	48
9. Bird's, Bridgend*	46
10. Woodham's, Barry	40

*This was the same yard, Bird's taking over c.August 1965

Castle

THE SIX 'CONVERSION' CASTLES were scrapped in the 1950s and although the pioneer 'pure' engines Nos.4073, 4074 were scheduled for withdrawal in 1955 they were both reprieved (until preservation from May 1960 and scrapping in May 1963 respectively). The dubious honour of being the first 'true' Castle to be withdrawn fell to No.5086 in November 1958 when it was only 21 years old. As the diesel-hydraulics took a hold on the West of England and Birmingham expresses, for 30 years the preserve of the Castles, the numbers of the elegant 4-6-0s dwindled, albeit slowly. 7 were condemned in 1960 and just 3 in 1961, but in 1962 the real blow fell when over the year an average of one engine a week was being taken out of traffic. 97 engines in stock at the end of 1962 were almost exactly halved in 1963 and a dozen worked into 1965, based at Tyseley (3), Oxley (5) and Gloucester Horton Road (4). Final survivor, of course, was No.7029, withdrawn for preservation in December 1965.

Apart from Swindon (32 Castles cut up), three private yards dominate the class's demise. Cashmore's at Newport took 37 and the firm's sister yard at Great Bridge 36: purchases were made from all over the WR, including Old Oak, Oxford, Worcester and Didcot, and from Oxley on the LMR. Hayes at Bridgend cut swathes through the South Wales engines, principally from store at Llanelly, but also from Newport, Cardiff and Carmarthen, and the firm also went farther afield to Southall, Reading and Swindon itself to accumulate 19 of the class. Cohen's of Morriston took 8, Bird's of Risca and King's, Norwich, 5 each, while Cooper's cut up 4 at Sharpness. Three Castles apiece went to Bird's, Bridgend and Cox & Danks, Oldbury while Bird's of Morriston had 2. Four single sales are most interesting: No.7028 to Barlborough Metals at Briton Ferry, No.5015 to Central Wagon in Ince, Wigan (ex-Craven Arms), No.5018 to Cohen's at Kettering and No.7013 to Cox & Danks, Park Royal. Three engines were sold twice, once to Cooper's Metals and following that firm's cessation of operations at Sharpness docks, to Cashmore's, Newport. They were Nos.7009, 7015 and 7037, the last of the class.

LEFT: By 1962, Castle withdrawals were in full flood. This 12th August view shows a long line-up of engines crowding into Swindon Works C Shop, which is looking quite inadequate for the job. No.5024 *Carew Castle* still wears her plates after three months in store but No.5006 *Tregenna Castle,* withdrawn that April, has lost hers. Also visible are No.4085 *Berkeley Castle* and No.5090 *Neath Abbey* (both condemned May) and No.4086 *Builth Castle* (April). *Photo: A. A. G. Delicata*

County

ALTHOUGH THE DEMISE OF the angular Hawksworth 4-6-0s appears to have been sudden, in fact, study of the statistics reveals a slow and gradual extinction which should perhaps have facilitated preservation: 9 withdrawals in 1962, 13 in 1963 and the last condemnations the following year. Ones, twos and threes died in each of fifteen different months between October 1962 (3 locos) and November 1964 (No.1011 at Swindon). Only 3 Counties were cut up at Swindon and no private yard could compete with Cashmore's total of 13 at Newport. Cooper's at Sharpness, King's of Norwich, Cashmore's, Great Bridge and Hayes at Bridgend took 2 each and Bird's chopped up one at Risca. The disposal of the class, however, is enlivened by the real curiosity of 5 engines travelling to Attercliffe, Sheffield, for the attention of Ward's. Nos.1017, 1022 arrived there in December 1963 ex-store at Craven Arms and Nos.1002, 1016 followed the next month from Shrewsbury.

A Great Western profile deep in Norfolk. Two Counties were purchased by King's of Norwich from store at Didcot where they had languished for over a year (what a tragedy they are not at that shed today) and were cut up in November 1963. This is No.1007 *County of Brecknock;* sister No.1018 *County of Leicester* was also present. *Photo: Dr I. C. Allen*

Hall

THROUGHOUT THE REGIONS, THE mixed traffic locomotives withstood the assault of the diesels rather better than the express classes, simply because the newcomers seized the passenger traffic first. The Halls, therefore, lasted well and by the end of 1961 only 10 of the 256 had been condemned. As with the other GWR 4-6-0s, however, the year 1962 was a shocking one and the long knives fell on 73 Halls, most in private yards as Swindon's scrappings slackened. Just over 100 Halls were left at January 1964 but half of these had gone by year's end. 14

View from the gantry at Cashmore's Great Bridge yard in June 1965. The cutters have already started work on No.6906 *Chicheley Hall,* a Banbury engine condemned that April. Chalked on the cylinder casing are the words 'save chimney'. Note the cylinder blocks scattered in gay abandon, mineral wagons filling with engine bits, and sledgehammer and blow torch left on the running plate. The cutters will return soon. *Photo: Sunday Mercury, Birmingham via Cashmore's*

worked into 1965 and the last engines in traffic, condemned in December 1965, were Nos.4920 (preserved ex-Barry) and 5971, both at Oxford. Swindon took the lion's share (60 engines) but Cashmore's cut 51 at Newport and 31 at Great Bridge. This latter figure was equalled by Hayes at Bridgend and the balance of the class disappeared into a variety of smaller yards: Bird's, Risca (4), Cohen's, Morriston (12), King's, Norwich (10) and Friswell's at Banbury MPD (9) are noteworthy. No.5938 was cut up at Wolverhampton Works.

Modified Hall

THE 1944-INTRODUCED MODIFIED Halls were untouched until January 1963 when No.6962 succumbed and the class, logically, lasted slightly longer than their half-sisters. Only 6 were withdrawn in 1963, 22 more in 1964 leaving 43 at work as 1965 dawned. A mass withdrawal of Oxford's allocation of 16 in December 1965 marked the end of the ubiquitous class. Only 8 were cut up at Swindon and Cashmore's, Newport, inevitably, was well to the fore taking 20 engines, Great Bridge dealing with 8, the same number as Bird's at Risca. 7 went to Bird's, Bridgend, and the rest of the class in ones, twos and threes to ten other private yards. Worthy of note is another Sheffield visitor, No.6964 from store at Banbury, purchased in December 1965

'This one next, guv?' Newly shunted into the yard at Cashmore's Newport on 25th October 1965 is one of the 20 Modified Halls which died there, No.6973 *Bricklehampton Hall,* purchased from Barrow Road that month. Her tender and connecting rods have been brutely severed and vandals have smashed her cab side windows.
Photo: E. H. Sawford

Grange

THE GRANGES ALSO LASTED well. Penzance's No. 6801 was condemned in October 1960 and the following month became the first of only 15 to be cut up at Swindon. 2 more died in 1961, 1 in 1962, 5 in 1963 and then the inevitable: 26 in 1964 and final slaughter, liked the Modified Halls, at the end of 1965. Disposal patterns were similar, too: 12 to Cashmore's, Newport, 6 to Great Bridge, 8 to Bird's, Bridgend, 6 to Bird's at Morriston. A surprising total of 10 Granges went to Cohen's, Kettering – mostly LMR engines from Oxley and Tyseley, although No. 6844 rattled all the way from Llanelly. Four more LMR Granges vanished into Cohen's somewhat mysterious yard at Kingsbury, Gloucester.

The wreck of No.6861 *Crynant Grange* looks no better for having her safety valve bonnet balanced upside down on her chimney as she stands in Cohen's yard at Kettering on 6th March 1966. A longtime Tyseley engine, she was withdrawn in October 1965.
Photo: E. H. Sawford

Manor

ONLY ONE OF THE class went home to Swindon — Shrewsbury's No.7809, the first (by a long interval) to be withdrawn, in April 1963. 10 more followed in 1964, and 1965 saw the Manors join all the other GWR 4-6-0s in the history books, at least as far as an enlightened BR, (fully occupied with keeping recalcitrant diesel-hydraulics at minimal availability) was concerned. Cashmore's Great Bridge cutters played havoc with the 7 Manors ex-store from Tyseley and Oxford while a further trio went to their Newport yard. Bird's had the rest: 4 at Morriston, 2 each at Risca and Bridgend and 1 apiece at Long Marston and Bynea.

In even worse state is the pioneer Manor, No.7800 *Torquay Manor,* barely recognisable as the handsome, lightweight 4-6-0 she once was, at Cashmore's, Great Bridge, in October 1964.
Photo: Cashmore's

A very 'Woodhamesque' scene, this: one almost expects to see scavenging enthusiasts, consumed with mid-1970s preservationist fervour, picking over the remains of these GWR locomotives. But this view, in fact, was taken on 4th July 1964 at the Sharpness scrapping site of Cooper's Metals and not one of these locos was saved. Foreground is Collett 0-6-0 No.2245, from Gloucester Horton Road (which some records show as being cut up the previous May), the only member of the class to be cut up here. Also from Horton Road is the unidentified Mogul while the 3 Castles are from St Philips Marsh. When Cooper's ceased operations at Sharpness numerous engines were re-sold to Cashmore's, Newport. *Photo: W. Potter*

Mogul

THIS LARGE AND USEFUL class disappeared gradually over a period of 28 years. Of the first series (43XX built 1911-16) withdrawals commenced in February 1936 with No.4305 and no fewer than 88 engines had been disposed of by the outbreak of World War 2, at which point scrappings abruptly ceased. 11 survivors of the series were at work in 1945 and the last to go was No.4358 in August 1959. Interestingly, this was one of the earliest private scrap purchases, going to Cashmore's, Newport, some 23½ years after the first of the class had been withdrawn.

Of the 1916-20 built 53XX series, No.5342 was the first casualty in April 1937 and 11 more followed before the war. Last survivor of the series was Taunton's No.5336, in September 1964, a guest of Cohen's, Morriston.

Apart from No.6315, condemned in October 1945 after the Llangollen crash, first of the 63XX series of 1920-21 to be disposed of was No.6383 in May 1956 and the last 6 in traffic succumbed in November 1964.

The bias towards early withdrawal means that Swindon cut up the bulk of the Moguls. Of the private yards, Cashmore's, Newport, took 34 and Hayes, Bridgend, 16. Also high scoring were Bird's, Risca, with 15 and Cashmore's, Great Bridge, who managed 12. Woodham's denied preservation no fewer than 8 and small quantities went to other private yards, twos and threes in most cases. Sheffield saw 3 of the class, No.5319 at Ward's, Killamarsh, and Nos.7309, 7336 at their Broughton Lane yard. Wolverhampton Works took No.6307, Caerphilly Works No.6396.

22XX/32XX

CONDEMNATIONS WERE SPREAD OVER 6½ years, from December 1958 (No.2258) to June 1965 (Nos.2210, 2244) and were gradual and remarkably consistent. Just over a third of the 0-6-0 class was disposed of at Swindon. Cashmore's purchased 32, neatly divided between their two yards, while 14 went to Bird's at Risca and 10 to Hayes, Bridgend. King's of Norwich made BR an unrefusable offer for 6 and several other private yards sampled the class, including the Wigan yard of Central Wagon Co., who took No.3208, ex-Machynlleth. No.3202, through no fault of its own, proved too much for the cutters at Wolverhampton Works and travelled home to Swindon in several mineral wagons. C Shop finished the job.

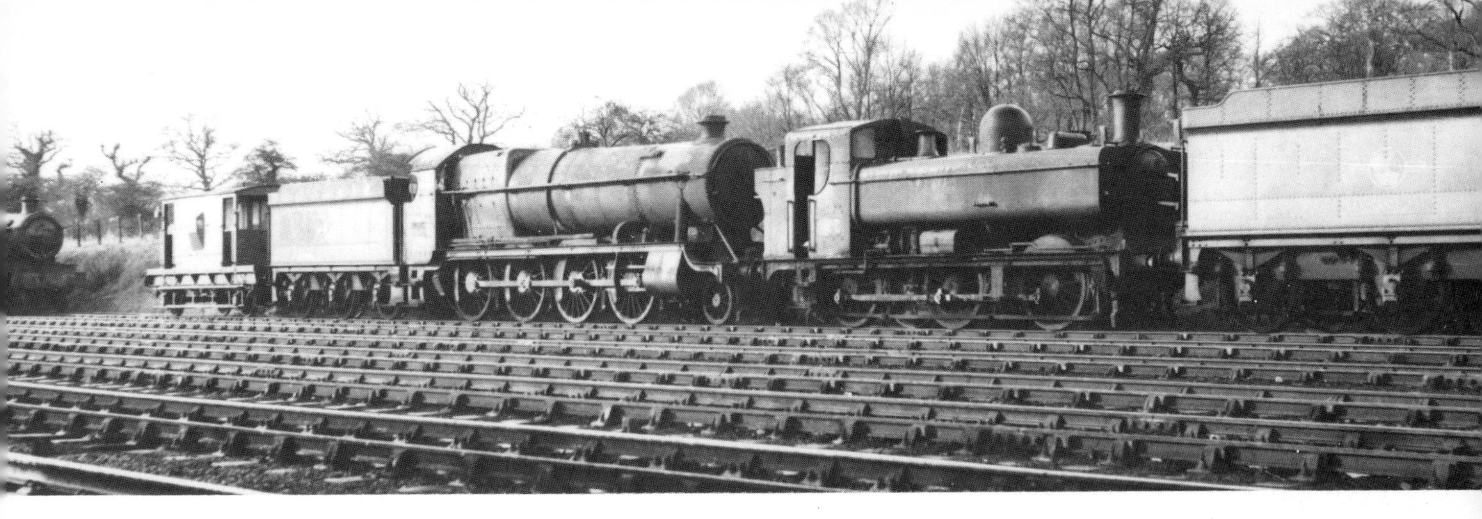

47XX

HERE IS ARGUABLY THE greatest oddity of the scrapping of the GWR classes: no fewer than 5 of these imposing 2-8-0s were cut up in Norwich by King's. Presumably, they quoted the best price for the type; undoubtedly each loco was not for the faint-hearted cutter. No.4700 from Southall was cut up in July 1964, and was joined by Old Oak's Nos.4705 (cut up April 1964) and 4703, 4704, 4707 (July 1964). No.4701 went to Cashmore's, Newport, after re-sale by Cooper's, Sharpness, and No.4708 went to Great Bridge. Nos.4702, 4706 were the Swindon disposals.

28XX/38XX

WHEN, IN 1958, THE new BR Standard 9F 2-10-0s began to appear at WR sheds they made a remarkable visual contrast with the Churchward 2-8-0s, elegant Edwardian solutions to the same design problem. They also precipitated the first withdrawals of the GWR engines, led by pioneer No.2800 in April 1958. Four more followed that year and by the end of 1960 only 118 locos were still in traffic, predominantly the later 1938-41 built series. The ranks thinned slowly however, more evidence that heavy freight was steam hauled for months or years after a district's passenger service had been monopolised by the diesels. The 35 1965 survivors were a remarkable vindication of the efficiency and robustness of the original 1903 design. Like most withdrawals in the period 1958-63, the Swindon disposals were predominantly engines passed to C Shop for scrapping after shopping had revealed defects not worth rectifying given the age of the engine and the approaching demise of steam. 39 of this class were cut up at Swindon and 2 more at Wolverhampton Works, less than a quarter of the class.

ABOVE: Pioneer 47XX 2-8-0 No.4700, in company with 57XX 0-6-0PT No.8752, has just arrived from Southall shed at the reception sidings for King's scrapyard, Norwich, in February 1964. Both engines will be cut up the following month. *Photo: Dr I. C. Allen*

BELOW: The very last GWR 2-8-0 to be scrapped was No.3817, seen here in March 1973, while being despatched by Woodham's, Barry. This contractor cut up only 2 steam locomotives in the 1970s (the great era of preservation purchases); the other was Standard Mogul No.76080, c.April 1972. *Photo: L. C. Jacks collection*

12 went to Bird's, Risca, 11 to Hayes, Bridgend, 8 to Cashmore's, Newport (the latter a surprisingly low figure) and numerous other yards lent a hand. Interesting early purchases in the first half of 1960 were Nos.2840, 2878, 2880 to Ward's, Killamarsh, Sheffield; No.2811 to Round Oak Steelworks, Brierley Hill; Nos.2843, 2848 at Hayes, Gloucester and Nos.2863, 2864, 2870 to Mahoney's at Newport. Oddest of all was No.2869, cut up by (of all people) the North Wales Wagon Company in June 1960.

Swindon dump on 28th June 1959. Class 28XX 2-8-0 No.2833 has come to the end of the line, after a working life of almost half a century had ended that March when she left Aberdare shed for the last time. Condemnation at Swindon followed.

Note that the cab fittings are still intact, complete even to the strip of white paper inserted behind the lubricator glasses to facilitate checking the oil flow.

The engine was outshopped at Swindon, (just a few hundred yards from where this, her last portrait, was taken) in 1911, when Britain still basked in the endless summer of Edwardian tranquillity.

This is a particularly interesting view as No.2833 was one of a batch of 7 28XXs to be sold to R. S. Hayes at Bridgend which left Swindon the following month. Photographs of engines involved in these early sales are scarce. The other 2-8-0s to go to Hayes at that date were Nos.2812, 2817, 2823, 2825, 2828, 2830. *Photo: T. W. Nicholls*

42XX/52XX

APART FROM THE 14 ENGINES rebuilt 1937-39 as Class 72XX 2-8-2T, withdrawals of these powerful 2-8-0Ts began with No.4224 in February 1959, a year which saw the end for 15 of the class. In the period 1960-62 there was a comparative lull but the torches flared in earnest 1963-64 and reduced the class to 18 engines. Predominantly South Wales locos all their lives, they died there when No.5235, the last in traffic, succumbed at Ebbw Junction in September 1965. The local yards gobbled up most of the dead engines — only 29 went to Swindon — Hayes taking no fewer than 34 and Cashmore's 21 at Newport. No.5205 went to King's at Norwich while No.4266 was disposed of in Caerphilly Works in February 1963.

Languishing in the sun at Hayes' yard, Bridgend, on 4th June 1965, is 52XX 2-8-0T No.5200, an Ebbw Junction stalwart withdrawn from that shed the previous April. *Photo: Michael Hale*

72XX

NOS.7224, 7241 FELL FIRST, in December 1962, and 13 sisters in 1963. 1964 saw the demise of 29 more and 10 South Wales survivors soldiered on, a final trio Nos.7205, 7248, 7252 lasting until June 1965. Messrs Hayes appear to have acquired a taste for these massive machines and indulged in 16, more than three times as many as their three nearest competitors put together: Bird's at Risca and Morriston and Cashmore's at Newport, who took 5 each. Only 6 of the class escaped from South Wales, Nos.7203, 7236 rumbled disconsolately all the way to King's at Norwich and just 4 achieving decent burial at Swindon.

Another of the surprisingly large number of GWR engines to be cut up in the wilds of Northants, courtesy of Cohen's at Kettering, and an interesting view of the internal configuration of the side tank of one of the massive 72XX 2-8-2 tanks, No.7218. Four of this class ended their days at Banbury shed; of the others Nos.7207 and 7221 were cut up on shed by Friswell's, while No.7236 was another purchase by King's at Norwich. This view, 31st January 1965. *Photo: E. H. Sawford*

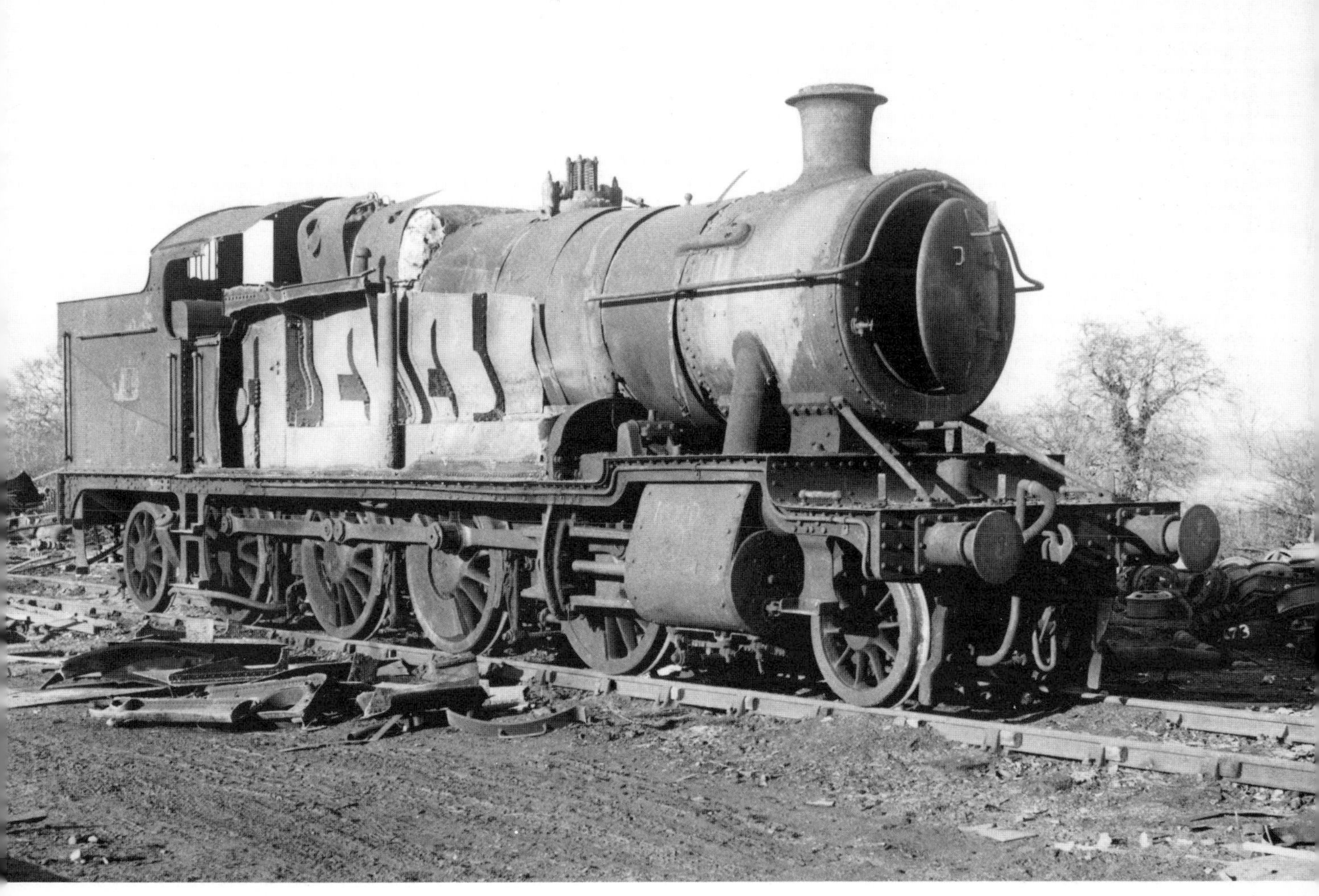

51XX/61XX

THE LARGE PRAIRIES WERE widely allocated, a fact reflected in their disposal patterns. A high proportion of the class disappeared into C Shop at Swindon in the period 1958-62, displaced by DMUs on the suburban services, but conversely some of the younger 61XX series survived into the last weeks of WR steam, shedded at Bristol Barrow Road, Gloucester (Horton Road), Oxford and Worcester. Cashmore's purchased 54 of the class (31 Newport, 23 Great Bridge), well ahead of the other contractors such as Bird's (14 to Risca, 11 to Bridgend). No fewer than 16 other yards took the class, including Ward's of Sheffield, who bought No.5170 on one of its spending sprees to Banbury shed, and No.5152 from Worcester. Three interesting minor yards who nibbled at a Large Prairie were L. C. Hughes of Bicester who purchased No.4105 after accident damage, Buttigieg's fledgling yard at Pontnewydd who took Nos.4130 and 6114, and Woodfields at Cadoxton, Barry, purchasers of No.6131. Also at Barry, and to the chagrin of the later preservationists, Woodham's demolished five of the class, including No.4156 as late as July 1980 during a lull in their wagon breaking contract with BR.

Sparks fly at the Long Marston, Warwicks, yard of Messrs Bird on 6th February 1966. One of Tyseley's large Prairies, No.4111, once a regular out of Snow Hill to Wolverhampton, Stourbridge, Stratford and Leamington Spa, was withdrawn the previous September, one of the last three engines of the class to go.
Photo: N. E. Preedy

45XX

THE EARLIEST MEMBERS OF this classic tank engine design, the 4500-54 series, were decimated in the early 1950s. No.4531 was the first casualty, in February 1950, and as the DMU replaced steam push-pull working in the Cardiff valleys from 1958, the auto-fitted engines fell in large numbers. Last survivor of the first series was No.4507, withdrawn October 1963. The later engines of the 4555-5574 series lasted an average of five years longer but condemnations were heavy 1958-60 as dieselisation took a hold. The demise of the class in the West Country, and elsewhere, was hastened by branch line closures and there were just 22 45XXs in stock at the end of 1962. The last quartet, Nos.5508, 5531, 5564, 5569, were condemned in December 1964, purchased from Southall shed in March 1965 by Cox & Danks and cut up the following month. 99 of the class went to Swindon, 2 to Wolverhampton Works and the rest to various private yards. Woodham's cut up 9.

Early days at Woodham's. August 1965 and 45XX No.5557 is disposed of at the firm's first cutting up area within the grounds of Barry Works at the back of the former carriage shops. This engine was purchased in January 1961 and her last shed was St Blazey. *Photo: P. Kearon*

56XX/66XX

IN COMPLETE CONTRAST TO the 45XXs, these 0-6-2Ts lasted well. Indeed, the 200-strong class was intact at December 1961, due almost entirely to their widespread use on coal traffic. During the period 1962-65, however, their numbers were roughly halved each year and Nos.5605, 6697 were the sole 1966 survivors, both withdrawn from Croes Newydd shed that May, No.6697 for preservation. Cashmore's, Newport, took a steady flow of these engines, assisted by Hayes at Bridgend, from store at Llanelly, Treherbert, Merthyr, Abercynon, Swansea and Cardiff (Radyr and East Dock) sheds, eventually totalling 34 and 33 engines respectively. Swindon took 29 and Cashmore's, Great Bridge, 20. With the exceptions of 4 cut up at Caerphilly Works, and 3 more sold to Cohen's, Kettering, the private South Wales yards, unsurprisingly, mopped up the rest. Woodham's cut up 4 of its 13 purchases.

Hayes, Bridgend, again: 56XX No.5693 is ex-Treherbert withdrawn January 1963; sister engine No.6670 is from store at Barry; 0-6-0PT No.9665, a Hereford regular; and No.7016 *Chester Castle,* for all her latter years a South Wales engine, and only 14 when she died. *Photo: Michael Hale*

The end of an era. The railmotor concept was introduced on the Stroud Valley line between Chalford and Stonehouse on 12th October 1903. How fitting, then, that the Chalford service was amongst the very last autotrain workings to survive the onset of the DMU. In November 1964, steam locos rendered redundant by the 31st October withdrawal of passenger services on the Hereford line, from Berkeley Road to Sharpness, and the Chalford shuttle, began to gather at Gloucester Barnwood shed. Photographed there on 15th November are 0-4-2Ts Nos.1453, 1458, 1472, 1420, the last of the class in service. Cashmore's introduced No.1453 to the cutters at Great Bridge, while Nos.1458, 1472 went to their yard at Newport. No.1420 was the one that got away; in January she made the long journey to safety on the Dart Valley Railway. *Photo: W. Potter*

14XX

THREE OF THESE PRETTY 0-4-2Ts, Nos.1404, 1425, 1460, were condemned as early as February 1956 and numbers fell steadily until the end of 1963 when a dozen survivors were at work. Last in traffic were Nos.1442, 1450, based at Exmouth Junction until May 1965. Swindon took most of the early withdrawals, but Nos.1404, disposed of at Caerphilly Works, and 1410, at Wolverhampton, were exceptions. A trio of engines were cut up within yards of each other at Barry, but oddly by different concerns — Nos.1461 (Barry Works July 1958); 1428 (Woodham's) and 1457 (J. O. Williams), both in November 1960. Another interesting early sale was No.1401, the 'Titfield Thunderbolt' star, which, having survived the memorable duel with Sid James' steam roller, succumbed to the cutters at Ward's, Briton Ferry, in November 1959.

Undoubtedly, however, the most significant casualty of the class was No.1469, whose place in the history of British steam is assured. This engine's humble and anonymous life, latterly in the bucolic idyll of the Exe Valley, was brought to its close in a corrugated iron shack at Caerphilly in April 1959, courtesy of scrap merchants I. & R. Morkot, who had purchased 7 0-4-2Ts. A photograph of the scrapping of No.1469 appeared in Vol.1 of this series and the photographer, Eric Mountford, subsequently wrote to me as follows: "Without doubt, No.1469 was the very first of the thousands of BR locos cut up by private contract under the new BR policy. Although five engines had been sold to Woodham Bros a few days earlier, they were all still intact at Barry Dock on 7th April 1959, the day that cutting up of No.1469 was completed at Caerphilly."

57XX

DETAILED ACCOUNTS OF THE disposal of large classes of humble tank engines are likely to make tedious reading for most enthusiasts, but the 57XX panniers have been included here as such large numbers give scope to examine the activities of the very small private scrapyards whose capabilities did not extend beyond a small, lightweight and simple locomotive. Here, then, we find such shadowy little outfits as J. O. Williams of Barry (6 engines), T. H. Jones of Newport (1), T. Jenkins of Port Talbot and Mumford's of Plaistow (6 each). Some pannier tanks travelled far and wide to meet their breakers, their last journey one of their longest, and doubtless they arrived wracked with hot boxes and thankful for the torch. Garnham, Harris & Elton took 3 in Chesterfield, Arnott Young at Bilston 2, Central Wagon, Wigan, no fewer than 16, King's of Norwich 8 and Ward's 2 at Killamarsh. No.3648, too far gone to travel another inch, was put out of her misery at Tondu shed.

At the other end of the scale the big boys hacked the little panniers to bits with contemptuous ease. No fewer than 165 of the 57XX class alone were swallowed by the gaping maw of Cashmore's Newport yard. Ward's took 76 at Briton Ferry, Hayes of Bridgend 48 and Cashmore's, Great Bridge, 40. A number of engines transferred to the SR were cut up at Eastleigh (4) and at Ashford (2), while those transferred to London Transport suffered curious fates: Nos.7741 and 7779 met their end at the LT depot, Neasden, in September 1967 and 1968 respectively. The last three LT 57XXs to be scrapped, Nos.5757, 7739, 7749, were cut up by Steelbreaking & Dismantling Co. of Chesterfield in January 1970, but they were not the last of the class to be scrapped. This honour goes to No.3663, sold to the NCB in January 1963, which was dismantled at NCB Bargoed Colliery later in 1970.

In all, the 860 57XX pannier tanks were disposed of in no fewer than 40 different locations, a statistic starkly revealing just how widespread locomotive scrapping once was.

ABOVE: An exceptionally interesting view of Swindon dump, taken on 1st March 1959. Just three weeks later BR Swindon despatched its first ever batch of engines to a private scrapyard.

From left to right: 57XX No.5777 (cut up at Cohen's, Morriston, in April 1959); Mogul No.5390 (Hayes, Bridgend, September 1959); Mogul No.5397 (Woodham's, December 1959); 57XX No.5733 (Swindon C Shop, March 1960); 55XX No.5502 (Cashmore's, Newport, April 1959); Mogul No.5392 (Woodham's, December 1959); 0-4-2T No.5801 (Morkot's, April 1959); 0-4-2T No.1469 (Morkot's, April 1959, and the very first BR loco to be cut up privately for scrap in the modernisation years); 0-4-2T No.1418 (Morkot's, April 1959).
Photo: W. Potter

RIGHT: Just a glimpse of the late surviving LT 57XXs, L98 (ex-7739) and L97 (ex-7749) at Steelbreaking & Dismantling Co, Chesterfield on 31st December 1970. They had arrived by road. *Photo: Peter Trushell*

Major Southern classes

OF ALL THE REGIONS, the Southern had the least dealings with the scrap metal industry. A Southern engine in a private scrapyard was a rare sight, a fact largely obscured because the SR type to suffer most in the private yards, the Bulleid Pacifics, were extensively photographed. The fate of these modern, late-surviving engines has already been recorded in detail, but the other express classes, the H15s, N15s, Nelsons and Schools, were withdrawn rather earlier and almost entirely cut up by BR. Eastleigh, with help from Ashford and to a lesser extent from Brighton, took the majority – sometimes entire classes – of most other types, particularly the pre-Grouping machines. Disposals on the Southern were, in fact, much more ordered, prompt and self-contained than on the other regions.

Apart from the pacifics, the only Southern types to suffer major sales to private yards were: S15 (40% sold), U (50%), Q1 (55%), N (56%) and Q (85%). Fewer than 20 purchasers were involved, the great majority in South Wales buying engines from store principally at Salisbury, Weymouth, Eastleigh, Nine Elms and Redhill. The leading yards were Cashmore's at Newport, whose most important purchases (apart from the Pacifics) were 15 Ns, 13 Us, 5 S15s and 5 Q1s, and Bird's at Morriston, Swansea, who took 18 Ns and 9 Q1s. Bird's other yards at Risca, Bynea and Bridgend lent a hand but the quantities were negligible, particularly compared withe the steady flow of GWR engines. Ward's, Briton Ferry, purchase of a full dozen M7 tanks is an important and very odd statistic.

Apart from the South Wales yards, notable SR sales were to Cohen's, Kettering (4 S15s, 3 Schools, 1 Q and 3 Q1s) and to King's of Norwich (4 Ns, 1 N1, 3 U1s, 3 Ks, 1 Q, 2 Q1s and even a Class H tank). The three private scrapyards in the southeast to purchase BR steam all took SR engines: the most notable sales to Wood's at Queensborough were 2 S15s, 4 Qs and 4 M7s while Ward's at Grays took 3 Us and 2 Qs and Cox & Danks cut up a single Q at Park Royal. One U went all the way to Slag Reduction at Rotherham, Yorkshire, and a quintet of disorientated Qs ended up at Ward's, Killamarsh, Sheffield.

King Arthur 4-6-0 Nos.30779 *Sir Colgrevance* (ex-Nine Elms) and 30780 *Sir Persant* on the scrap line at Eastleigh Works on 17th September 1959. At that time a number of N15 boilers were being recovered and this seems to be the case with No.30779: the cab and front frames together with smokebox have been cut away before the boiler is lifted by the rail mounted crane in the background. *Photo: M. K. Lewis*

N15

THE FIRST ENGINE FROM the earliest batch of LSWR N15s, Urie-designed Nos.30736-55, was condemned as early as 1953 and the series became extinct in March 1958 with the withdrawal of No.30738. The first SR King Arthurs, Nos.30448-57 and 30763-30792 of 1925, succumbed in the period October 1958 (30454) and November 1962 (30770). The 1926 series, Nos.30793-30806, was disposed of between April 1959 (30801) and August 1962 (30793). With the exception of Nos.30788 and 30804, cut up at Ashford, all the engines went home to Eastleigh.

H15

URIE'S FIRST 4-6-0s, THE 30482-91 series, were withdrawn between 1955 and 1959. With the exception of No.30331 (condemned March 1961) the first Drummond engines, later rebuilds, disappeared 1956-58 and the Maunsell designed machines Nos.30473-78, 30521-24 in 1959-61. At this comparatively early stage of disposals, Southern types were cut up promptly after withdrawal, long periods in store being unusual, and most of the H15s disappeared without trace within a month or so of their fires dying, all at Eastleigh Works.

Lord Nelson

HARD AT WORK RIGHT till the end of 1960, the Nelsons were withdrawn in 1961 and 1962, six and ten engines respectively. Eastleigh took 13, Ashford two (Nos.30852, 30863) and No.30850 was preserved after lengthy store in locations as diverse as Fratton and Carnforth.

One of Feltham's S15s, No.30507, has Schools No.30935 *Sevenoaks* for company at Cohen's Kettering yard in May 1964. This contractor purchased 4 S15s and 3 Schools and all 7 engines arrived at the site in March 1964. In the foreground is the cutting up road, littered with fascinating fragments including the unmistakable wheel from a Bulleid Q1 (probably No.33016), one of a quartet of the small Bulleids cut up here. The LT underground stock provides contrast and what appears to be the *engine* scrap tonnage has been painted, oddly, on the *tender* of the steam locomotives. *Photo: G. D. King*

S15

THESE EFFICIENT 4-6-0s WERE late survivors; at December 1963 only four engines from the 45-strong class had been condemned and since by that date the BR works were reducing their intake of redundant locos many of the S15s were sold to the private scrapyards. Cashmore's, Newport, took 5; Cohen's, Kettering 4, while 2 apiece went to Bird's, Morriston; Bird's, Risca and Wood's, Queenborough. Woodham's cut up Nos.30512 and 30844 (their other five purchases surviving). Buttigieg's took No.30833. Last year for the S15s was 1965 with only six engines at work, although No.30837 worked two specials in January 1966 prior to sale to Cashmore's. Many members of the class spent several months stored dead at Feltham shed.

Schools

DISPLACED BY THE 1960 electrification of the Kent coast line, the Schools, capable and well liked but not the easiest engines for which to find work, never found a new role and met an early demise, withdrawals commencing in February 1961. By December 1962 it was all over for the powerful 4-4-0s. The last batch to go were a trio of Nine Elms engines Nos. 30902/21/35 in December 1962. They were not disposed of at once, and after a period in store they went to Cohen's Yard at Kettering in the spring of 1964. This late disposal date ensured that they would not go to a BR works for cutting and were the only ones which didn't.

T9

35 OF THE ELEGANT 'GREYHOUNDS' remained in service at January 1957 but by the end of 1959 the total had fallen to 14. Twelve months later only one more engine had been withdrawn but 1961 saw the virtual extinction of the class, only the nationally preserved engine, No.30120, remaining nominally on booked stock. Throughout 1962 and up to July 1963 she was the solitary surviving working British 4-4-0; only three years previously there had been 315 engines of that once common wheel arrangement in service.

Most members of the Southern classes described above met their fate in BR works. When, however, we examine the younger, smaller mixed traffic SR engines we find greatly increased involvement by the private scrapyards, for despite increasing SR electrification there was still plenty of work for the more humble and economic steam classes and the various classes of Moguls, particularly, stayed in traffic well into the 1960s and many outlasted the cessation of scrappings at Eastleigh and Ashford.

N

BIRD'S, MORRISTON, TOOK 18 engines and Cashmore's, Newport, 15 while six other private yards made purchases, including King's of Norwich (4 engines). Nos.31850 and 31866 were demolished on shed by cutters from Cohen's, at Redhill and Eastleigh respectively. Electrification displaced the Kent engines by January 1962 and the Ns useful and prolonged work on the 'Withered Arm' west of Exeter ended in September 1964 with the mass condemnation of the Exmouth Junction stud. At January 1965 only a dozen Ns remained in stock, all Guildford engines working the Reading-Redhill services.

N1

THIS CLASS WAS RENDERED extinct in two batches of three in October and November 1962 and all the locos were stored — five at Stewarts Lane, the class's last shed — for lengthy periods, over a year in most cases. Five of the six engines went to Eastleigh but No.31822 travelled all the way to King's, Norwich, as late as April 1964.

U

THE PICTURE HERE IS similar to the Ns: Cashmore's, Newport, taking the private yard record with 13 engines. Interesting sales were No.31793 to Slag Reduction, Rotherham, and in Grays, Essex, Ward's turned the torches on three Us, rare purchases for this yard.

TOP: Eastleigh's cutters descend on newly arrived T9 4-4-0 No.30718, one of a trio of the class withdrawn from Exmouth Junction shed in March 1961. This view was taken on 12th April 1961. *Photo: Christopher Fifield*

BOTTOM: Numerous Southern Moguls, Ns and U1s, ended their days in store at Redhill shed. Several were sold to King's at Norwich, others went to Eastleigh and Cashmore's, Newport, took 1. Class N No.31850 was deemed unfit to travel and after three months rusting in the sun was cut up on the shed by cutters from Cohen's. She is seen here on 5th April 1964. *Photo: H. N. James*

U1

AGAIN, EASTLEIGH AND KING'S, Norwich, were involved, the latter yard taking Nos.31893, 31894, 31996 from Stewarts Lane. The last surviving U1s were Brighton based.

K

LIKE THE N1s AND U1s, the Ks were decimated at the end of 1962. The first 8 members of the class were withdrawn that November and the following month, at a stroke, the K was rendered extinct with a mass condemnation of 9 engines. The whole class was latterly based on two sheds, Brighton and Three Bridges, and following store for anything from one to sixteen months the Ks ended their days at Eastleigh or King's, the latter yard taking 3. No.32347 was cut up at Stewarts Lane shed.

Q

UNLIKE THE OLDER SOUTHERN 0-6-0s such as the 700 Class and the C Class (all cut up by BR at Eastleigh and Ashford) the comparatively modern 1938-built Qs were denied a BR burial. Eastleigh only took 2 and, interestingly, it required nine private yards to dispose of the other 17 engines (No.30541, a Woodham's purchase, is preserved). Oddly, 5 Qs went all the way to Sheffield for breaking, at Ward's of Killamarsh in the second half of 1964.

ABOVE: Class K Mogul No.32337 in King's yard, Norwich, in late April 1964, recently arrived in a train comprising a GWR 2-8-0T, GWR 0-6-0 and three SR Moguls. The coach frames in the foreground for cutting up are from Wymondham on the disused branch to Forncett where it was King's practice to burn off redundant stock's coachwork, horrifying enthusiasts and irritating local residents. *Photo: Dr I. C. Allen*

LEFT: Tucked away beside the River Swale near Queenborough in Kent, Messrs Wood cut up a small but interesting selection of SR engines in bleak and scruffy sidings owned by Settle, Speakman & Co Ltd. This rare view of the site shows Class Q 0-6-0s Nos.30534, 30540, 30537. No.30531 was also a Wood purchase. *Photo: C. G. Deario*

Q1

MUCH THE SAME THING happened to the Bulleid Q1s: Bird's, Morriston, took no fewer than 9; King's, Norwich, 7 and four other private yards purchased these ugly but characterful 0-6-0s. Cohen's flying cutters descended on Eastleigh shed and reduced No.33015, too sick to travel, to its component parts.

700

Withdrawals of these Drummond 0-6-0s were spread from September 1957 (No.30688) to December 1962 when seven survivors were condemned en masse. No.30368 was partially dismantled at Eastleigh in 1960 but subsequently fitted with parts from No.30687 to enable it to work on to become one of the last batch in traffic.

TOP: More scrap for King's: 3 of the 7 Q1s for this contractor in the reception sidings at Norwich in October 1964. The engines are Nos.33003, 33030, 33040, from store at Nine Elms. *Photo: Dr I. C. Allen*

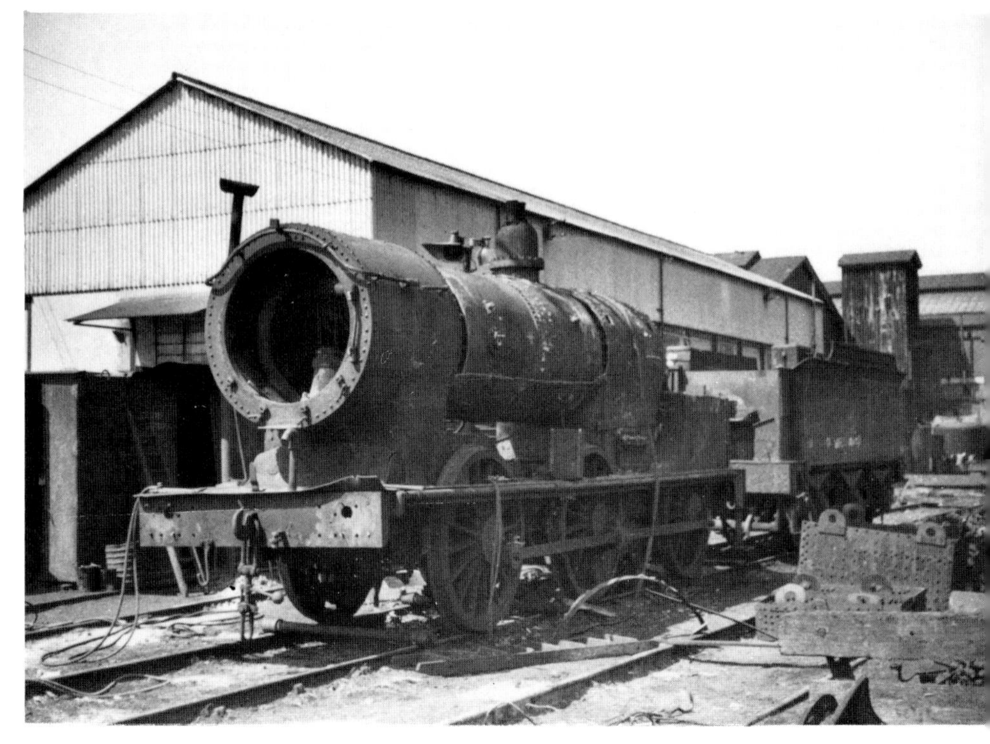

RIGHT: The last Class 700 0-6-0 in existence, No.30700, is scrapped at Eastleigh Works in April 1964. With the exception of a trio of engines cut up at Ashford Works, Eastleigh took this whole class of 30. *Photo: R. E. Rosendale*

M7

UBIQUITOUS ON THE WESTERN Division of the SR, the ancient M7s lasted fairly well but the dreaded DMU was not to be denied and by the end of 1962 only 35 members of the class of 103 were still in stock. 14 survivors worked in the class's last year, 1964, before extinction that May with the condemnation of 9 locos at Bournemouth and Salisbury. Unsurprisingly, Eastleigh took the lion's share of these LSWR tanks but Ward's of Briton Ferry, very oddly took a full dozen. Wood's of Queenborough purchased 4 and one engine apiece died at Cashmore's, Newport, and Brighton Works.

Another view of Wood's at Queenborough, with a trio of headless M7s, Nos.30249, 30035, 30320, taken on 11th July 1964. This yard also despatched No.30032 of the class. *Photo: Arthur G. Wells*

H

THESE HANDSOME SECR ENGINES were largely replaced by the EMUs on the Central and Eastern Divisions and the numbers dwindled gratifyingly slowly; three (Nos.31263, 31518, 31551) lasted into January 1964. Ashford took most of the class with Eastleigh 8; Ward's, Briton Ferry 3 and Wood's, Queenborough and King's, Norwich, one each.

E4/E4X

AN EXCLUSIVE BR DISPOSAL job was performed on these LBSCR 0-6-2 tanks. Of the 58 engines in stock at January 1957, Ashford took 40, Eastleigh 13 and Brighton 4. A very similar picture applied to the other classes of pre-Grouping tanks and small tender engines, the comparatively early withdrawals precluding the private scrapyard's involvement.

Two representatives of the scores of SR locos cut up at Ashford Works. Photographed on the scrapline, 30th August 1955, are Class E4 0-6-2T No.32501 and one of the quartet of rebuilds from Class E5, reclassified E5X, 0-6-2T No.32576. *Photo: Tony Copas*

Major LMS classes

THE REPRESENTATIVE LMS classes which follow were disposed of at no fewer than 75 different private scrapyards, or around four times as many as purchased SR engines. Clearly, there were many more steam locos on the LMR to dispose of, but the most important factor to note here is the very high percentage of small yards: around 57 of the total took fewer than 20 engines and the overall picture is notably less organised than on any other region. However, the larger, more efficient yards redressed the balance somewhat and here we find some of the most prolific purchasers of British steam. The top ten purchasers of the LMS classes we consider here were:

1. Cashmore's, Great Bridge	605
2. Draper's, Hull	354
3. Motherwell Machinery & Scrap	182
4. Ward's, Beighton	169
5. Ward's, Killamarsh	137
6. Cohen's, Kettering	120
7. Buttigieg's, Newport	115
8. Cashmore's, Newport	96
9. Central Wagon, Wigan	82
10. Campbell's, Airdrie	60

Buttigieg's total includes no fewer than 92 8Fs (they were the third biggest purchasers of the class) and MM&S took 101 Black Fives. Ward's two big Sheffield yards were consistent across the classes and respecters of none, and Cohen's total is almost entirely composed of Black Fives (73) and 8Fs (29). Some of the Newport disposals were LM types withdrawn from the WR and SR.

Geographically, the spread of yards was wide indeed, from the major Scottish contractors like MM&S, Campbells and McWilliams to the north-eastern purchaser Hughes Bolckow at North Blyth. In the south, Cohen's at Kettering and Bird's of Long Marston were joined by Bird's at Morriston, Risca and Bridgend and even King's of Norwich sampled a few LMS engines.

BR made inroads into the earlier withdrawals, LMS engines being cut up at Crewe, Derby, Horwich, Inverurie, Gorton, Darlington, Cowlairs, Swindon, Doncaster and Kilmarnock, plus one or two at Stratford and Eastleigh. Major contributions were 83% of the Patriots, 60% of the Scots, most of the 4P and 2P 4-4-0s plus the bulk of the Pacifics, as recorded in Vol.2. Later surviving engines fared very differently and BR despatched only 33% of the Horwich Crabs, 15% of the Ivatt Moguls, 4% of the Black Fives and just 2% of the 8Fs.

ABOVE: Because of its location and the hazardous operations which went on within, the interior of Crewe Works Scrap Shop are understandably sparse. On 11th August 1964, the scene inside is captured, but the only identifiable object is the bunker of Stannier 2-6-2T No. 40135, with at least 8 boilers lined up behind it. Taken in the poor lighting conditions that make such views rare, this gives a good impression of the size of the shop, far larger than C Shop which performed the same function at Swindon Works. *Photo: Keith Till*

RIGHT: Once a locomotive was sold, its purchaser and destination were normally indicated on a tag attached to her handrail. Occasionally, more immediately legible means were used, as seen here on LMS 'Jinty' 0-6-0T No. 47549 at Central Wagon's Wigan yard on 14th February 1965. *Photo: A. D. Nugent.*

Patriot

NOT ONE OF THE unrebuilt Patriots was sold by BR but 9 of the Ivatt rebuilds, withdrawn on average 2-3 years later, came well into the era of the private scrapyards, seven contractors — predominantly Scottish — being involved, buying one or two engines each. The last trio of survivors, Nos.45512, 45530, 45531 were all Kingmoor engines: the first two went to Motherwell Machinery & Scrap and No.45531 to Campbell's at Airdrie. No.45530 was the last of this greatly mourned class to cling to its existence, finally succumbing in July 1966.

Royal Scot

THIRTY SCOTS FELL IN the first casualty year, 1962, 15 more in 1963, 21 in 1964 and only five lasted into 1965. Like their near sisters, the Patriots, the survivors were shedded at Kingmoor, last shed for so many fine engines. The pattern of disposal for the Scots is similar to the Patriots; ones and twos to ten different yards, plus 7 locos to McWilliams, Shettleston. Two went all the way to South Wales: No.46148 to Bird's, Morriston, and No.46163 to Bird's, Risca, fascinating movements both.

BELOW: Farewell to the Patriots. Stored beneath the charred roof girders of the burnt out running shed at Preston MPD, No.45543 *Home Guard* is captured on 8th June 1963 awaiting its final movement that August to Crewe Works for cutting up. *Photo: John Stretton*

ABOVE: A grim sight for admirers of the Scots: No.46112 *Sherwood Forester* is in a terrible state at Cashmore's, Great Bridge, in September 1964 following condemnation at Annesley shed that May. The front end damage was not the work of the cutters and precipitated her withdrawal. *Photo: Cashmore's*

ABOVE: Jubilee No.45598 *Basutoland* at Ward's Beighton yard on 27th March 1965, with an Ivatt Mogul and WD 2-8-0 for company. The sign, left foreground, states with fine irony 'Engines must not pass this point'. *Photo: A. D. Nugent*

Jubilee

FIRST JUBILEE TO BE withdrawn was, of course, No. 45637 wrecked in the horrific double collision at Harrow & Wealdstone on 8th October 1952. Limited scrapping commenced in September 1960, largely due to the lack of replacement boilers, but it was 1962 before the handsome and popular 4-6-0s began to lose their grip on their traditional workings, 41 engines being condemned in that year, the Eastern and Scottish regions losing their allocations entirely. By high summer 1964 the last WR Jubilees had gone and at that year's end just four dozen LMR locos soldiered on. Surprisingly, the class lasted right through 1965 and 1966 and the final rearguard action was fought by 15 engines in 1966 and 8 the following year, latterly shedded in the Leeds, Bradford and Wakefield areas. Disposal of the Jubilees makes very odd reading indeed. Apart from the dominance of Crewe Works (57 engines), it was the private yards which bore the brunt of disposal. Cashmore's with 37 took the most, but with the exception of Draper's, Hull (14) and Ward's, Beighton (11), no other yard achieved double figures with the class. Indeed, the balance of 67 engines was cut up at no fewer than 23 different sites: 20 private contractors and Cowlairs (9), Horwich (4) and Darlington (2) works.

TOP: Buffered up to the Central Wagon Co's only Pacific, No. 46243 *City of Lancaster*, on 15th March 1965 is Jubilee No. 45631 *Tanganyika*, which some observers have recorded as a Cashmore's purchase. One of 7 Jubilees to be cut up at Wigan, she was a Longsight engine for much of her life. *Photo: H. L. Holland*

BOTTOM: Though Draper's yard at Hull took 14 Jubilees, views of the class at this location are rather rare: This view shows one of the last 8 Jubilees to last into 1967, Low Moor's No. 45565 *Victoria*, waiting her fate on 18 June 1967. *Photo: N. B. Collin*

4P Compound

SCRAPPING OF MIDLAND ENGINES was particularly heavy in the period 1955-59 and the graceful and interesting Compounds had been decimated from 153 engines at the end of 1954 to just 19 only four years later. The great majority of these went home to Derby for disposal with a handful each to Crewe, Doncaster, Kilmarnock and Gorton, but it is fascinating to note that all the 4P Compounds in stock at the end of 1958 were sold to the private yards, significant purchases at that early stage of sales for scrap. Most notable are the 6 locos bought by Ward's, Killamarsh. Two engines, Nos.40936, 41168, lasted in stock but out of use at Monument Lane into 1961. They went eventually to Cashmore's, Great Bridge, and Derby Works respectively.

A last look at Class 4P No.41106 waiting in the reception siding at McLellan's, Langloan, scrapyard on 18th June 1959 after arrival from Crewe where she had been in store for nearly a year. This was one of the very first 4Ps to be sold for scrap, other sad pioneers in 1959 being Nos.40931, 41068, 41078, 41119, 41156, 41163/4/7 and 41193. Also seen here is Johnson 0-6-0 No.43742. *Photo: J. L. Stevenson*

2P

BY CONTRAST, THE 2Ps survived through the 1950s and serious inroads into their ranks were not made until 1959 during which year 42 fell. A slight lull in 1960 saw further slaughter in 1961 reducing the class to 15 members, including 6 much-recorded engines still working the S&D line. Derby took most, with Inverurie, Crewe, Gorton, Doncaster, Horwich and Cowlairs all lending a hand. 74 2Ps were sold to private contractors, including 18 to Loom's at Spondon, regular purchasers of Derby's overspill. 17 also went to Connell's at Calder and 15 to Cashmore's, Great Bridge. Noteworthy were No.40332 which travelled mutely all the way from Klondyke Sidings, Derby, to Hayes at Bridgend for disposal in February 1960 and No.40396, a Burton engine and rare purchase by Cohen's small yard at Kingsbury.

Standing in the pouring rain at Gorton Works on 22nd January 1961, Class 2P No.40588 provides a talking point for a party of visiting enthusiasts. 9 of this class succumbed at Gorton, this engine travelling from Bank Hill for disposal. *Photo: John Corkill*

'Black Five'

A VIOLENT COLLISION BETWEEN two freight trains at Warrington in October 1961 precipitated premature withdrawal of the two engines involved: Jubilee No.45630 and Edge Hill 'Black Five' No.45401, the latter engine taking its place in history as the first of the 842-strong class to be condemned. Throughout the first half of the 1960s, the efficient and ubiquitous 'Fives' regularly replaced older and often more powerful classes of pre-Grouping origin as withdrawals accelerated: there always seemed something for Stanier's superbly successful workhorse to do. Its numbers dwindled slowly and by the close of 1962 No.45401 had been joined in oblivion by only 21 of her sisters. 31st December 1963 saw 791 of the class still at work; the same day in 1964, 724, and as 1965 drew to a close one in five of the steam locos in service on BR was a 'Black Five', 627 engines out of 2,989 on booked stock. Surely, over thirty years after their introduction the class could have no finer testimonial? It couldn't last, of course. 171 engines fell in 1966 and a grim 305 the following year. At December 1967, 151 'Black Fives' were in stock and their percentage share of the steam fleet had leapt to an impressive (but heavily distorted) 42%. Then they were gone altogether.

ABOVE: This miserable object was once a Black Five. Motherwell Machinery & Scrap's Wishaw yard took no fewer than 101 of the class, the third highest yard total. 4th September 1967. *Photo: Keith Romig*

BELOW: A pair of Fives share a grim fate at Cohen's, Kettering. Left is No.44878, right No.45353, both July 1968 withdrawals from Lostock Hall. Note the tearful face. The date is 1st March 1969; BR had been steam-free for 7 months but some engines still clung precariously to life in a few private scrapyards. *Photo: H. L. Holland*

8F

THE DISPOSAL OF THIS class is extremely interesting. While the 842 'Black Fives' met their fate in no fewer than 38 different scrapyards, the 663 8Fs were disposed of in only 18 locations and of these, six yards cut up a single 8F apiece. The statistics here are distorted by the amazing dominance of Cashmore's yard at Great Bridge which, as already recorded in this series, hacked its way through 219 8Fs. Also hard at work were Draper's, Hull (who managed 156); Buttigieg's, Newport (92); Ward's, Beighton (59) plus 29 to Cohen's, Kettering, and 25 each to Ward's, Killamarsh, and Cashmore's, Newport. First of the class to go was No.48616, condemned w/e 22nd October 1960 after being severely damaged in a runaway accident between Turvey and Olney on 17th June that year. The class remained otherwise intact until 1963 when just two engines were condemned, Nos.48009 and 48407. Thereafter, inevitably, the death rate increased its momentum: 26 engines in 1964, 95 in 1965, 162 in 1966, 231 in 1967. By the end of that year, the 8F, now purely an LMR engine, became the unsung hero of steam's last months and the 150 survivors became stars of an obsessive photographic binge by dozens of camera-toting Colin Gifford disciples to whom an 8F in silhouette, (preferably trailing a mile-high specially arranged exhaust) became symbolic of steam's twilight days. Twenty 8Fs were still active and (thanks to roving bands of voluntary polishers) often cleaner than they had been for years in the last week of all, shedded at Lostock Hall and Rose Grove.

ABOVE: 8F No.48375 at Rose Grove MPD on 7th March 1968. Severely damaged in a collision and derailment at Copy Pit in October 1967, she languished at Rose Grove, minus rods and pony truck, until April 1968 when Maudland Metals cut her up on the spot. *Photo: John Corkill*

BELOW: Apparently complete in every respect, including the tablet catcher for working the single line northern extension of the S&D line, S&D 7F 2-8-0 No.53807 waits for the torch at Cashmore's Newport yard on 16th April 1965, the last of the class to be withdrawn and the last to be scrapped. *Photo: Michael Hale*

S&D 7F

FIRST OF THE ELEVEN Bath-shedded S&D 7Fs to be condemned was the pioneer engine, No.53800, in July 1959, which became the only engine of the class to be cut up at its birthplace, Derby Works. Subsequent withdrawals were as follows: Nos.53802 (withdrawn March 1960, cut up at Doncaster Works); followed by four locos disposed of at Crewe Works: Nos.53805 (March 1961), 53801 (July 1961) and 53803, 53804 (February 1962). No.53810, condemned in December 1963, was the first 7F sale to Cashmore's and was followed to Newport by No.53806 (withdrawn January 1964) and No.53807 (October 1964). The pair of Woodham's purchases Nos.53808, 53809, were withdrawn in March 1964 and June 1964 and purchased for preservation in October 1970 and December 1975 respectively.

'Horwich Crab'

AN AMAZING (AND SOMEWHAT puzzling) total of 37 scrapyards cut up the 245 'Crabs': Horwich (53) naturally taking most, Crewe (17); Cowlairs (4); Darlington and Derby (3 each); Gorton and Swindon (1 apiece), plus thirty private contractors, of which a full dozen managed only a single example. Apart from seven engines which reached South Wales, disposals were concentrated on northern English yards, notably Central Wagon at Ince, Wigan, which took 29, and in Scotland where McWilliams', Shettleston, held the private yard record with 30. Scrappings spanned the years 1961 (3 only) to January 1967 when Nos.42727, 42942 were withdrawn.

Cowlairs Works: cutters are hard at work on Crab No.42830, 27th March 1964. Amazingly, this engine had been withdrawn as long ago as November 1962 from Carlisle Kingmoor where she had languished in store until removal to Cowlairs in April 1963. *Photo: A. D. Nugent*

Ivatt Mogul

THESE MODERN AND EFFICIENT machines lasted well. Over 100 of the 128 engines were still at work at the start of 1965 and in their last year of service, 1967, the 42 survivors were all LMR engines. Swindon, Doncaster, Darlington and Crewe all helped dispose of the class and of the private yards the chief culprits were Cashmore's, Great Bridge (40); Ward's, Killamarsh (30); Motherwell Machinery & Scrap (29); and Draper's, Hull (27). 6 went to King's at Norwich but the only South Wales yards involved were Cashmore's, Newport (14) and Buttigieg's, Newport (5).

Ex-store at Newton Heath, this is Ivatt Mogul No.46485 in Buttigieg's Newport yard in May 1968. This contractor purchased numerous LMR engines from the northwest in the last 12 months of steam and took a considerable time to cut them up. *Photo: D. K. Jones*

LMS 2-6-4T

ANOTHER CLASS DECIMATED BY Cashmore's at Great Bridge, where 107 of the class ended their days. Other private yards to wage war on this class of 645 included Draper's, Hull (42); Motherwell Machinery & Scrap (35); Central Wagon, Ince (32); and Ward's, Killamarsh (21). Thirty-three other yards were involved while BR participated as follows: Crewe (118); Derby (71); Doncaster (37); Horwich (27); Darlington (3); Cowlairs (2) and Stratford (1). Two oddities were No.42234 cut up at Willesden shed in November 1964 and No.42325 which slowly vanished at Scratchwood Sidings, London, at the hands of a shadowy contractor whose identity is unknown. The large class of four designs were withdrawn over eight years — an ususually long period for a comparatively modern type which reflected their widespread allocation and the differing timescale of changeover to modern traction in the regions. Peak year for withdrawals of the LM 2-6-4Ts was 1962 when 152 engines died.

A woebegone assemblage rumbles through Manchester Victoria, bound from Southport to Ward's yard at Beighton, Sheffield, on 10th June 1965. The LMS 2-6-4Ts are Nos.42551, 42662, both minus chimney and rods. The spacer wagons (which may also be condemned) are to spread the weight of the train. A WD 2-8-0 was in charge. *Photo: H. L. Holland*

Ivatt 2-6-2T

HERE IS ANOTHER INTERESTING case of a yard dominating proceedings. Cohen's of Morriston, Swansea, bought 29 of this class, including the S&D engines, and topped even Crewe's effort (22), a fact which must be explained by their sharp tender for the type. Apart from these two yards and Cashmore's, Great Bridge (12); the rest of the 130-strong class were disposed of in small handfuls by 18 other widespread yards (including Nos.41248 and 41303 by Woodham's) plus Horwich Works (5); Derby (1) and Eastleigh (7). The eight 1967 survivors were all SR engines.

One of the Southern's Ivatt 2-6-2Ts, No.41319, purchased from store as far away as Weymouth in February 1968 has arrived at its proud new owners, King's of Norwich, that March. A cutter makes preliminary investigations. *Photo: Dr I. C. Allen*

Major LNER classes

This mid-February 1963 view of Blaydon shed yard shows the lifeless forms of numerous LNER engines: on the left, J39 No.64852, V3 No.67657/67687 and J39 No.64864; in the centre is A2 Pacific No.60521 *Watling Street,* ex-Gateshead and Tweedmouth and in store at Blaydon since October 1962. The Pacific survived the savage winter of 1962-3 before going home to Doncaster where, as spring turned to summer, she ceased to exist. *Photo: John Stretton*

THE SMALLER PRE-GROUPING tank and tender engines were predominantly dealt with by BR at their works of origin, and they also took most of the earlier Pacific withdrawals. If we are to find serious inroads by the private yards in this the third busiest region for the private yards, we must look primarily to the B1s (72% sold), K1/K2/K3 (14%) and Q6 (58%), The biggest private purchaser of LNER types was Draper's of Hull who probably took more LNER engines than all other private yards put together – some 378 members of the classes which follow. A long way behind them was Hughes Bolckow's of North Blyth with some 21% of Draper's total. MM&S took several dozen, mainly Scottish based 0-6-0s, but all the other private yards involved, some 50 in number, took ones and twos, or perhaps a dozen or so, of LNER engines. Sales to South Wales were virtually unknown, the great bulk being cut up in Scotland and northern England.

Norwich, 26th October 1964. Dwarfed by the 6' 8" driving wheels of A3 No.60063 *Isinglass,* King's cutter attacks the engine's centre splasher. Everything above the running plate of this New England engine has vanished. *Photo: H. N. James*

A3 Pacific

IN DECEMBER 1959 THERE occurred an event which the RCTS described at the time as 'shattering': the withdrawal of the first of the Gresley A3s. No.60104 of Kings Cross shed was found to have a severely cracked and broken frame and while no A3s were then scheduled for withdrawal No.60104 was not judged worthy of the expense of repair. She was cut up with decent haste at Doncaster Works the following month. Happily, the following year was free of A3 condemnations but in 1961 six more were to go, in April (1 engine), September (4) and November (1). The withdrawn total doubled the following year but the rot really set in in 1963 with 33 engines withdrawn. At January 1964 the 26 remaining A3s were concentrated at St Rollox, St Margarets, Darlington, Gateshead and New England sheds, and by year's end they had virtually gone, with the exception of a lucky trio, Nos.60041, 60052, 60100. Last in traffic was No.60052 condemned in January 1966 at St Margarets. Doncaster Works, predictably, dominated scrapping of the A3s, taking 35; Darlington had 9, Inverurie 2, Cowlairs 1. First sale to a private yard took place in June 1964 when Henderson's of Airdrie purchased their only A3, No.60094 from St Rollox. In the same month, Arnott Young at Carmyle bought Nos.60037, 60057, 60087, 60099 and 60101, all from store at Bathgate shed, and No.60096 from Parkhead; they later took three more A3s. Draper's managed 8 at their Hull yard, King's of Norwich 6, Hughes Bolckow's of North Blyth 4 and Motherwell Machinery & Scrap and McLellan's, Langloan 1 apiece.

ABOVE: Inside Cowlairs Works on 4th August 1966, No. 60041 Salmon Trout, penultimate A3 in traffic, is cannabalised for spares for the preserved *Flying Scotsman.* Photo: D. N. Creasey

ABOVE: Sister A3 No.60054 *Prince of Wales* was also ex-34E and arrived at King's in September 1964, in company with *Isinglass.* In this view, again taken on 26th October 1964, with the exception of the coal shute and part of the front sheet, the Pacific's tender has been stripped to its chassis. A magnetic crane is loading bits into a rake of mineral wagons. *Photo: H. N. James*

RIGHT: A quick snapshot over the fence at the Carmyle yard of Arnott Young records A3 No.60099 *Call Boy,* just arrived from Bathgate. This firm took 6 A3s in June 1964, this view being taken on the 29th. *Photo: J. L. Stevenson*

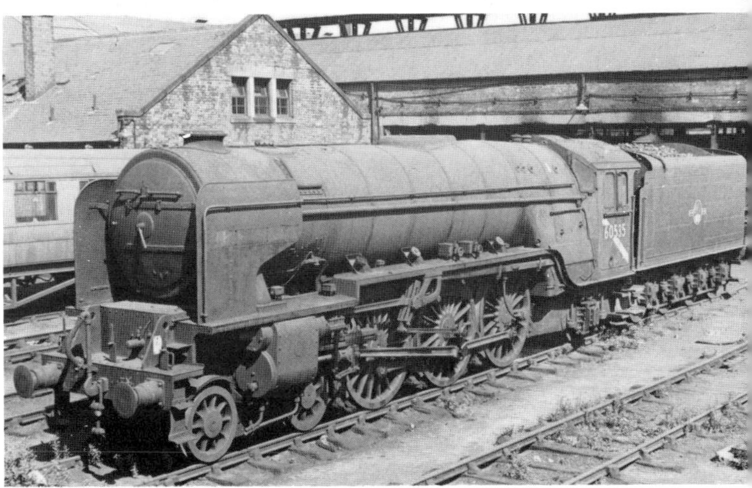

A2 Pacific

THE THOMPSON A2s DIED hard; the A2/1s between August 1960 and February 1961; the A2/2s November 1959-July 1961 and the A2/3s succumbed between November 1962 and June 1965. The Peppercorn engines fared a little better, going between November 1962 and the end of 1966. With the demise of the last New England locos in July 1963 the A2s became purely Scottish Region engines and helped eclipse the region's Coronation Pacifics. The last A2 in traffic, No.60532, was the last British LNER Pacific in service, succumbing in December 1966. 29 A2s died at Doncaster, the other 10 in private yards in Scotland: Motherwell Machinery & Scrap (6); Campbell's, Airdrie (3) and McWilliam's, Shettleston (1).

TOP LEFT: The scrap line at Doncaster Works in late 1959. Still carrying its full set of plates, Thompson A2/2 No.60503 *Lord President* stands in the rain awaiting scrapping. She was one of the first two LNER Pacifics to be condemned, the other being sister engine No.60505 *Thane of Fife.* Both were November 1959 casualties, from York and New England respectively. *Photo: Geoffrey King*

TOP RIGHT: The same location on 18th September 1960 and the fire has died for the last time in Thompson A2/1 No.60509 *Waverley,* also still wearing plates. Withdrawn, ex-Haymarket, the previous month she is less than 16 years old. *Photo: N. Joseph*

ABOVE LEFT: The remains of Thompson A2/3 No.60513 *Dante* at Doncaster Works in May 1963. *Photo: T. Middlemass*

ABOVE RIGHT: 161 tons of prime scrap metal stand ready for a purchaser on Polmadie shed in August 1965. Shortly afterwards, the buyer from Motherwell Machinery & Scrap tendered successfully for Peppercorn A2 No.60535 *Hornets Beauty* and in September she travelled dead to Wishaw for disposal. *Photo: John Corkill*

A1 Pacific

Withdrawals commenced in July 1962 with No.60153 and continued with four more that October. The end of year stock totals declined more slowly than those of the older A3s and the last survivors were Darlington's Nos.60124 and York's 60145, the latter the last English LNER Pacific. A high proportion of A1s were sold off: Draper's had 10; Ward's, Killamarsh managed 7; Hughes Bolckow's, North Blyth 6; and Ward's at Beighton took 3. Interesting sales were two to the little yard of Cox & Danks at Wadsley Bridge and No.60152, all the way from York to Cashmore's, Great Bridge. No.60129, a Heaton engine, was King's only A1 while two locos went to the obscure yard of Clayton & Davie of Dunstan-on-Tyne. W. George managed to cut up two A1s at their very cramped site adjacent to the station at Wath upon Dearne. The last A1 in existence was No.60145 cut up at Draper's, Hull, in September 1966; the preservationists were too late.

RIGHT: Ward's scrapyard at Killamarsh, Sheffield, in March 1966. Transcending the squalor of her surroundings, A1 No.60146 *Peregrine,* for so long a York engine, maintains that aura of power and dignity intrinsic to her class. *Photo: Tony Wakefield*

BELOW: One-time Heaton engine, ex-store at Tyne Dock, this is A1 No.60116 *Hal O'the Wynd* surrounded by the debris of destruction in the quayside yard of Hughes Bolckow's at North Blyth. The stately, menacing cranes were not that familiar with steam locomotives: to them even a lordly Pacific was small fry. For years, Bolckow's cut their way through Britains's naval and merchant fleets (a forlorn remnant of which is in the background) and the cranes feasted on the entrails of ocean liners, cruisers and destroyers. *Photo: R. Anderson*

B1

FORTY-TWO DIFFERENT YARDS involved here, the yard record going to Doncaster Works with 49 engines cut. Darlington was one engine behind and the remaining 310 scrapped B1s were disposed of in widely disparate locations in Scotland and England (the only member of the class to be sent to South Wales, No.61264, was a Woodham's survivor). Ten private yards took one apiece, several took 2 and many others managed only a handful. The only private yards to take more than ten B1s were Draper's, Hull (37); Hughes Bolckow's, North Blyth and Cashmore's, Great Bridge (27 each); Central Wagon at Wigan and Motherwell Machinery & Scrap (18 each); King's of Norwich and Shipbreaking Industries, Faslane, both had 16 and Garnham, Harris and Elton cut up 14 at their Chesterfield premises. The BR works at Cowlairs (15) and Inverurie (3) also lent a hand. The first B1 to be condemned was another accident casualty, No.61057, in April 1950 while the first life-expired engine was No.61085 in December 1961. From that date on the decline was dramatic. The last trio, Nos.61030, 61306, 61337 were all Low Moor engines; No.61306 was preserved.

Q6

THE CLASSIC RAVEN 0-8-0 heavy freight engines took a lot of killing off. Despite their vintage (introduced 1913) 17 of the 120 engines lasted into the last 12 months of BR steam. Consett's No.63372 was the first to go, in May 1960, followed by No.63457 in December 1961. Annual withdrawals were subsequently remarkably consistent, the pace of condemnations actually slackening in 1964 and 1965, but the class was extinct at September 1967. Most Q6s went home to Darlington (51 engines) and only Hughes Bolckow's yard at North Blyth (23) made much impression on the rest. Twelve other private yards, all unsurprisingly in the north-east of England, disposed of the balance of the class.

Q7

ALTHOUGH SLIGHTLY YOUNGER THAN the Q6s, the Q7s faded fast. Tyne Dock was the last shed for the entire class of 15 and they were condemned en masse in November/December 1962 during the NER's biggest withdrawal spree. Apart from the preserved engine, No.63460, all were cut up at Darlington Works between December 1962 and May 1963.

TOP: B1 No.61375, renumbered as departmental locomotive No.24 and used for steam heating purposes until April 1966, was photographed at Bird's yard, Long Marston, on 23rd July 1966 in company with Moguls Nos.43116 and 46496 and 'Jinty' No.47453. Judging by the brightness of the B1's leading wheels, she has just arrived. *Photo: Michael Hale*

ABOVE: More effectively than any technical description, this view in Darlington Works scrapyard conveys the massive simplicity, even crudity, of the steam locomotive. Looking back from the high-tech eighties it seems astonishing that such machines should still, in the decade man walked on the moon, play a fundamental role in Britain's transport system. Class Q6 0-8-0s No.63370 and 63345 were pictured on 25th July 1964. *Photo: A. Brown*

K1/K2/K3/K4

THE GENERAL PATTERN IN the disposal of these LNER Moguls shows the dominance of Doncaster Works: 7 K1s, the solitary K1/1, 15 K2s and no fewer than 133 K3s. The engines' Scottish tradition is reflected in scrapping figures for Cowlairs (2 K1s, 19 K2s, 26 K3s); Inverurie (3 K2s, 1 K3, 1 K4) and Kilmarnock (4 K2s), and the Scottish private yards were similarly involved. Oddities are no fewer than 9 K3s cut up at Cashmore's, Great Bridge; 2 K4s disposed of at Halbeath Wagon Works and K3 No.61864 which ended its days at King's of Norwich following store at New England shed.

Locomotives poured into Cashmore's Great Bridge yard from all points of the compass. These LNER Class K3 Moguls, photographed on 2nd March 1963, came from Colwick. Somewhat rare, this: the great bulk of the class went to Doncaster Works during 1961-3.
Photo: Michael Hale

J6/J10/J11/J19/J20/J21/ J35/J36/J37/J38/J39

THESE ANONYMOUS AND USEFUL 0-6-0s declined but slowly. Maids of all work, sturdy and economical, they were less vulnerable to the onslaught of the diesel-electrics than their bigger, more glamorous sisters. Nevetheless, the 0-6-0 on the LNER, as on the other regions, was extinct by the end of 1966. The LNER engines tended to end their days at BR works; notable disposal feats including: Inverurie (32 J35s, 33 J37s, 31 J36s, 9 J39s); Cowlairs (5 J35s, 2 J37s, 8 J36s, 48 J39s); Darlington (76 J39s, 10 J21s); Gorton (all 37 J10s) and Doncaster (102 J26s). Most notable effort in the private yards: 42 J37s cut up at Motherwell Machinery & Scrap.

Throughout their lives, the Gresley Class J38 0-6-0s were Scottish based, normally overhauled at Cowlairs, and No.65913 has returned there to be scrapped, 12th September 1964. The last surviving pair of the 35-strong class was condemned in April 1967.
Photo: J. L. Stevenson

BR Standard classes

ONLY 24 OF THE 999 BR Standards were scrapped in a BR works. They were:

Britannia	70007	Crewe
Clan	72000/1/2/3/4	Darlington
9F	92177	Crewe
Class 5	73166	Eastleigh
Class 2 Mogul	78009	Swindon
	78015	Darlington
Class 4 2-6-4T	80040/44/56/129	Crewe
	80103	Stratford
Class 3 2-6-2T	82002/8/43	Eastleigh
Class 2 2-6-2T	84012/21/22/23/24/27	Crewe

The remainder were cut up throughout the scrapyards, their last destination usually — but by no means always — within reasonable distance of their last shed. The top ten yards involved were:

1.	Cashmore's, Newport	165
2.	Motherwell Machinery & Scrap	91
3.	Campbell's, Airdrie	65
4.	Cashmore's, Great Bridge	59
5.	Ward's, Beighton	54
6.	Draper's, Hull	50
7.	Buttigieg's, Newport	45
8.	Shipbreaking Industries, Faslane	44
9.	Ward's, Killamarsh	34
10.	Bird's, Risca	23

The record for one class went to Cashmore's, Newport, with a staggering total of 73 Class Fives, followed by Draper's 39 9Fs, Ward's, Beighton, 36 9Fs and Campbell's tidy total of 33 9Fs cut up at Airdrie.

RIGHT: Gaunt portrait of 9F No.92093 at Motherwell Machinery & Scrap, Wishaw, in February 1968, revealing the internal configuration of single blastpipe and chimney. In that month, no fewer than 8 9Fs were cut up in this yard, all but one being Kingmoor engines. *Photo: Trevor Rees*

BELOW: One of the September 1967 withdrawals, 9F No.92127, travelled from store at her last shed, Birkenhead, to Buttigieg's yard in Newport, South Wales, arriving in November. By the date of this view, 10th March 1968, little work has been done on her, a not unusual state of affairs at this yard. *Photo: N. E. Preedy*

9F

FIVE DAYS BEFORE CHRISTMAS 1953, a correspondent in the 'Railway Observer' noted the first 9F, No.92000, outside the paint shop at Crewe Works, resplendent in shining black paint. "At a quick glance," he recorded, "it would almost pass for a Britannia." Thus cursorily dismissed, No.92000 left Crewe for active service on 7th January. Just 11 years later, the first of the class were withdrawn.

While the study of the disposal of BR steam must remain objective and unsentimental, it is difficult to examine the disposal statistics of the handsome, efficient and ill-used 9Fs without continuous pangs of regret and the occasional stab of genuine anger. By 1964, it was becoming increasingly difficult to accommodate steam in a rapidly evolving diesel and electric railway, where maintenance, crew training and rostering were not only changing to suit the new motive power but also being severely pruned in accordance to the Beeching Plan. Nevertheless, surely the planners could have found better utilisation of the 9Fs, purpose-built as they were for heavy freight which was steam-hauled (in places) right to the end? Their demise is littered with examples of waste.

The first six engines to be axed were Nos.92170, 92175, 92177 from Doncaster and 92171, 92176 from New England. All had a pitifully short working life of between 6 years 2 months and 6 years 5 months, but as the grim attrition of their sisters gathered momentum it became clear that their youth would not be untypical. In fact, 122 9Fs (almost exactly half the class) had a working life of less than a decade, 32 working for less than seven years and 7 (Nos.92198, 92199, 92207, 92210, 92214, 92216, 92219) shared with the immortal 92220 a working life of little more than five years. Elder statesmen of the class, the longest lived, were Nos.92004 (14 years 3 months) and 92009 (14 years 1 month) which were both withdrawn from Carnforth shed in March 1968 and ended up at Cashmore's yard in Newport. The same shed hosted the last 9Fs in stock (Nos.92167, 92077, both condemned in July 1968). A BR 9F could expect an average life of 9 years 2 months: a statistic which, perhaps more than any other, exemplifies the inevitable waste of the modernisation years.

Only one 9F was cut up by BR, No.92177 at Crewe Works in mid-1964 (aged 6 years) and 9 still exist today. 23 private yards hacked their way through the remainder of the 251-strong class. A 140 ton 9F was not a particularly welcome object at the 'three men and a dog' smaller yards (six yards took one apiece and lived to tell the tale) and it was the larger, more professional outfits which disposed of Riddles' giants. Three contractors cut up 42% of the class between them: Campbell's of Airdrie had 33; Ward's, Beighton 34 and Draper's lured a record 38 to Hull. Also hard at work were Cashmore's, Newport (21) and Ward's, Killamarsh (16) but only nine yards achieved double figures with the 9Fs. Notable casualties were No.92250, the 7331st and last steam locomotive to be built at Crewe Works (cut up without ceremony in July 1966 by Cashmore's, Newport), and also the Woodham's disposals; No.92232 in March 1965 and the celebrated and lavishly photographed late demise of No.92085 in July 1980.

Standard 5

ONE OF THE GREAT fascinations inherent in the study of disposals is the occasional revelation of a perplexing statistic. Turning to the Standard Fives, we find that Cashmore's, Newport, purchased no fewer than 73 engines, some 42% of the class total. Only two other yards achieved double figures: Cashmore's sister yard at Great Bridge (27) and Motherwell Machinery & Scrap (19). The Newport yard was buying Fives from three regions and widely disparate locations: SR engines from Eastleigh and Salisbury — even as far away as Guildford and Nine Elms — and the S&D engines from Bath Green Park; WR engines from Croes Newydd and LMR locos from Bolton and Patricroft, to list but a few. Such was Cashmore's appetite that a team of their cutters travelled to Weymouth goods yard to demolish No.73170, unfit to travel, in January 1967, while of the series 73014-73035 (22 engines), Cashmore's gobbled up all but one.

Other notable disposals were No.73164, cut up at Banbury MPD by Friswell's and No.73041, disposed of at Eastleigh shed by Cohen's. A lucky loco was No.73050, withdrawn by WR in April 1964, reinstated the following month by the LMR and purchased for preservation from Patricroft shed following a second withdrawal in June 1968.

OPPOSITE, TOP:
With a tragically short life of just 86 months behind her, 9F No.92179 awaits the cutters' favours at Hughes Bolckow's at North Blyth on 11th July 1966. A New England engine until January 1965, she was withdrawn from Colwick shed in November 1965, following a brief sojourn at Langwith Junction, whose shed code she still carries. *Photo: A. Brown*

OPPOSITE, BOTTOM:
Another view of the mechanical havoc at Motherwell Machinery & Scrap, 24th November 1966. Surrounded by rail mounted crane, bundles of tubes, assorted junk and Ivatt Mogul No.46460, this is Standard Five No.73107, withdrawn just down the line at Motherwell shed that September. Long believed to have been sold to Arnott Young at Old Kilpatrick, she was in fact a MM&S purchase. *Photo: Keith Romig*

ABOVE:
There is something particularly poignant about this photograph. The date is February 1969, nearly seven months after the end of regular steam working on BR and the locomotive, Standard Five No.73069, will be a familiar friend to the many dedicated enthusiasts who in 1968 chased and cherished the last handful of steam locomotives clinging to life in the dying steam sheds of the northwest. The last of her class at work, she was also one of the last quartet of Standards to survive (the other three were Class Fours) and worked numerous specials in the last months of BR steam.

This, the engine's last portrait, may also appeal to the Running Foreman at Patricroft shed. In June 1968 "dismayed at what was happening all around him" he was appalled when six of his last seven Standard Fives were condemned, despite his conviction that they "were good for another twenty years." Patricroft shed closed on 1st July, but the seventh Five, No.73069, was the best of the bunch and transferred to Carnforth where she survived until the last week of steam, being withdrawn in August 1968.

After a full six months in store at Lostock Hall she departed, towed dead, on the long melancholy journey to South Wales and became the very last BR steam loco to be cut up at Cashmore's Newport yard. Behind her, the legendary 'engine bits' mountain – the rise and fall of which we have remarked upon before in this series – is at a low ebb and diluted with general scrap while one of the flail-equipped army tanks has been uncovered again.

Cashmore's didn't initiate the destruction of the steam locomotive but they played a pivotal role. Now, as the steam age ended, they would look elsewhere for scrap. *Photo: D. Short*

TOP: Photographed in the Chesterfield yard of Garnham, Harris & Elton in January 1968 is Standard Four 4-6-0 No.75055, one of two of the class cut up here. The other was No.75050; both were Stoke engines, withdrawn in June 1967 and November 1966 respectively. LNER Class K1 Mogul No.62048 is in the foreground. *Photo: Graham Wignall*

ABOVE: This unfortunate pile of bits and pieces is not a giant K's Kit but Standard Four 2-6-0 No.76053. Purchased by Cashmore's, Newport, but unfit to travel she was cut to pieces in Weymouth goods yard, seen here in August 1967. *Photo: A. Coleman*

Standard 4 4-6-0

IN COMPLETE CONTRAST TO the Standard Fives, the Fours were cut up all over the place. This is decidedly odd for, despite being smaller than the Fives it is unlikely that they were easier to cut up; the facts, however, speak for themselves. 21 different yards (all private contractors) helped rid BR of the angular 4-6-0s, ranging from Motherwell Machinery & Scrap (2 engines), one of four Scottish yards involved, to King's of Norwich (3), to Draper's of Hull (2), to Ward's at Killamarsh (8). 7 Welsh yards also lent a hand but, curiously, Cashmore's purchased only 5: perhaps they were too busy with the Fives? The yard record here is also perplexing: Bird's of Long Marston, a relatively minor yard not noted for unusual scrapping feats, took a full dozen of the class. Ward's of Beighton was the only other purchaser to achieve double figures, with 10. The same firm also cut up Nos.75072, 75073, both from store at Templecombe shed, at Ringwood in Hampshire, a most unusual location.

The first condemnations were on the SR:

Nos.75067 (Eastleigh, October 1964) and 75001 (Yeovil, December 1964), although the former engine subsequently served as a stationary boiler at Redbridge sleeper works for twelve months. These were the only 1964 withdrawals, but condemnations — 11 in 1965, 21 in 1966, 36 in 1967 — accelerated thereafter. Ten engines worked into 1968 and Nos.75009, 75019, 75020, 75027, 75048 were still nominally in stock at the August 1968 finale.

Standard 4 2-6-0

A SIMILAR PICTURE HERE to the 4-6-0s. Cashmore's, Newport, did better, however, and took the yard record with 22. The other 89 scrapped engines went to 21 different contractors, 10 firms taking just 1 engine. Although the type was never allocated to the WR, 7 South Wales scrapyards helped in its demise (another delightfully inexplicable statistic). By mid-1967 the class had suffered rather more badly than the 4-6-0 Fours and only six survivors were in stock, all shedded at Springs Branch, Wigan. Of these, one (No.76079) was preserved, 2 were cut up in Newport (No.76075 at Buttigieg's, 76081 at Cashmore's) and 3 were sold to Woodham's, Nos.76077, 76079, 76080, the latter engine being cut up by April 1972.

Standard 2 & 3 Moguls

ANOTHER MIXED BAG OF private yards involved here, ranging from McLellan's at Bo'ness to Bird's, Morriston, to Draper's at Hull. Since the classes spent most of their working lives in NE England and Scotland the bulk of the class was cut up in the northern yards, Motherwell Machinery & Scrap taking most (15), although, as so often, Cashmore's Great Bridge yard did their bit (12). Small quantities elsewhere, ones and twos, with 2 engines going to BR works (No.78009 Swindon, cut up December 1964; No.78015, Darlington, cut up January 1964).

TOP: Following withdrawal at Croes Newydd in September 1966, Standard Four 2-6-0 No.76086 was stored for some six months at her last shed before moving to Burnt Mill Sidings near Sutton Bridge Junction, Shrewsbury. The engine, showing every sign of her enforced idleness, was pictured there on 4th March 1967; soon after, Cohen's purchased her and she ended her days at Morriston, Swansea, two months later. The 'Jinty' is No.47677. *Photo: M. C. Embrey*

BOTTOM: Also from store at Shrewsbury (6D) was Standard Two Mogul No.78017 which was another purchase by Cashmore's, Newport. Seen here in Dock Street reception sidings in August 1967, this was one of four of the class condemned at 6D in December 1966. *Photo: M. Sheppard*

Standard 4 2-6-4T

MOST NOTABLE LOCO HERE, at least in the scrapping statistics, is No.80103, the first of the class to be withdrawn (September 1962) following electrification of lines from Fenchurch Street and subsequently cut up at Stratford. The real carnage commenced some two years later as the diesel onslaught cut into local passenger workings and by the end of 1965 the class was concentrated in Scotland and on four SR sheds. Disposals reflect the Scottish factor with Motherwell Machinery & Scrap (29 engines) and Shipbreaking Industries, Faslane (26) taking the lion's share. Cashmore's, Newport, wrought havoc with the SR engines (18) and the class, in fact, died on the Southern, the last survivors being based at Bournemouth, Eastleigh and Nine Elms. There were several interesting disposals: a quartet of locos to Crewe Works, the obscure yard of Steel Supply, West Drayton, took Nos.80031 and 80148 in April 1965 and Woodham's demolished No.80067 in September 1965. Three, too sick to travel, were cut up by private firms on a BR site: Nos.80096 and 80102 at Ringwood goods yard in March 1966 and No.80132 to following month at Eastleigh shed, all 3 by workers from Cohen's.

Standard 3 2-6-2T

THE MOST NOTABLE SCRAPPINGS here are the trio cut up at BR, Eastleigh Works: Nos.82002, 82008, 82043. Cashmore's, Newport, held the yard record (13) and three quarters of the class were disposed of in South Wales.

Standard 2 2-6-2T

A MOST INTERESTING DISPOSAL here is No.84007 which was purchased by the important, early yard of Loom's at Spondon: that firm's only BR Standard. Six members of this underused and short lived class went to Crewe for disposal.

TOP: Cashmore's, Newport, yet again and a rare glimpse of one of the big 80XXX series 2-6-4Ts, No.80138, a SR engine ex-store at Salisbury. Tubes are bundled in the foreground and the 'bits mountain' reaches a new and precarious peak in this February 1967 view. *Photo: M. Sheppard*

BOTTOM: Two of only four Standards cut up at SR works, Class Three 2-6-2Ts Nos.82002 and either 82008 or 82043 are seen at Eastleigh Works where they were disposed of in April-June 1964. *Photo: R. E. Rosendale*

WDs

WD 2-10-0

THE STORY HERE, SIMPLY told, is dominated by BR: seven engines to Cowlairs and a dozen to Darlington. Campbell's at Shieldhall (5) and Airdrie (1) helped dispose of this predominantly Scottish-based class.

WD 2-8-0

EXAMINATION OF THE SCRAPPINGS of the army of Riddles 2-8-0s (733 strong at January 1957) reveals a pageant of destruction which stretched the cutters to the limit. It wasn't just the large yards who were involved, everyone who could wield a torch or sledgehammer and were within bidding distance of a depot clogged with unwanted Austerities dragged the filthy, silent monsters within their gates. Or so it seemed. In the north of England (very few WDs were cut up in the south) they were all at it: small firms whose origins and fate remain a mystery and who cut up very few engines; Maden & McKee, Carrex Metals, Butler's of Otley, Routledge of Bootle, Willoughby's of Choppington and Arnold Young of Dinsdale to name but six. Several yards got to grips with the WDs and achieved double figures, eight cutting 10-20, six 20-40. Draper's of Hull, though, apparently became addicted: the gates of their yard swallowed 25,778 tons of WDs, 205 engines. They all came out again, of course, but they were in very small pieces.

While partly due to the final geographical allocations of the class, Draper's domination of disposal of the WDs parallels Cashmore's lion's share of the LMS 8Fs, already recorded, and reflects either that the big, efficient and prosperous yards were bidding very competitive prices for engines whose construction they knew and were used to, or that they were bidding low but undertaking to take large quantities.

BR was also heavily involved with the earlier WD withdrawals: Crewe took 50, Darlington 47, Doncaster 27, Gorton 12, Horwich 11, Cowlairs 10, Stratford 9 and Inverurie 7.

TOP: Eight of the WD 2-10-0s were stored at Grangemouth, their last shed, for many months from withdrawal in December 1962. Of these, five were purchased by Campbell's at Shieldhall between November 1963 and January 1964. One went to Cowlairs, one to Darlington, and this engine, No.90774, was sold to Campbell's of Airdrie. No.90757 is also visible in this 18th May 1963 view. *Photo: John Corkill*

ABOVE: George H. Campbell's yard at Shieldhall, Glasgow, on 25th January 1964. Under the cranes is WD 2-8-0 No.90505, an engine withdrawn over 18 months previously from Ardrossan shed, where she was stored until movement to Campbell's in November 1963. *Photo: J. L. Stevenson*

Chapter Eight

The Final Analysis

THE STEAM LOCOMOTIVE'S massive construction and the comparative ease of replacing damaged parts meant that, at least until the twilight years of steam, it was rare for an engine to be scrapped as the result of a accident. Indeed, extraordinarily elaborate methods were sometimes used to recover derailed engines, notably in the case of Princess Royal Pacific No.46207 *Princess Arthur of Connaught* which landed on its left hand side at the foot of a low embankment after derailment of the 8.20 am Liverpool-Euston express at Weedon on 21st September 1951. Extrication of the 94½ ton locomotive and 27 ton tender from a field of soft, unstable earth beyond the reach of rail-mounted cranes called for remarkable ingenuity by BR and recovery on 28th October was achieved using a combination of ramps, steel piles, outriggers, cranes from Willesden and Crewe and no fewer than five 8F freight engines acting as stabilisers.

LEFT: More humble engines, clearly, were not worth such strenuous or costly efforts and the SDJR 'Bulldog' No.76 which nosedived into the mud of the Somerset Levels following a collision on 26th August 1949 was cut up where it lay – but not completely. Difficult working conditions meant that parts of the engine stayed where they were, to be recovered quite recently for preservation. By the 1960s, however, even a costly express passenger engine was dispensible, Jubilee No.45695 *Minotaur*, for example, being cut up at Broadheath Goods Yard close to the site of her rear end collision with a freight train between Cinderland Crossing and Broadheath (Altrincham) on 18th January 1964. Her executioner was scrap merchant J. F. Parker of Broadheath, who took several weeks to accomplish the task.
Photo: L&GRP, courtesy David & Charles

RIGHT: On 10th November 1964 LMS Ivatt Mogul No. 43072 was working a twenty-one empty wagon train from Ardsley at Bradford when it went out of control at Listerdyke. It careered into Adlolphus Street goods yard at an estimated 50 mph, its crew throwing themselves clear. Demolished buffer stops and crashed through a wall to fall thirty feet into the road below. At this late date she was deemed not worth saving and scrap merchant G. W. Butler of Bradford bought the Ivatt – and cut it up on the spot. The photograph was taken on the day of the accident, and shows No. 43072 being 'copped' by a quartet of policemen. *Photo: Gavin Morrison*

BELOW: While working a York-Scarborough train at Haxby on 2nd July 1960, LNER Class B16/1 4-6-0 No. 61456 blew out her right hand cylinder. Photographed at York on 1st August, with her self inflicted wound very evident, she was sent subsequently to Darlington. In 1960, steam engines which disgraced themselves were asking for trouble – nine of No. 61456's sisters had already been withdrawn and she was summarily condemned and cut up the following month.
Photo: N. E. W. Skinner, via Ken Hoole

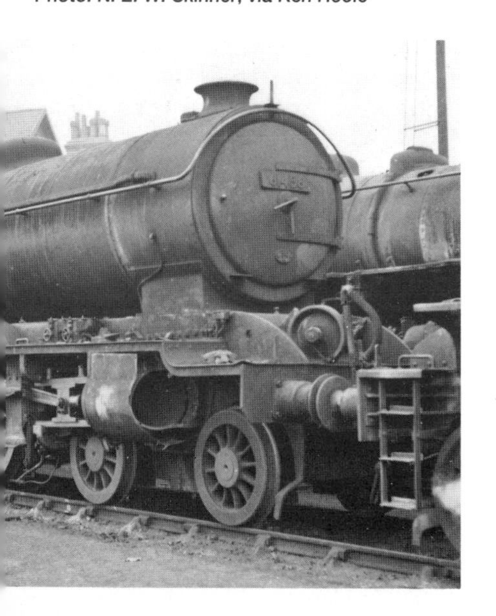

PART SEVEN

Enthusiasts at work

IN THE MID AND late 1960's, the railway preservation movement was incomparably less robust than it is today and the gricers and spotters could only make their presence felt by minor, but touching, displays of affection for the steam locomotive in its death throes. Outposts of steam, the last sheds, the last turns — each was sought out, recorded and saluted. Engines were groomed for their last journey — if they could not be saved, at least they could bow out looking presentable.

TOP: Unofficial cleaning at Draper's scrapyard, Hull. LNER Class B16/3 4-6-0 No.61420 received the attention of enthusiasts during the bitter weather of January 1964 and was recorded on the 12th. The first of this class to be condemned, No.61474, left a local shed, Hull (Botanic Gardens) as early as February 1958, while thirteen engines lasted into 1964 based at Hull (Dairycoates) and York. The last to go was No.61435 and most of the class were cut up at Darlington, many after up to eighteen months in store, but Drapers took nine of the 1964 survivors. *Photo: Ken Hoole*

BOTTOM: During September 1967, after a period in store at Nine Elms, Bulleid West Country Pacific No.34002 *Salisbury* departed, towed dead, for Cashmore's yard at Newport. At Coaley Junction she developed a hot box and was stopped at Horton Road MPD for attention. While there, she was descended upon by a gang of enthusiasts determined that she should look her best for her visit to South Wales. Apart from a thorough polishing, 34002 received white painted buffers and lamp brackets and had her name, crest and smokebox number artistically reinstated. The photographer recorded these endeavours on 21st September and the following day the engine left for Cashmore's, where the cutters were suitably impressed. *Photo: N. E. Preedy*

In all the history of British steam, no group of locomotives was so passionately followed as the LMR engines which remained active into the last week of steam in August 1968. Shedded at Carnforth (10A), Lostock Hall (10D) and Rose Grove (10F) they comprised 31 'Black Fives', twenty 8F's, three Standard 4's, one Standard 5 and one Britannia: a total of 56 engines. They were chased, noted, counted and cheered: they were photographed, drawn, painted, polished and covered with chalked slogans. More positively, sixteen of the LMR 1968 survivors were purchased for preservation.

This view sums up those last few weeks in the north west: from the top of the defunct coaling plant at Rose Grove shed, Burnley, it was taken on 4th August 1968, one day after regular steam working had ceased on BR. All that was left was that day's railtours and the following week, on the 11th, the famous 'Farewell to Steam' tour. Visible are, from right: 'Black Five' No.45397 and 8F's Nos.48451, 48191, 48666. Foreground are 8F's Nos.48278, 48257, 48448. Note the chalked inscriptions on the tenders of Nos.48191 and 48278. *Photo: N. E. Preedy*

THE PRESERVATION MIRACLE

IN THE MARCH 1967 edition of the *Railway Magazine*, an editorial stated 'It is said that 'the British are never so keen on keeping something as when they have lost it, and this is certainly true about steam locomotives.' At that time steam was in full retreat, with hundreds of locomotives being cut up throughout Britain. Ostensibly, steam had just over a year left to live. There was great bitterness at the demise of some well-loved engines, as might be expected when time-honoured servants are suddenly and illogically made redundant. But it was the sight of the Standard Class locomotives, some barely five years old, being cut up which caused the greatest ferour. A couple of thousand quid was the asking price, and though that sum would barely buy a decent second-hand car today, twenty-five years ago it was an impossible sum to realise. Yet, many groups and a few private individuals believed they could raise the asking price and save a locomotive from the scrap heap. To the vast majority of railway enthusiasts, these were just pipe dreams.

True, many of the ambitious schemes did fail, and one by one the objects of preservation plans faded and died. Yet some succeeded, and slowly but surely the preservation movement began to grow. Though several locomotives had been preserved long before August 1968, to most of us these were just a part of a rag bag selection of shining museum pieces - engines which would never feel the breath of steam again. Alan Pegler's preservation of the A3 Class *Flying Scotsman* showed what could be done. True, there were problems but, where there was a will, a way could be found. Willingly, hundreds of enthusiastic volunteers set about that way, and fund raising events, appeals and a variety of other money raising schemes came to our notice. However, as steam clung to its tenuous life-line in the North-west, Cashmore's, Cohen's, Draper's and the like devoured, with a voracious appetite, all the locomotives which became available. Time was fast running out.

Yet, like in all good fairy stories, a miracle was about to happen. It is doubtful whether Dai Woodham would have ever cast himself in the role of the fairy god-mother, but it was his magic wand which allowed the preservationists time to get their act together. By showing remarkable restraint, and far sighted vision, as well as astute business acumen, the management of the yard left rows and rows of silent locomotives sitting on the sidings. However, though they were, to all intents and purposes, depreciating, rusting hulks, they were a sound investment in the re-birth of British steam. I travelled to Barry on business in 1971, and took the opportunity to visit the yard: on my arrival, I was fortunate to witness the departure of No.34092 *City of Wells* to the Worth Valley Railway. I felt somewhat incredulous that this useless object could ever be made to run again, yet just a decade later and I was privileged to observe the restored locomotive in action on its first main line outing up the Settle & Carlisle line. More by accident than design, I found myself at Newbiggin Station, where a small group of assembled photographers drew my attention; I was just in time to watch the West Country class thrash through - as it disappeared towards Carlisle in a welter of spray incredulity turned to belief.

In the years that have followed 65 engines have been brought back to life, a figure made up of 33 GWR engines, 11 SR locos., 11 of LMS parentage and 10 BR Standards. The only noticeable absentee being ex-LNER locomotives, but few of this type were sent to Woodhams, which is a great pity. The only survivor being Class B1 No.61264 which was removed to the Great Central Railway at Loughborough in 1976. There are a few quotable statistics that should be mentioned in passing, such as the newest locomotive to be preserved No.92219 (built in January 1960) and the oldest No.2807 which dates from 1905. Whilst No.5553 stayed at he yard over 28 years, No.43924 was there for only 35 months. The breakdown of the survivors clearly shows their parentage, 98 GWR, 41 Southern, 35 LMS, 1 LNER and 38 BR. There will be no more now, the yard is devoid of locomotives - the preservationists must now look further afield, perhaps to Turkey were a number of ex-WD Stanier 8Fs are languishing.

So, as the story comes to an end, it is again to the Keighley & Worth Valley Railway that I must return. Of all the ongoing projects involved in restoring engines from Barry, the one which has just been completed as the book goes to press is that of Standard Class 2MT 2-6-0 No.78022. I saw this hulk resting in the rose-bay willow herb covered sidings in March 1975, and took a picture of what appeared to be yet another useless piece of junk - yet on Friday 15th October 1992 I stood on the footplate of the same engine in the yard at Howarth. However, this was not quite the same engine, for the machine on which I stood was a fully restored and mechanically superb railway engine; its fire-box alive with glowing coals and its boiler awaiting testing and inspection as a final step before it returned to revenue earning duties. Once more I took a photograph of it - to compare with my original view, reflecting that miracles really do happen. All power to Woodham Bros. and the many enthusiasts who have turned nightmares into dreams and dreams into reality!

Looking at this picture you may be forgiven for assuming that the Barton-Wright 0-6-0 tank engine is destined for the scrap, not so, in fact it is two diesel shunters behind it at Bolton MPD that are awaiting the chop. This marvellous old engine started life in Queen Victoria's days as an 0-6-0 tender engine, they were later rebuilt as saddle-tanks and enjoyed a relatively successful if not glamorous life on shunting duties around the old L&YR system. This view on 25th April 1968 sees the 0-6-0ST in transit between Parsonage Colliery and Heap Bridge Sidings for the L&YR Saddle-tanks Fund.
Ian G. Holt

This is the sort of sight that inspired the preservationists, rows of locomotives, unwanted and with no home to go to. This view is taken at Barry Docks on 2nd September 1968, days after the end of BR main line steam. They are (from right to left):-
Row 1; Nos.42968*, 47298*, 3855*, 3817, 45379*;
Row 2; Nos.45699*, 44932*, 34067*, 34081*,
Row 3; Nos.46521*, 78022*, 75079*, 35029*
Row 4; Nos. 7812*, 7820*, 7927*,
Row 5; Nos.34092*, 4561*, 5527, 4566*.
And if you had told anybody back then that some of these engines might yet be saved, who would have given you favourable odds - yet, those engines with an asterisk against their number, well they're still around almost a quarter of century on.
A. J. Sommerfield

With the legend 'Long Live Dai', the last survivor at the Barry scrapyard is pictured on 2nd January 1986. Exactly two years later the ex-GWR 2-6-2T, No.5553, left for the Forest of Dean after spending 28 years in the yard - the great steam preservation movement had achieved its goal.
A. J. Sommerfield

I had seen this Standard Class 2MT 2-6-0 many times as it worked around the Sheffield area in my youth, before it was eventually purchased by Woodham Bros. in March 1967. However, on my visit to Barry in April 1975, it was sad to see what eight years of neglect had done to her. This picture was taken just a few weeks before No.78022 was removed from Barry by the Standard Four group, destined for the Keighley & Worth Valley Railway, and rebuilding.
Alan Earnshaw

Make a new tender, add a virtually completely rebuilt engine, and you have a locomotive ready for entering service once again. Thousands of pounds and millions of man hours went in to the project, but it was a proud team who saw No.78022 raise from the grave on Friday 16th October 1992. I was privileged to be there to witness it.
Alan Earnshaw

INDEX TO LOCOMOTIVE PHOTOGRAPHS CONTAINED IN COMPENDIUM VOLUME

PRE-NATIONALISATION LOCOMOTIVES

EX-GWR LOCOMOTIVES

EX-SOUTHERN RAILWAY LOCOMOTIVES

EX-LONDON MIDLAND & SCOTTISH RAILWAY LOCOMOTIVES

EX-LONDON & NORTH EASTERN RAILWAY LOCOMOTIVES

EX-WAR DEPARTMENT/BRITISH RAILWAY STANDARD LOCOMOTIVES

In conclusion....a scene reminiscent for all of us who tramped round isolated depots in the closing years of steam, as No.57441 stands outside Forfar MPD on 17th February 1962 ready for its final journey - to the scrapyard!
Gerald T. Robinson.